Democracy, Minorities and International Law

This work examines the contribution that international law may make to the resolution of cultural conflicts – political disputes between the members of different ethno-cultural groups – in democratic States. International law recognises that persons belonging to minorities have the right to enjoy their own culture and peoples have the right to self-determination, without detailing how these principles are to be put into effect. The emergence of democracy as a legal obligation of States permits the international community to concern itself with both the procedure and the substance of 'democratic' decisions concerning ethno-cultural groups. Democracy is not to be understood simply as majority rule. Cultural conflicts in democratic States must be resolved in a way that is either acceptable or defensible and defeasible to all citizens, including persons belonging to ethno-cultural minorities. *Democracy, Minorities and International Law* examines the implications of this recognition.

STEVEN WHEATLEY is Senior Lecturer in Human Rights Law and International Law at the University of Leeds.

Democracy, Minorities and International Law

Steven Wheatley
University of Leeds

CAMBRIDGE
UNIVERSITY PRESS

CAMBRIDGE UNIVERSITY PRESS
Cambridge, New York, Melbourne, Madrid, Cape Town, Singapore, São Paulo

CAMBRIDGE UNIVERSITY PRESS
The Edinburgh Building, Cambridge, CB2 2RU, UK

Published in the United States of America by Cambridge University Press,
New York

www.cambridge.org
Information on this title: www.cambridge.org/9780521848985

First published 2005

Printed in the United Kingdom at the University Press, Cambridge

A catalogue record for this book is available from the British Library

ISBN-13 978-0-521-84898-5 hardback
ISBN-10 0-521-84898-9 hardback

for Katherine Louise

Contents

Acknowledgments

The author would like to thank the following who have commented on parts of the work: James Crawford, Colin Harvey, Dominic McGoldrick, Rachel Murray, Brian Thompson and Alexandra Xanthaki. The usual disclaimer applies. He would also like to thank the University of Liverpool Research Development Fund for its support in enabling the author to spend some time in 2002 at the Lauterpacht Research Centre for International Law, Cambridge University, where part of the research was undertaken. He would also like to thank the staff at the Centre for their hospitality. The author remains grateful to his parents, Michael Wheatley and Rosaleen Wheatley, and his immediate family, Katherine, Ben and Francesca, for their encouragement and forbearance during the writing of this book.

Table of cases

International Court of Justice

Case Concerning Military and Paramilitary Activities in and Against
Nicaragua (Nicaragua v. United States) Merits, ICJ Reports (1986)
p. 14, 132

Legal Consequences for States of the Continued Presence of South
Africa in Namibia (South West Africa) Notwithstanding Security
Council Resolution 276 (1970), ICJ Reports (1971), p. 16, 49 ILR 2, 68

Legal Consequences of the Construction of a Wall in the Occupied
Palestinian Territory, International Court of Justice, Advisory
Opinion 9 July 2004, 43 ILM (2004) 1009, 12, 19, 77, 79, 125

Western Sahara Case, ICJ Reports (1975), p. 12, 59 ILR 13, 72

Human Rights Committee

Aärelä and Näkkäläjärvi v. Finland, Communication No. 779/1997, UN
Doc. CCPR/C/73/D/779/1997, 7 November 2001, 17, 151

Aduayom et al. v. Togo, Communications Nos. 422/1990, 423/1990 and
424/15 1990, UN Doc. CCPR/C/57/D/422/1990, 19 August 1996, 146

Altesor v. Uruguay, Communication No. 10/1977, UN Doc. CCPR/C/15/D/
10/2 1977, 19 March 1982, 140

Ballantyne and Davidson, and McIntyre v. Canada, Communication
Nos. 359/1989 and 385/1989, UN Doc. CCPR/C/47/D/359/1989, 5 May
1993, 14, 17, 108

Barzhig v. France, Communication No. 327/1988, UN Doc. CCPR/C/41/D/
327/1988, 6 May 1991, 12

Clement Boodoo v. Trinidad and Tobago, Communication No. 721/1996,
UN Doc. CCPR/C/74/D/721/1996, 2 April 2002, 14

African Commission on Human and Peoples' Rights

European Court of Human Rights

International Criminal Tribunal for Rwanda

United States

Canada

Table of treaties

Table of UN resolutions and OSCE and other documents

General Assembly resolutions

Security Council resolutions

OSCE documents

Other documents

Abbreviations

CEDAW	Committee on the Elimination of Discrimination against Women
CSCE	Conference on Security and Co-operation in Europe
EC	European Community
GA	General Assembly
ICCPR	International Covenant on Civil and Political Rights
ICESCR	International Covenant on Economic, Social and Cultural Rights
OSCE	Organization for Security and Co-operation in Europe
SC	Security Council
SFRY	Socialist Federal Republic of Yugoslavia
UN	United Nations
UNESCO	United Nations Educational, Scientific and Cultural Organization
US	United States

Introduction

The period following the end of the Cold War has seen an 'increasing clash of cultures',[1] most notoriously with the attacks on 11 September 2001 by Islamic terrorists on the twin towers of the World Trade Center in New York, the pre-eminent symbols of Western global capitalism.[2] Immediately following the attacks, the United Nations Educational, Scientific and Cultural Organization (UNESCO) adopted a Universal Declaration on Cultural Diversity.[3] The Declaration proclaims that the 'defence of cultural diversity is an ethical imperative, [implying] a commitment to human rights and fundamental freedoms, in particular the rights of persons belonging to minorities and those of indigenous peoples'.[4]

[1] Dru Gladney, 'Introduction: making and marking majorities', in Dru Gladney (ed.), *Making majorities: constituting the nation in Japan, Korea, China, Malaysia, Fiji, Turkey, and the United States* (Stanford: Stanford University Press, 1998), p. 1, at p. 3.

[2] The terrorists also attacked the Pentagon in Washington DC, the symbol of American military power.

[3] UNESCO Universal Declaration on Cultural Diversity, adopted unanimously by the General Conference of the United Nations Educational, Scientific and Cultural Organization, 2 November 2001. UNESCO's Director-General, Koïchire Matuura, expressed the hope that the Declaration might 'one day ... acquire the same force as the Universal Declaration of Human Rights': see 'Foreword', 'Universal Declaration on Cultural Diversity' (UNESCO: 2002).

[4] Article 4, *ibid*. The term 'culture' in the Declaration refers to the 'set of distinctive spiritual, material, intellectual and emotional features of society or a social group'. Culture encompasses 'lifestyles, ways of living together, value systems, traditions and beliefs': *ibid*., preamble. See also GA Res. 55/2, adopted 8 September 2000, 'Millennium Declaration', para. 6: human beings must 'respect one another, in all their diversity of belief, culture and language'. Additionally, the member States of the United Nations resolved to 'strengthen the capacity of all our countries to implement the principles and practices of democracy and respect for human rights, including minority rights': *ibid*., para. 25.

The purpose of this book is to examine the position of cultural minorities in international law, with a particular focus on democratic States.[5] For the purposes of the work, the term 'ethno-cultural' will be applied to cultural groups, given the inter-generational aspect of group identity. Ethno-cultural groups are groups of persons, predominantly of common descent, who think of themselves as possessing a distinctive cultural identity, which may be based on a particular religion and/or language, and who evidence a desire to transmit their culture to succeeding generations. In this context, 'culture' is a synonym for identity.[6] Cultural conflicts involve disputes (violent and other) between different identity groups.[7] Cultural conflicts exist primarily between the State authorities and ethno-cultural minorities. The cultural identity of the State is reflected, inter alia, in citizenship laws, language laws and practices, education policy, and in the adoption of public symbols and choice of public holidays.[8] This 'national identity', reflecting the cultural values, beliefs and practices of the dominant/majority ethno-cultural group, is imposed on minority cultures.[9]

---

[5] The rights of minorities in a democracy have been the subject of much writing in political theory and political science. See, for example, Brian Barry, *Culture and equality: an egalitarian critique of multiculturalism* (Cambridge, MA: Harvard University Press, 2001); Seyla Benhabib, *The claims of culture: equality and diversity in the global era* (Princeton, NJ: Princeton University Press, 2002); Seyla Benhabib (ed.), *Democracy and difference: contesting the boundaries of the political* (Princeton, NJ: Princeton University Press, 1996); John Dryzek, *Discursive democracy: politics, policy and political science* (Cambridge: Cambridge University Press, 1990); John Dryzek, *Deliberative democracy and beyond: liberals, critics, contestations* (Oxford: Oxford University Press, 2000); Will Kymlicka, *Multicultural citizenship: a liberal theory of minority rights* (Oxford: Clarendon Press, 1995); Will Kymlicka, *The rights of minority communities* (Oxford: Oxford University Press, 1995); James Tully, *Strange multiplicity: constitutionalism in an age of diversity* (Cambridge: Cambridge University Press, 1995); and Iris Marion Young, *Inclusion and democracy* (Oxford: Oxford University Press, 2000).

[6] Benhabib, *The claims of culture*, p. 1.

[7] See Avishai Margalit and Joseph Raz, 'National self-determination', in Will Kymlicka (ed.), *The rights of minority cultures* (Oxford: Oxford University Press, 1995), p. 79, at p. 86. See also Will Kymlicka, *Liberalism, community and culture* (Oxford: Clarendon Press, 1989), p. 178.

[8] Will Kymlicka, 'Western political theory and ethnic relations in Eastern Europe', in Will Kymlicka and Magda Opalski (eds.), *Can liberal pluralism be exported? Western political theory and ethnic relations in Eastern Europe* (Oxford: Oxford University Press, 2001), p. 13, at p. 49. See also Martti Koskenniemi, 'National self-determination today: problems of legal theory and practice' (1994) 43 *International and Comparative Law Quarterly* 241, 263; and James Tully, *Strange multiplicity: constitutionalism in an age of diversity* (Cambridge: Cambridge University Press, 1995), p. 68.

[9] Charles Taylor, 'The politics of recognition', in Amy Gutmann (ed.), *Multiculturalism: examining the politics of recognition* (Princeton, NJ: Princeton University Press, 1994), p. 25, at p. 43.

Explicitly cultural values may be given legal force in constitutional and/or other legislative provisions. In 2004, for example, France legislated to ban the wearing of conspicuous religious symbols or clothing by pupils in schools.[10] The law is intended to affirm the principle of *laïcité* (roughly, secularism) against Islamic religious/cultural values, beliefs and practices (the wearing of the *hijab* or *foulard* by Muslim girl children).[11] It is unlikely that there will be a single group perspective on this or any other issue of culture. The recognised 'leaders' or 'representatives' of the 'community' might demand respect for the cultural practice. Other members of the group may consider a legal proscription on the wearing of the *hijab* as empowering girl children in discussions with their parents. Others might see it as an unjustified interference in the individual rights to freedom of religion and moral autonomy (both in respect of the parents and the child). Individuals have a multiplicity of identities relating to their gender, and other interests and commitments.[12] Identity is not constituted by group membership.[13] There is no single group position with which the State may engage. Cultures are the result of contested, and contestable, narratives.[14] The uncritical

[10] *Loi No. 2004-228 du 15/3/2004 encadrant, en application du principe de laïcité, le port de signes ou de tenues manifestant une appartenance religieuse dans les écoles, collèges et lycées publics*, Article 1. The European Court of Human Rights has translated the provision as 'In State primary and secondary schools, the wearing of signs or dress by which pupils overtly manifest a religious affiliation is prohibited': *Leyla Sahin* v. *Turkey*, App. No. 44774/98, judgment, 29 June 2004, para. 54.

[11] See generally Benhabib, *The claims of culture*, pp. 94–100. See also Human Rights Committee, General Comment No. 04, Article 3 (Equal right of men and women to the enjoyment of all civil and political rights), adopted 30 July 1981, reprinted in 'Compilation of General Comments and General Recommendations adopted by Human Rights Treaty Bodies', UN Doc. HRI/GEN/1/Rev.7, 12 May 2004, p. 127, at paras. 13 and 21. See *Hudoyberganova* v. *Uzbekistan*, Communication No. 931/2000, UN Doc. CCPR/C/82/D/931/2000, 18 January 2005.

[12] Young, *Inclusion and democracy*, p. 137. See also Jane Mansbridge, 'What does a representative do? Communicative settings of distrust, uncrystallized interests, and historically denigrated status', in Will Kymlicka and Wayne Norman (eds.), *Citizenship in diverse societies* (Oxford: Oxford University Press, 2000), p. 99, at p. 108; and Peter Leuprecht, 'Minority rights revisited: new glimpses of an old issue', in Philip Alston (ed.), *Peoples' rights* (Oxford: Oxford University Press, 2001), p. 111, at p. 124.

[13] For communitarians, individual identity is constituted by the values, beliefs and practices of the community: 'communality or groupness is a necessary condition of existence': Ronald Garet, 'Communality and existence: the rights of groups' (1982/3) 56 *Southern California Law Review* 1001, 1066. See also Rainer Forst, 'The rule of reasons: Three models of deliberative democracy' (2001) 14 *Ratio Juris* 345, 353.

[14] See Amy Gutmann, 'The challenge of multiculturalism in political ethics' (1993) 22 *Philosophy and Public Affairs* 171, 174–5; and Thomas Franck, *The empowered self: law and society in the age of individualism* (Oxford: Oxford University Press, 2001), pp. 250–1.

acceptance of the position of community leaders or community representatives ignores the possibility that other perspectives may exist within the group. Moreover, the values and practices of ethno-cultural groups (majorities and minorities) are often influenced by internal hierarchies, in particular those based on gender (men/women) and age (adults/children), with female children being particularly vulnerable to being the victims of multiple discriminations and harmful cultural practices.[15] Democratic governments cannot seek to respond to the fact of cultural conflict by concluding bargains with the putative representatives of ethno-cultural minorities.

In the majority of instances, no specific legislation is required for the imposition of cultural norms: the majority's language will be used in public institutions, and its holidays recognised as public holidays, etc.[16] The values of the majority pervade all aspects of public life, the media, schools, the courts, the government and other official bodies, where they are replicated and reinforced, exerting a powerful influence on the standards of behaviour that are accepted as the 'norm' within the State.[17] For members of the majority ethno-cultural group, '[p]ublic life is understandable and meaningful to them – familiar and comfortable'.[18] They are able to approach the ideal of a self-determined life

---

See also Rodolfo Stavenhagen, 'Cultural rights: a social science perspective', in Halina Niec (ed.), *Cultural rights and wrongs* (Paris: UNESCO Publishing, 1998), p. 1, at p. 6; and Benhabib, *The claims of culture*, p. 3.

[15] See, for example, Vienna Declaration and Programme of Action (1993), ILM 32 (1993) 1661, para. I(21): 'National and international mechanisms and programmes should be strengthened for the defence and protection of children, in particular, the girl-child.' The leading example is the practice of female genital mutilation. See Article 24(3) of the Convention on the Rights of the Child; Article 21(1)(a) of the African Charter on the Rights and Welfare of the Child, adopted 11 July 1990, in force 29 November 1999, OAU Doc. CAB/LEG/24.9/49 (1990), reprinted in (2002) 9 *International Human Rights Reports* 870; and Committee on the Elimination of Discrimination against Women, General Recommendation No. 14, 'Female circumcision', adopted 2 February 1990, reprinted in 'Compilation of General Comments and General Recommendations adopted by human rights treaty bodies', UN Doc. HRI/GEN/1/Rev.7, 12 May 2004, p. 241.

[16] Will Kymlicka, 'Introduction: an emerging consensus?' (1998) 1 *Ethical Theory and Moral Practice* 143, 149. Many disputes between majority and minority populations concern symbolic issues. Jacob Levi traces the break up of Czechoslovakia to the refusal by the national Parliament to insert a hyphen into the name of the State (i.e. Czecho-Slovakia): Jacob Levi, *The multiculturalism of fear* (Oxford: Oxford University Press, 2000), pp. 154–5. Cf. Rex Adhar, 'Indigenous spiritual concerns and the secular State: some developments' (2003) 23 *Oxford Journal of Legal Studies* 611, 636.

[17] Amy Gutmann, 'The challenge of multiculturalism in political ethics' (1993) 22 *Philosophy and Public Affairs* 171, 185.

[18] Alan Patten, 'Democratic secession from a multinational state' (2002) 112 *Ethics* 558, 569.

largely by relying on the human right 'to be free from unjustified interferences in one's personal life'. For members of ethno-cultural minorities, the 'context for thought and action is often much less congenial'.[19]

Ethno-cultural groups manifest themselves in political life in opposition to laws and regulation that conflict with the cultural values, beliefs and practices of the group.[20] As Seyla Benhabib explains, the concern should be 'less on what the group *is* but more on what the political leaders of such groups *demand* in the public sphere'.[21] The concern of this work is to consider the extent to which international law supports the claims of culture. The rights of ethno-cultural minorities are recognised in international instruments concerning 'minorities',[22] 'national minorities',[23] 'indigenous peoples'[24] and 'peoples'.[25] Where the demand is for cultural security, the group makes references to international instruments concerning the rights of minorities, and, in Europe, national minorities. For a number of ethno-cultural groups, the desire for political self-government forms part of the collective identity of the group. They consider themselves nations or peoples (including indigenous peoples). These groups demand the application of the right of peoples to self-determination to them.

The work is divided into three substantive chapters. Chapter 1 examines the right of persons belonging to minorities to enjoy their own culture, to profess and practise their own religion, and to use their own language. The position of national minorities in Europe is also considered. Chapter 2 examines the right of peoples to self-determination. It reviews briefly the application of the principle of equal rights and self-determination of peoples in the process of decolonisation, before considering self-determination 'beyond coloni-alism'. Two aspects are identified: an external aspect which provides the people with the right to determine the international status of the

---

[19] Perry Keller, 'Re-thinking ethnic and cultural rights in Europe' (1998) 18 *Oxford Journal of Legal Studies* 29, 39.

[20] Michael Hechter, *Containing nationalism* (Oxford: Oxford University Press, 2000), p. 70.

[21] Benhabib, *The claims of culture*, p. 16 (emphasis in original).

[22] Article 27 of the International Covenant on Civil and Political Rights, and the UN Declaration on Minorities.

[23] The Framework Convention on National Minorities, and OSCE Copenhagen Document.

[24] ILO Convention No. 169 concerning Indigenous and Tribal Peoples in Independent Countries, and the Draft Declaration on the Rights of Indigenous Peoples.

[25] Article 1 of the International Covenant on Civil and Political Rights, and the African Charter on Human and Peoples' Rights.

territory, and an internal aspect, which is concerned with the right of peoples to self-government. The external aspect is enjoyed by the peoples of trust and non-self-governing territories, the peoples of sovereign and independent States, peoples excluded from public life, and the peoples of the units of an ethnic federation in the process of dissolution. The internal aspect of the right of peoples to self-determination is enjoyed by the peoples of sovereign and independent States, and groups recognised as indigenous peoples and peoples by the State. Chapters 1 and 2 demonstrate that the international community has failed to agree detailed rules for the implementation of the rights of minorities to cultural security and the rights of peoples to self-determination. Detailed commitments will emerge from domestic decision-making procedures.

The traditional position of international law has been to regard the system of government and the process for making decisions as falling within the reserved domain of sovereign and independent States. The emergence of democracy as a legal obligation of States changes this: the international community may concern itself with both the procedure and the substance of decisions in areas of reserved competence in democratic States. Chapter 3, on democracy, considers the importance of procedural inclusion for persons belonging to national or ethnic, religious and linguistic minorities, and the measures necessary to ensure that the interests and perspectives of persons belonging to minorities are included in relevant decision-making processes. The limits of procedural inclusion are recognised, and the chapter considers arguments that certain ethno-cultural minorities should be permitted to share power in a consociational democracy. The work rejects these arguments and considers alternative integrative and deliberative understandings of democracy. The work concludes by examining the implications of recognising the deliberative nature of contemporary democracy for the regulation of cultural conflict.

1   The rights of minorities

This chapter examines the protection afforded by international law to ethno-cultural minorities.[1] Central to this discussion is Article 27 of the International Covenant on Civil and Political Rights. The scope of application and content of the minority rights provided by Article 27 are examined, including the requirement for the State to take positive measures to maintain and support minority cultures. The regime concerning national minorities in Europe is considered, to the extent that it illuminates relevant debates at the universal level.

---

[1] Ethno-cultural majorities are protected, inter alia, by the Convention on the Prevention and Punishment of the Crime of Genocide, adopted by General Assembly Resolution 260 A (III), 9 December 1948, in force 12 January 1951, and by the right of all peoples to self-determination. On the rights of minorities, see Patrick Thornberry, *International law and the rights of minorities* (Oxford: Clarendon Press, 1991). See also Gudmundur Alfredsson and Erika Ferrer (eds.), *Minority rights: a guide to United Nations procedures and institutions* (London: Minority Rights Group and Raoul Wallenberg Institute of Human Rights and Humanitarian Law, 1998); Bill Bowring and Deidre Fottrell (eds.), *Minority and group rights in the new millennium* (The Hague: Martinus Nijhoff, 1999); Peter Cumper and Steven Wheatley (eds.), *Minority rights in the 'new' Europe* (The Hague: Kluwer Law International, 1999); Thomas Franck, *The empowered self: law and society in the age of individualism* (Oxford: Oxford University Press, 2001); Kristin Henrard, *Devising an adequate system of minority protection: individual human rights, minority rights, and the right to self-determination* (The Hague: Martinus Nijhoff, 2000); Yoram Dinstein (ed.), *The protection of minorities and human rights* (Dordrecht: Martinus Nijhoff, 1992); Natan Lerner, *Group rights and discrimination in international law* (Dordrecht: Nijhoff, 1991); Alan Phillips and Allan Rosas (eds.), *Universal minority rights* (Turku/Åbo: Åbo Akademi University Institute for Human Rights, 1995); Javaid Rehman, *The weaknesses in the international protection of minority rights* (The Hague: Kluwer Law International, 2000); Jay A. Sigler, *Minority rights: a comparative analysis* (Westport, CT: Greenwood, 1983); and Gnanapala Welhengama, *Minorities' claims: from autonomy to secession: international law and state practice* (Aldershot: Ashgate, 2000).

The League of Nations' minorities regime

Throughout the history of international law, examples existed of protective treaties concluded for the benefit of minority groups, often on the basis of some bond of religion, nationality or culture between the protecting power and the protected minority.[2] The most notable example was the inter-governmental system of the League of Nations. In the aftermath of the First World War, the new and greatly enlarged States of Central and Eastern Europe were compelled either to sign minority protection treaties, or to make declarations guaranteeing various rights for their minority groups.[3] The rights of minorities included not only the right to equality under the law, but also certain cultural, educational and language rights.[4] The League of Nations' scheme provided for the protection of certain minorities in certain States,[5] but did not recognise any general rights of minorities.[6] Absent of treaty obligations, no duty to protect the distinctive identities of minority groups existed for States in international law.[7]

---

[2] Patrick Thornberry, *International law and the rights of minorities* (Oxford: Clarendon Press, 1991), p. 25. See generally chapter 2, *ibid.*

[3] Nathaniel Berman, '"But the alternative is despair": European nationalism and the modernist renewal of international law' (1993) 106 *Harvard Law Review* 1792, 1822. The League of Nations minorities regime concerned treaties concluded between the Principal Allied Powers and Poland, Austria, the Serb-Croat-Slovene State, Czechoslovakia, Bulgaria, Romania (all 1919) and Hungary (1920); a treaty on the protection of minorities in Greece (1920), treaties between Poland and Danzig on the minorities in the Free City of Danzig (1920), and between Sweden and Finland on the preservation of Swedish traditions in the Aaland Islands (1921); declarations made to the League concerning minorities, respectively by Albania (1921), Lithuania (1922), Latvia (1923), Estonia (1923) and Iraq (1932); a German–Polish convention relating to Upper Silesia (1922), a treaty of peace regarding the protection of minorities in Turkey and Greece (1923), and a convention concerning minorities in the territory of Memel (1934). See Thornberry, *International law and the rights of minorities*, pp. 40–2. See generally Julius Stone, *International guarantees of minority rights* (London: Oxford University Press, 1932).

[4] Berman, 'But the alternative is despair', 1823.

[5] The application of minority treaties was not only restricted to Europe: the dividing line was between 'big and small states'. Obligations were imposed on defeated Austria, Hungary and Bulgaria, but not on Germany. Obligations were also imposed on '"victorious" new states' (Czechoslovakia, Poland) and the aggrandised States of Greece and Romania, but not on Italy: Josef Kunz, 'The present status of international law for the protection of minorities' (1954) 48 *American Journal of International Law* 282, 283.

[6] Attempts to introduce a general provision concerning minorities into the Covenant of the League of Nations were 'repulsed': Thornberry, *International law and the rights of minorities*, p. 39.

[7] Ifor Evans, 'The protection of minorities' (1923/4) 4 *British Year Book of International Law* 95, 102. The Third Assembly of the League of Nations did 'express the hope' that

The Polish Minorities Treaty,[8] the first adopted under the League of Nations' scheme, served as a model for the other treaties.[9] Poland undertook to 'assure full and complete protection of life and liberty to all inhabitants of Poland without distinction of birth, nationality, language, race or religion';[10] to recognise the 'free exercise of any creed, religion or belief';[11] and to recognise that all Polish nationals 'shall be equal before the law and shall enjoy the same civil and political rights without distinction as to race, language or religion'.[12] No restriction was to be imposed on the 'free use by any Polish national of any language in private intercourse, in commerce, in religion, in the press or in publications of any kind, or at public meetings', and adequate facilities were to be given to Polish nationals of non-Polish speech for the use of their language, either orally or in writing, before the courts.[13] Polish nationals who belonged to racial, religious or linguistic minorities were entitled to 'establish, manage and control at their own expense ... schools and other educational establishments, with the right to use their own language and to exercise their religion freely therein'.[14] In towns and districts in which a considerable proportion of the citizens spoke minority languages, the Treaty provided that 'adequate facilities for ensuring that in the primary schools the instruction

States not bound by any legal obligations to the League with respect to minorities would nevertheless observe in the treatment of their own racial, religious or linguistic minorities 'at least as high a standard of justice and toleration as is required by any of the treaties': see Evans, *ibid.*, 121.

[8] Treaty of Peace with Poland ('Polish Minorities Treaty'), adopted at Versailles, 28 June 1919. Treaty of Peace Between the United States of America, the British Empire, France, Italy, and Japan and Poland, reprinted in (1919) 13(4) Supplement, *American Journal of International Law* 423. See generally Theodore S. Woolsey, 'Editorial comment: the rights of minorities under the treaty with Poland' (1920) 14 *American Journal of International Law* 392.

[9] Thornberry, *International law and the rights of minorities*, p. 42.

[10] Article 2 of the Polish Minorities Treaty. Under Article 3, Poland was obliged to recognise as 'Polish nationals *ipso facto* and without requirement of any formality German, Austrian, Hungarian or Russian nationals habitually resident [in the territory of Poland]'. The application of Polish citizenship was not automatic: the relevant persons were entitled to 'opt for any other nationality which may be open to them'. Where an individual did opt for another citizenship, they were required to 'transfer within the succeeding twelve months their place of residence to the State for which they have opted': *ibid.*

[11] Article 2, *ibid.*

[12] Article 7, *ibid.* 'Differences of religion, creed or confession shall not prejudice any Polish national in matters relating to the enjoyment of civil or political rights, as for instance admission to public employments, functions and honours, or the exercise of professions and industries': Article 7, *ibid.*

[13] Article 7, *ibid.*   [14] Article 8, *ibid.*

shall be given to the children of such Polish nationals through the medium of their own language'.[15]

The United Nations era

The limited protection afforded under the League system ended in the immediate aftermath of the Second World War – a consequence of the fundamental change of circumstances between 1939 and 1947.[16] The United Nations Charter makes no specific mention of minorities. The emphasis is on individual human rights.[17] The Universal Declaration of Human Rights, adopted by the General Assembly on 10 December 1948, recognises the human rights to equality,[18] freedoms of thought, conscience and religion,[19] opinion and expression,[20] association,[21] freedom of choice in the education of children,[22] and the freedom to 'participate in the cultural life of the [but not 'their'] community'.[23] The Declaration does not contain a provision directly concerning minorities.[24] According to the General Assembly, it was considered 'difficult to adopt a uniform solution of this complex and delicate question, which has special aspects in each State in which it arises'. Given the 'universal character of the Declaration of Human

---

[15] Article 9, *ibid.*

[16] See UN Secretariat, 'Study of the legal validity of the undertakings concerning minorities', UN Doc. E/CN.4/367, 7 April 1950, referred to in Kunz, 'The present status of international law for the protection of minorities', 284. On the collapse of the minority protection system under the League of Nations, see Berman, 'But the alternative is despair', 1901.

[17] See Charter of the United Nations, adopted 26 June 1945, in force 24 October 1945, preamble, and Articles 1(3), 13(1)(b), 55(c), 62(2), 68 and 76(c).

[18] Articles 2 and 7 of GA Res. 217 (III) A, adopted 10 December 1948, 'Universal Declaration of Human Rights'.

[19] Article 18, *ibid.*   [20] Article 19, *ibid.*   [21] Article 20(1), *ibid.*   [22] Article 26(3), *ibid.*

[23] Article 27(1), *ibid.*

[24] A proposal to include the following 'minorities' clause was rejected: 'In States inhabited by a substantial number of persons of a race, language or religion other than those of the majority of the population, persons belonging to such ethnic, linguistic or religious minorities shall have the right, as far as compatible with public order and security to establish and maintain schools and cultural or religious institutions and to use their own language in the Press, in public assembly and before the courts and other authorities of the State'. See Report Submitted to the Commission on Human Rights, UN ESCOR, Commission on Human Rights, 1st Session, at 13, UN Doc. E/CN.4/52 (1947), referred to in Johannes Morsink, 'Cultural genocide, the Universal Declaration, and minority rights' (1999) 21 *Human Rights Quarterly* 1009, 1017–18. See generally Thornberry, *International law and the rights of minorities*, chapter 13.

Rights', it was decided 'not to deal in a specific provision with the question of minorities'.[25]

The International Covenants

The human rights recognised in the Universal Declaration were given legal force in the International Covenant on Civil and Political Rights and the International Covenant on Economic, Social and Cultural Rights, adopted by the General Assembly on 16 December 1966.[26] The rights in the Covenants are to be enjoyed by all individuals 'without distinction of any kind', included on grounds such as race, colour, language and religion.[27] The International Covenant on Economic, Social and Cultural Rights recognises the rights to work,[28] to social security[29] and to an adequate standard of living,[30] and requires that the 'widest possible protection and assistance should be accorded to the family'.[31] Article 15 recognises the right of everyone to 'take part in cultural life'.[32] Culture includes the idea of culture as a way of life.[33] The provision requires States parties to take measures to preserve and foster minority and indigenous cultures.[34]

The International Covenant on Civil and Political Rights provides: 'All persons are equal before the law and are entitled without any discrimination to the equal protection of the law.'[35] States parties are required to prohibit, by law, any discrimination, and to guarantee to all persons equal and effective protection against discrimination on any ground such as race, colour, sex, language, religion and national

---

[25] GA Res. 217 (III) C, adopted 10 December 1948, 'Fate of Minorities'.

[26] GA Res. 2200A (XXI), adopted 16 December 1966, 'International Covenant on Economic, Social and Cultural Rights, International Covenant on Civil and Political Rights and Optional Protocol to the International Covenant on Civil and Political Rights'. International Covenant on Economic, Social and Cultural Rights, in force 3 January 1976; International Covenant on Civil and Political Rights, in force 23 March 1976.

[27] See Article 2(1) of the International Covenant on Civil and Political Rights, and Article 2(2) of the International Covenant on Economic, Social and Cultural Rights.

[28] Article 6(1) of the International Covenant on Economic, Social and Cultural Rights.

[29] Article 9, *ibid.*   [30] Article 11(1), *ibid.*   [31] Article 10(1), *ibid.*   [32] Article 15(1)(a), *ibid.*

[33] Roger O'Keefe, 'The right to take part in cultural life under Article 15 of the ICESCR' (1998) 47 *International and Comparative Law Quarterly* 904, 916–17.

[34] *Ibid.*, 918. The International Covenant on Economic, Social and Cultural Rights does not proscribe the promotion of a distinctive national (i.e. State) identity, by for example limiting the influence of foreign media and multi-national corporations, or the funding of particular cultural activities and events, or recognising as public holidays the important religious days of the dominant/majority religion: *ibid.*, 917.

[35] Article 26 of the International Covenant on Civil and Political Rights.

origin.[36] A number of rights in the International Covenant are of direct importance to persons belonging to minorities: the right to be informed 'in a language which he understands' of the nature and cause of a criminal charge;[37] the right to have the free assistance of an interpreter 'if he cannot understand or speak the language used in court';[38] and the right of every individual not to be subject to arbitrary or unlawful interference with their privacy, family or home.[39] Further, all persons enjoy the rights to freedom of religion,[40] expression,[41] and association.[42] The enjoyment of these rights may be restricted only on specific and limited grounds.[43]

The International Covenant on Civil and Political Rights recognises the liberty of parents 'to ensure the religious and moral education of their children in conformity with their own convictions'.[44] This right is contained in a number of international human rights documents and may be regarded as a rule of general international law.[45] Children may

---

[36] *Ibid.*

[37] Article 14(3)(a) of the International Covenant on Civil and Political Rights.

[38] Article 14(3)(f), *ibid.* This is not a minority right. Article 14 'is concerned with procedural equality; it enshrines, inter alia, the principle of equality of arms in criminal proceedings'. There is no obligation to provide an interpreter where a person is 'capable of understanding and expressing himself or herself adequately in the official language': *Barzhig* v. *France*, Communication No. 327/1988, UN Doc. CCPR/C/41/D/327/1988, 6 May 1991, para. 5.5.

[39] Article 17(2) of the International Covenant on Civil and Political Rights.

[40] Article 18(1), *ibid.*   [41] Article 19(2), *ibid.*   [42] Article 22(1), *ibid.*

[43] See, for example, Articles 18(3), 19(3), 21 and 22(2), *ibid.* The International Court of Justice has pointed out that it is 'not sufficient that such restrictions be directed to the ends authorized; they must also be necessary for the attainment of those ends ... ' [They] 'must conform to the principle of proportionality' and 'must be the least intrusive instrument amongst those which might achieve the desired result': *Legal Consequences of the Construction of a Wall in the Occupied Palestinian Territory*, International Court of Justice, Advisory Opinion, 9 July 2004, 43 ILM (2004) 1009, para. 136.

[44] Article 18(4) of the International Covenant on Civil and Political Rights.

[45] See Article 26(3) of the Universal Declaration of Human Rights (1948); Article 13(3) of the International Covenant on Economic, Social and Cultural Rights; Article 14(2) of the American Convention on Human Rights, adopted 22 November 1969, in force 18 July 1978, 1114 UNTS 123; Article 2 of the Protocol to the Convention for the Protection of Human Rights and Fundamental Freedoms, adopted at Paris, 20 March 1952, in force 18 May 1954, ETS No. 9; Article 17 of the African Charter on Human and Peoples' Rights, adopted at Nairobi, 27 June 1981, in force 21 October 1986, 21 ILM (1982) 58; Article 5(1)(b) of the Convention against Discrimination in Education, adopted by the General Conference of the United Nations Educational, Scientific and Cultural Organization, 14 December 1960, in force 22 May 1962; and Article 5(2) of GA Res. 36/55, adopted 25 November 1981, 'Declaration on the Elimination of All Forms of Intolerance and of Discrimination Based on Religion or Belief'. See also Articles 3(1), 5, 12(1), 14 and 29

not be inculcated into a value system against the wishes of their parents.[46] A complementary right is recognised in the International Covenant on Economic, Social and Cultural Rights: parents may establish private educational institutions, provided that they comply with international and national educational standards.[47] There is no obligation for States parties to fund minority schools.[48]

Language and religion are the key signifiers of ethno-cultural difference. Any interference with the practice of speaking a minority language would be likely to infringe the right to freedom of expression,[49] in particular when read with the non-discrimination provision.[50] The potential grounds for limiting the exercise of the right[51] could not justify a prohibition on the teaching and learning of a minority language.[52] The State may prescribe one (or more) official or working language(s) for the State, but it may not dictate the language(s) to be used in the wider public sphere.[53] No obligation for the State to communicate with individuals in their own language is recognised, although an instruction to civil

of the Convention on the Rights of the Child, adopted by General Assembly Resolution 44/25, 20 November 1989, in force 2 September 1990.

[46] See, for example, Article 5(2) of GA Res. 36/55, adopted 25 November 1981, 'Declaration on the Elimination of All Forms of Intolerance and of Discrimination Based on Religion or Belief': the child 'shall not be compelled to receive teaching on religion or belief against the wishes of his parents . . . , the best interests of the child being the guiding principle'.

[47] See Articles 13(3) and (4) of the International Covenant on Economic, Social and Cultural Rights; Article 29(2) of the Convention on the Rights of the Child; and Article 5(1)(b) of the UNESCO Convention Against Discrimination in Education. The Convention Against Discrimination in Education recognises the right of members of national minorities to maintain their own schools, including the possibility of the using of, or the teaching in, the minority language: Article 5(1)(c), ibid.

[48] See also Committee on Economic, Social and Cultural Rights, General Comment No. 13, 'The Right to Education (Article 13)', adopted 8 December 1999, reprinted in 'Compilation of General Comments and General Recommendations adopted by human rights treaty bodies', UN Doc. HRI/GEN/1/Rev.7, 12 May 2004 (hereafter 'Compilation of General Comments and General Recommendations'), p. 71, para. 30.

[49] Article 19 of the International Covenant on Civil and Political Rights.

[50] Article 2(1), ibid. See also Article 26, which provides for a prohibition on discrimination, inter alia, on the ground of 'language'. Cf. S.G. v. France, Communication No. 347/1988, UN Doc. CCPR/C/43/D/347/1988, 15 November 1991, para. 5.2.

[51] The exercise of the rights to freedom of expression may 'be subject to certain restrictions, but these shall only be such as are provided by law and are necessary . . . (b) For the protection of national security or of public order (ordre public), or of public health or morals': Article 19(3), ibid.

[52] See also the non-discrimination provisions: Articles 2(1) and 26 of the International Covenant on Civil and Political Rights.

[53] 'A State may choose one or more official languages, but it may not exclude, outside the spheres of public life, the freedom to express oneself in a language of one's

servants not to communicate with individuals in a minority language (where they are capable of doing so) constitutes a violation of the non-discrimination provision (Article 26).[54]

Article 18 of the International Covenant on Civil and Political Rights recognises that everyone has the right to freedom of thought, conscience and religion.[55] The right to freedom of religion may be subject only to such limitations as are 'prescribed by law and are necessary to protect public safety, order, health, or morals or the fundamental rights and freedoms of others'.[56] The right includes the freedom, 'individually or in community with others and in public or private, to manifest his religion or belief in worship, observance, practice and teaching'.[57] In its General Comment on Article 18, the Human Rights Committee determined that the right to freedom of religion extends to the protection of ritual and ceremonial acts giving expression to religious belief, the building of places of worship, the use of ritual formulae and objects, the display of symbols, and the observance of holidays and days of rest. The right further extends to such customs as the observance of dietary regulations, the wearing of distinctive clothing or head coverings, and the use of a particular language customarily spoken by a group.[58]

Article 27 of the International Covenant on Civil and Political Rights

The effective guarantee of economic, social and cultural rights and civil and political rights is essential for the protection of the rights of persons belonging to minorities. These human rights are available to all persons, 'without distinction of any kind'.[59] Further, all persons

choice': *Ballantyne and Davidson, and McIntyre* v. *Canada*, Communication Nos. 359/1989 and 385/1989, UN Doc. CCPR/C/47/D/359/1989, 5 May 1993, para. 11.4.

[54] *Diergaardt et al.* v. *Namibia*, Communication No. 760/1997, UN Doc. CCPR/C/69/D/760/1996, 6 September 2000, para. 10.10.

[55] Article 18(1) of the International Covenant on Civil and Political Rights.

[56] Article 18(3), *ibid*. Human Rights Committee, General Comment No. 22, 'The Right to Freedom of Thought, Conscience and Religion (Article 18)', adopted 30 July 1993, reprinted in 'Compilation of General Comments and General Recommendations', p. 155, para. 8.

[57] Article 18(1), *ibid*. See also Article 18(2): 'No one shall be subject to coercion which would impair his freedom to have or to adopt a religion or belief of his choice.'

[58] See generally Human Rights Committee, General Comment No. 22, 'The Right to Freedom of Thought, Conscience and Religion', para. 4. See, for example, *Clement Boodoo* v. *Trinidad and Tobago*, Communication No. 721/1996, UN Doc. CCPR/C/74/D/721/1996, 2 April 2002, para. 6.6.

[59] Article 2(2) of the International Covenant on Economic, Social and Cultural Rights, and Article 2(1) of the International Covenant on Civil and Political Rights.

are 'equal before the law and are entitled without any discrimination to the equal protection of the law'.[60] The major innovation of the International Covenant on Civil and Political Rights was the recognition, in Article 27, of the rights of persons belonging to minorities beyond the issues of individual moral autonomy and the non-discrimination norm:

In those States in which ethnic, religious or linguistic minorities exist, persons belonging to such minorities shall not be denied the right, in community with the other members of their group, to enjoy their own culture, to profess and practise their own religion, or to use their own language.

The formulation is repeated in a number of international human rights instruments,[61] and may be regarded as a rule of general international law.[62] This is the position of the Human Rights Committee.[63] It is more difficult to argue that Article 27 reflects a peremptory norm of

---

[60] Article 26 of the International Covenant on Civil and Political Rights.

[61] See Article 30 of the Convention on the Rights of the Child; Vienna Declaration and Programme of Action (1993), ILM 32 (1993) 1661, para. I(19); and Article 2(1), GA Res. 47/135, 'Declaration on the Rights of Persons Belonging to National or Ethnic, Religious and Linguistic Minorities', adopted 18 December 1992.

[62] Yoram Dinstein, 'Collective human rights of minorities' (1976) 25 *International and Comparative Law Quarterly* 102, 118. See also S. James Anaya, 'The capacity of international law to advance ethnic or nationality rights claims' (1990) 75 *Iowa Law Review* 837, 841. See also Inter-American Commission on Human Rights, Resolution No. 12/85, Case No. 7615, 5 March 1985, reprinted in 'The Human Rights Situation of the Indigenous People in the Americas', OAS, IACHR, OEA/Ser.L/V/II.108, 20 October 2000, p. 131, at p. 136: 'That international law in its present state, and as it is found clearly expressed in Article 27, International Covenant on Civil and Political Rights, recognizes the right of ethnic groups to special protection on their use of their own language, for the practice of their own religion, and, in general, for all those characteristics necessary for the preservation of their cultural identity.' Cf. Patrick Thornberry, *International law and the rights of minorities*, p. 246.

[63] Human Rights Committee, General Comment No. 24, 'Issues Relating to Reservations Made upon Ratification or Accession to the Covenant or the Optional Protocols Thereto, or in Relation to Declarations under Article 41 of the Covenant', adopted 4 November 1994, reprinted in 'Compilation of General Comments and General Recommendations', p. 161, para. 8. Cf. Human Rights Committee, General Comment No. 29, 'Derogations During a State of Emergency (Article 4)', adopted 31 August 2001, reprinted in 'Compilation of General Comments and General Recommendations', p. 184, para. 13(c): 'The Committee is of the opinion that the international protection of the rights of persons belonging to minorities includes *elements* that must be respected in all circumstances. This is reflected in the prohibition against genocide in international law, in the inclusion of a non-discrimination clause in Article 4 itself (paragraph 1), as well as in the non-derogable nature of Article 18 [concerning the right to freedom of thought, conscience and religion]' (emphasis added).

international law:[64] 'a norm accepted and recognized by the international community of States as a whole as a norm from which no derogation is permitted.'[65] Upon accession to the International Covenant, France declared that: '[A]rticle 27 is not applicable so far as the Republic is concerned.' The declaration was not objected to by other States parties.[66] The Human Rights Committee concluded that the declaration constituted a valid reservation, and that it was 'not competent to consider complaints directed against France concerning alleged violations of Article 27 of the Covenant'.[67]

In its General Comment on Article 27, the Human Rights Committee confirmed that the 'minorities' provision of the International Covenant on Civil and Political Rights establishes and recognises a right which is conferred on individuals belonging to minority groups, and 'which is distinct from, and additional to, all the other rights which, as individuals in common with everyone else, they are already entitled to enjoy under the Covenant'.[68] The following sections consider the content and scope of Article 27, drawing on the General Comments and Opinions of the Human Rights Committee, a body recognised as providing an authoritative interpretation of State party commitments under the International Covenant.[69]

---

[64] Cf. Conference on Yugoslavia Arbitration Commission: Opinions on Questions Arising from the Dissolution of Yugoslavia, 31 ILM 1488 (1992), Opinion No. 1, para. 1(e), which refers to the 'rights of peoples and minorities' as 'peremptory norms of general international law'.

[65] Article 53 of the Vienna Convention on the Law of Treaties, adopted 23 May 1969, in force 27 January 1980, 1155 UNTS 331.

[66] *H.K.* v. *France*, Communication No. 222/1987, UN Doc. CCPR/C/37/D/222/1987, 8 December 1989, para. 8.5.

[67] *Ibid.*, para. 8.6. See also the reservation of Turkey to Article 27 of the International Covenant on Civil and Political Rights. France, Turkey and Venezuela have issued reservations in respect of the 'minorities' clause (Article 30) of the Convention on the Rights of the Child. In its Concluding Observations on the State party report by France, the Committee made the following point: 'The mere fact that equal rights are granted to all individuals and that all individuals are equal before the law does not preclude the existence in fact of minorities in a country, and their entitlement to the enjoyment of their culture, the practice of their religion or the use of their language in community with other members of their group': Human Rights Committee, Concluding Observations on France, UN Doc. CCPR/C/79/Add.80, 4 August 1997, para. 24.

[68] Human Rights Committee, General Comment No. 23, 'Rights of Minorities (Article 27)', adopted 8 April 1994, reprinted in 'Compilation of General Comments and General Recommendations', p. 158, para. 1.

[69] Brad Roth, *Governmental illegitimacy in international law* (Oxford: Oxford University Press, 2000), pp. 334–5.

Minorities

In contrast to other provisions, which apply to '[e]veryone' and '[a]ll persons',[70] and which are to be enjoyed without distinction of any kind,[71] the personal scope of application of Article 27 is persons belonging to 'ethnic minorities', 'religious minorities' and/or 'linguistic minorities'. No definition of the relevant terms is provided, although their use, according to the Human Rights Committee, indicates 'that the persons designed to be protected are those who belong to a group and who share in common a culture, a religion and/or a language'.[72] Minorities are collectivities defined by ethnic, religious and/or linguistic identity.

The scope of application of Article 27 is not normally contentious in individual complaints to the Human Rights Committee under the Optional Protocol.[73] In Opinions concerning the Finnish Sami, the Committee simply notes that it is 'undisputed that the authors are members of a minority culture'.[74] In *Mahuika* v. *New Zealand*, the Committee accepted that it was 'undisputed that the authors are members of a minority [the Maori] within the meaning of Article 27 of the Covenant'.[75] *Ballantyne* v. *Canada* is the only Opinion in which the scope of application of Article 27 is directly addressed, where the Committee concluded that the English-speaking minority in Quebec could not be considered a minority for the purposes of Article 27, given that the

---

[70] Cf. Articles 1 (peoples), 6(5) (children and pregnant women), 13 (aliens), 24 (children) and 25 (citizens) of the International Covenant on Civil and Political Rights.

[71] Article 2(1), *ibid.*

[72] Human Rights Committee, General Comment No. 23, 'Rights of Minorities (Article 27)', para. 5.1.

[73] Optional Protocol to the International Covenant on Civil and Political Rights, adopted by General Assembly Resolution 2200A (XXI), 16 December 1966, in force 23 March 1976. The General Comment on Article 27 does not consider the question of definition: Human Rights Committee, General Comment No. 23, 'Rights of Minorities (Article 27)'.

[74] See *Äärelä and Näkkäläjärvi* v. *Finland*, Communication No. 779/1997, UN Doc. CCPR/C/73/D/779/1997, 7 November 2001, para. 7.5; *Länsman et al.* v. *Finland (No. 1)*, Communication No. 511/1992, UN Doc. CCPR/C/52/D/511/1992, 8 November 1994, para. 9.2; and *Länsman et al.* v. *Finland (No. 2)*, Communication No. 671/1995, UN Doc. CCPR/C/58/D/671/1995, 22 November 1996, para. 10.2. In *Kitok* v. *Sweden*, the State party accepted that the Sami 'form an ethnic minority in Sweden', and that persons belonging to this minority are entitled to protection under Article 27 of the Covenant: *Kitok* v. *Sweden*, Communication No. 197/1985, UN Doc. CCPR/C/33/D/197/1985, 10 August 1988, para. 4.2.

[75] *Mahuika et al.* v. *New Zealand*, Communication No. 547/1993, UN Doc. CCPR/C/70/D/547/1993, 15 November 2000, para. 9.3.

Anglophone community was not a minority in Canada as a whole.[76] Groups that regard themselves as indigenous peoples, such as the Sami and Maori, enjoy the protection of Article 27. Majority groups do not. Nor do groups that define themselves by reference to economic rather than cultural activities.[77]

In any consideration of the meaning of the term 'minority', reference is invariably made to the following definitions, proposed respectively by Francesco Capotorti and Jules Deschênes:

A group numerically smaller to the rest of the population of the State, in a non-dominant position, whose members – being nationals of the State – possess ethnic, religious or linguistic characteristics differing from those of the rest of the population and show, if only implicitly, a sense of solidarity, directed towards preserving their culture, traditions, religion or language.[78]

A group of citizens of a State, constituting a numerical minority and in a non-dominant position in that State, endowed with ethnic, religious or linguistic characteristics which differ from those of the majority of the population, having a sense of solidarity with one another, motivated, if only implicitly, by a collective will to survive and whose aim to achieve equality with the majority in fact and in law.[79]

The Capotorti definition is the most widely cited in the literature.[80] Patrick Thornberry has concluded that any acceptable international definition is unlikely to depart greatly from this line of approach.[81] The definitions share a number of common criteria, which may provide a framework of analysis for the concept of 'minority': (1) the relevant group constitutes a numerical minority of the population; (2) its members are in a non-dominant position; (3) they are citizens of the State; (4) they are different from the rest of the population, and these

---

[76] *Ballantyne and Davidson, and McIntyre* v. *Canada*, Communication Nos. 359/1989 and 385/1989, UN Doc. CCPR/C/47/D/359/1989, 5 May 1993, para. 11.2. The Opinion was accompanied by strong dissenting opinions and may not be followed in future Opinions of the Human Rights Committee: Patrick Thornberry, *Indigenous peoples and international law* (Manchester: Manchester University Press, 2002), p. 53.

[77] See *Diergaardt et al.* v. *Namibia*, Communication No. 760/1997, UN Doc. CCPR/C/69/D/760/1996, 25 July 2000, especially the Concurring Individual Opinion by Elizabeth Evatt and Cecilia Medina Quiroga.

[78] Francesco Capotorti, 'Study on the rights of persons belonging to ethnic, religious and linguistic minorities', UN Doc. E/CN.4/Sub.3/384/Add.1–7 (1977), para. 568.

[79] Jules Deschênes, 'Proposal concerning a definition of the term "minority"', UN Doc. E/CN.4/Sub.2/1985/31 (1985), para. 181.

[80] Patrick Thornberry, *International law and the rights of minorities*, p. 6.   [81] *Ibid.*, p. 7.

differences relate to language, religion and/or ethnicity/culture; and (5) the group manifests a sense of 'self', and a desire to maintain its difference(s) from the majority population.

Numerical size

The first issue is the question of numerical size. Capotorti refers to a 'group numerically smaller to the rest of the population of the State', Deschênes to a group 'constituting a numerical minority'. No minimum threshold is specified. The Human Rights Committee has recognised the Sami of Sweden,[82] a group comprising just 0.2 per cent of the total population,[83] as a minority for the purposes of the International Covenant on Civil and Political Rights. All ethnic, religious and linguistic minorities enjoy the protection of Article 27. Majority groups, that is, those comprising at least 50 per cent plus one of the total population, are excluded from the scope of application of the provision. It is not possible to read a provision which refers to 'persons belonging to minorities' as encompassing persons belonging to majorities.[84]

Where no group constitutes a numerical majority of the population,[85] all ethnic, religious or linguistic groups within the State, including the largest, are 'numerically smaller to the rest of the population of the State' (Capotorti). In many cases, the largest group will exercise decisive political control, and its values, practices and beliefs will determine the social culture. These groups do not need the protection of Article 27. In other cases, the culture of the largest group will not determine the social culture. There is no reason to exclude, a priori, the largest group from the protection of the right to cultural security provided in Article 27. The right of persons belonging to ethnic, religious or linguistic minorities to enjoy their own culture, to profess and practise their own religion, or to use their own language, is the right of cultural security in the face of

[82] See *Kitok* v. *Sweden*, Communication No. 197/1985, UN Doc. CCPR/C/33/D/197/1985, 10 August 1988.

[83] Minority Rights Group (ed.), *World directory of minorities* (London: Minority Rights Group International, 1997), p. 179.

[84] See Article 31(1) of the Vienna Convention on the Law of Treaties: a 'treaty shall be interpreted in good faith in accordance with the *ordinary meaning* to be given to the terms of the treaty in their context and in the light of its object and purpose' (emphasis added). The Convention represents customary international law in this respect: *Legal Consequences of the Construction of a Wall in the Occupied Palestinian Territory*, International Court of Justice, Advisory Opinion, 9 July 2004, 43 ILM (2004) 1009, para. 94.

[85] Examples include Ethiopia, Guinea-Bissau, Liberia, Angola, Cameroon, Congo, Kenya, Gabon, Malawi, Mauritania and Togo.

a dominant culture. All groups are entitled to this right to cultural security, including the largest group in the State, provided that it does not constitute a majority.

Non-dominance

Both the Capotorti and Deschênes definitions refer to groups 'in a non-dominant position'. Reference to 'non-dominance' has led to some debate, with two perspectives emerging.[86] According to some writers, the expression is taken to refer to the size of the group. Reference to 'numerically non-dominant minorities' is tautologous. It adds nothing to the debates concerning the definition of the term 'minority'. Alternately, dominance is taken to refer to economic, cultural and social domination. According to José Bengoa, 'when a minority is not in a state of dependence and subordination, it cannot be considered to be in a minority situation. The minority issue appears to be inevitably bound up with a status of inferiority in relation to the majority.'[87]

A focus on economic, cultural and/or social discrimination fails to distinguish sufficiently between racial discrimination and the position of ethno-cultural minorities. Racism involves the attachment, by others, of significance to irrelevant factors, usually with negative consequences. In the majority of cases, the criteria concern inherited, group-based, visible characteristics.[88] The International Convention on the Elimination of All Forms of Racial Discrimination is not concerned with defining the concept of 'race',[89] but with racial discrimination: discrimination on the grounds of 'race, colour, descent, or national or ethnic origin'.[90] The Convention requires that States parties 'prohibit

---

[86] See generally Eyassu Gayim, *The concept of minority in international law: a critical study of the vital elements* (Rovaniemi: University of Lapland Press, 2001), pp. 20–33.

[87] José Bengoa, 'Existence and recognition of minorities', UN Doc. E/CN.4/Sub.2/AC.5/2000/WP.2, 3 April 2000, para. 17 (reference omitted).

[88] See generally Report of the World Conference against Racism, Racial Discrimination, Xenophobia and Related Intolerance (January 25, 2002), UN Doc. A/CONF.189/5, 41 ILM (2002) 772. Racism can also include discrimination against members of communities based on forms of social stratification, such as caste and analogous systems of inherited status. See Committee on the Elimination of Racial Discrimination, 'General Recommendation XXIX, on Article 1, paragraph 1 (Descent)', adopted 1 November 2002, reprinted in 'Compilation of General Comments and General Recommendations', p. 226, preamble.

[89] Thornberry, *International law and the rights of minorities*, p. 160. See also William Schabas, *Genocide in international law* (Cambridge: Cambridge University Press, 2000), pp. 122–3.

[90] See Article 1(1) of the International Convention on the Elimination of All Forms of Racial Discrimination, adopted by GA Res. 2106 (XX), 21 December 1965, in force 4 January 1969. Racial discrimination is defined as 'any distinction, exclusion,

and bring to an end … racial discrimination by any persons, group or organization'.[91] Discrimination on the ground of race is contrary to the Charter of the United Nations.[92] It is proscribed by the United Nations' human rights instruments,[93] and the regional human rights treaties;[94] the issue is addressed in the International Convention on the Elimination of All Forms of Racial Discrimination.[95] The prohibition on discrimination on the ground of race is a rule of customary international law. It is a norm of *jus cogens*.[96]

The remedy in cases of racial discrimination is the effective application of the equality principle: equal treatment, equal respect and equal opportunities. The International Convention on the Elimination of All Forms of Racial Discrimination requires that States parties, when the circumstances so warrant, take 'special and concrete measures' for the purpose of guaranteeing the full and equal enjoyment of human rights and fundamental freedoms.[97] Special and concrete measures are introduced to facilitate the achievement of de facto equality. This must be done in conformity with the principle of proportionality in order to avoid a violation of the rights of others. Special and concrete measures must not extend, in time or scope, beyond what is necessary in order to achieve the aim of full and effective equality.[98] Their introduction may

restriction or preference … which has the purpose or effect of nullifying or impairing the recognition, enjoyment or exercise, on an equal footing, of human rights and fundamental freedoms in the political, economic, social, cultural or any other field of public life': Article 1(1), *ibid.*

[91] Article 2(1)(d) of the International Convention on the Elimination of All Forms of Racial Discrimination.

[92] One of the purposes of the United Nations is to promote and encourage respect for human rights and for fundamental freedoms for all without distinction as to race, sex, language or religion: Article 1(3) of the UN Charter (1945). See also Articles 13(1), 55 and 76(c). See GA Res. 1904 (XVIII), adopted 20 November 1963, 'United Nations Declaration on the Elimination of All Forms of Racial Discrimination'.

[93] See Articles 1 and 2 of the Universal Declaration of Human Rights (1948). Also, Articles 2 and 26 of the International Covenant on Civil and Political Rights.

[94] See Article 2 of the African Charter on Human and Peoples' Rights (1981); Article 1(1) of the American Convention on Human Rights (1969); and Article 14 of the Convention for the Protection of Human Rights and Fundamental Freedoms (as amended), adopted at Rome, 4 November 1950, in force 3 September 1953, ETS No. 5, and Protocol No. 12 to the Convention for the Protection of Human Rights and Fundamental Freedoms, adopted at Rome, 4 November 2000, in force 1 April 2005, ETS No. 177.

[95] International Convention on the Elimination of All Forms of Racial Discrimination.

[96] Maurizio Ragazzi, *The concept of international obligations erga omnes* (Oxford: Clarendon Press; 1997), p. 120.

[97] Article 2(2) of the International Convention on the Elimination of All Forms of Racial Discrimination.

[98] Article 1(4), *ibid.*

'in no case entail as a consequence the maintenance of unequal or separate rights for different racial groups after the objectives for which they were taken have been achieved'.[99]

The recognition of 'minority rights' does not seek to eliminate difference, but to maintain (cultural) difference. The demand for different treatment is not made by the dominant/majority population ('racial discrimination'), but by the minorities themselves. Persons belonging to minorities are aware of their differences to the dominant/majority cultural group, and they wish to maintain those differences. They are minorities by choice.[100] The basis of any legal regime for the protection of minorities is the concurrent recognition of the right of persons belonging to minorities to full equality with members of the majority, and their right to preserve their separate identity.[101] The right to equality is recognised in the international instruments concerning minorities,[102] national minorities[103] and indigenous populations.[104] It is implicit in the right of peoples to self-determination.[105] The primary concern of the international instruments concerning ethno-cultural groups is not, however, the recognition of the equality principle, but the recognition of difference.

The International Covenant on Civil and Political Rights provides that: 'All persons are equal before the law and are entitled without any discrimination to the equal protection of the law.'[106] Additionally, the International Covenant recognises that persons belonging to

---

[99] Article 2(2), *ibid*.

[100] See Thornberry, *International law and the rights of minorities*, pp. 9–10; and John Packer, 'Problems in defining minorities', in Bill Bowring and Deidre Fottrell (eds.), *Minority and group rights in the new millennium* (The Hague: Martinus Nijhoff, 1999), p. 223, at p. 254.

[101] Yoram Dinstein, 'Collective human rights of minorities' (1976) 25 *International and Comparative Law Quarterly* 102, 116.

[102] Article 4(1) of GA Res. 47/135, adopted 18 December 1992, 'Declaration on the Rights of Persons belonging to National or Ethnic, Religious and Linguistic Minorities'.

[103] Article 4(1) of the Framework Convention for the Protection of National Minorities, adopted at Strasbourg, 1 February 1995, in force 1 February 1998, ETS No. 157.

[104] Article 3(1) of the Indigenous and Tribal Peoples Convention (1989) (No. 169), adopted by the General Conference of the International Labour Organization, 27 June 1989, in force 5 September 1991.

[105] The right of self-determination recognises a right of all citizens to participate in the government of the State on the basis of equality: James Crawford, 'State practice and international law in relation to secession' (1998) 69 *British Year Book of International Law* 85, 113–14.

[106] Article 26 of the International Covenant on Civil and Political Rights. See also Article 2(1), *ibid*.

minorities enjoy the right 'to enjoy their own culture, to profess and practise their own religion, or to use their own language'.[107] The Human Rights Committee, in its General Comment on Article 27, commented: 'Some States parties who claim that they do not discriminate on grounds of ethnicity, language or religion, wrongly contend, on that basis alone, that they have no minorities.'[108] The absence of ('racial') discrimination does not preclude the recognition of groups as (ethnic, religious and/or linguistic) minorities for the purposes of Article 27. 'Dominance', in the sense of economic, cultural and/or social discrimination, is not relevant in defining the term minority. Where an ethno-cultural group manifests a distinct cultural identity, it is a minority for the purposes of Article 27.

The inclusion of 'non-dominance' in the definition of minorities denies racist minority governments, such as the apartheid regime in South Africa (1948 to 1990/1), any potential claim to legitimacy from the international instruments concerned with the protection of minorities. The rights of persons belonging to minorities form one part of the international human rights regime recognised in the International Covenant on Civil and Political Rights. These rights may not be exercised 'in a manner or to an extent inconsistent with the other provisions of the [International Covenant]'.[109] The systematic oppression and domination of the members of one group by those of another is not compatible with the International Covenant. If reference to non-dominance is required in any definition of the term minority, it is to be understood in relation to a dominant social culture: persons belonging to a minority group that defines the dominant social culture have no requirement for the introduction of positive measures to protect their ethno-cultural identity. Nonetheless, the group is a minority for the purposes of Article 27, and persons belonging to this group have the right to enjoy their own culture, to profess and practise their own religion, or to use their own language.

---

[107] Article 27, *ibid.*

[108] Human Rights Committee, General Comment No. 23, 'Rights of minorities (Article 27)', para. 4

[109] *Ibid.*, para. 8. See also Human Rights Committee, General Comment No. 04, 'Equal right of men and women to the enjoyment of all civil and political rights (Article 3)', adopted 30 July 1981, reprinted in 'Compilation of General Comments and General Recommendations', p. 127, paras. 5 and 32; also, Article 4(2) of GA Res. 47/135, adopted 18 December 1992, 'Declaration on the Rights of Persons belonging to National or Ethnic, Religious and Linguistic Minorities'.

Citizenship

The Capotorti definition refers to a 'group ... whose members [are] nationals of the State'. Deschênes' definition refers to a 'group of citizens of a State'. The terms 'national' and 'citizen' are coterminous for these purposes. Where some, but not all, of the members of a particular group are not citizens, it is not clear whether the group should be denied recognition as a minority, or whether those members of the group who are not citizens should be excluded from the personal scope of application of Article 27.[110] Either interpretation would be contrary to the object and purpose of the International Covenant on Civil and Political Rights: the protection of the cultural security of persons belonging to minorities in States parties.

The rationale for restricting the scope of application of Article 27 to citizens is not clear in an age of universal minority rights protection.[111] For John Packer, the definition of a minority group is inextricably linked to the democratic principle: a minority is 'a group of people who freely associate for an established purpose where their shared desire differs from that expressed by the majority rule'.[112] The rights of political

---

[110] The Advisory Committee on the Framework Convention has noted that a restriction on the personal scope of application of the Framework Convention for the Protection of National Minorities to citizens would, in all likelihood, exclude some but not all of the members of a particular national minority, 'creating arbitrary or unjustified distinctions within these minorities': Opinion on Sweden, ACFC/INF/OPI(2003)006, para. 16.

[111] The regime of the League of Nations often concerned minorities in one State who shared an ethno-cultural identity with the majority/titular population of a neighbouring State. The loyalties of persons belonging to minorities were expected to lie with the State of which they were citizens, and not the neighbouring State. The Third Assembly of the League of Nations noted the duty of minorities to 'co-operate as loyal fellow-citizens with the nations to which they now belong': reprinted in Ifor Evans, 'The protection of minorities' (1923/4) 4 British Year Book of International Law 95, 120. Cf. UN Secretariat, 'Definition and classification of minorities', UN Doc. E/CN.4/Sub.2/85, 27 December 1949, referred to in Josef Kunz, 'The present status of international law for the protection of minorities' (1954) 48 American Journal of International Law 282, 286.

[112] John Packer, 'On the definition of minorities', in John Packer and Kristian Myntti (eds.), The protection of ethnic and linguistic minorities in Europe (Turku/Åbo: Institute for Human Rights, Åbo Akademi University, 1993), p. 23, at p. 45. In later writings, Packer makes clear that he is concerned with issues concerning human dignity and individual identity, and not all 'minorities' in a democratic State: John Packer, 'Problems in defining minorities', p. 272. Cf. Eric Heinze, 'The construction and contingency of the minority concept', in Bill Bowring and Deidre Fottrell (eds.), Minority and group rights in the new millennium (The Hague: Martinus Nijhoff, 1999), p. 25.

participation, contained in Article 25 of the International Covenant on Civil and Political Rights, are restricted to citizens, ipso facto, the rights of minorities, reflected in Article 27, may only be enjoyed by citizens.[113] Minorities exist, however, in States that cannot be regarded as democratic, and where the principle of majority rule is not recognised. Moreover, whilst citizenship is a relevant criterion when determining rights of political participation, the framework of rights and responsibilities that emerges from the process of political deliberation is applied to all individuals within the territory of a State party and/or subject to its jurisdiction 'without distinction of any kind', inter alia, on grounds such as race, language, religion, national origin, birth or other status.[114]

The International Covenant refers variously to 'anyone', including references to 'everyone' and 'no one',[115] and 'any person', or 'all persons'.[116] The expressions 'everyone' and 'all persons' both refer to natural legal persons.[117] Article 27 refers to 'persons' belonging to minorities. It is to be interpreted in accordance with the ordinary meaning to be given to the term 'person'. Neither the text of Article 27, nor the object and purpose of the International Covenant, admits an interpretation to exclude non-citizens. The Human Rights Committee, in its General Comment on Article 27, is clear on the issue: a State party may not 'restrict the rights under Article 27 to its citizens alone'.[118] Citizenship is not a relevant criterion in determining the scope of the

---

[113] John Packer, 'Problems in defining minorities', p. 266.

[114] Article 2(1) of the International Covenant on Civil and Political Rights.

[115] Articles 6–9, 11, 12, 14–19 and 22 of the International Covenant on Civil and Political Rights.

[116] Articles 2, 10, 14–16 and 26 of the International Covenant on Civil and Political Rights. In contrast, Article 13 refers to the right of an 'alien' lawfully residing in the State to be expelled only in accordance with the law following a decision by a competent authority.

[117] Article 7, for example, provides that 'No one' shall be subjected to torture; Article 10 that 'All persons' deprived of their liberty shall be treated with humanity. Article 16 of the International Covenant on Civil and Political Rights provides that '*Everyone* shall have the right to recognition everywhere as a *person* before the law' (emphasis added). See Article 1(2) of the American Convention on Human Rights: 'For the purposes of this Convention, "person" means every human being.'

[118] Human Rights Committee, General Comment No. 23, 'Rights of minorities (Article 27)', para. 5.1. See also Human Rights Committee, General Comment No. 15, 'The position of aliens under the Covenant', adopted 11 April 1986, reprinted in 'Compilation of General Comments and General Recommendations', p. 140, para. 7: 'where aliens constitute a minority within the meaning of Article 27, [they shall not be denied the protection of the provision].'

application of Article 27, and no reading of the International Covenant can support such a restrictive understanding.

'Ethnic', 'religious' and 'linguistic' minorities

The personal scope of application of Article 27 concerns persons belonging to ethnic, religious or linguistic minorities. There is no great controversy regarding the definition of religious minorities and linguistic minorities.[119] A linguistic group is one whose members share a common language, and a religious group is one whose members share the same religion, denomination or mode of worship.[120] There may be questions concerning the distinction between languages and dialects,[121] and controversies regarding the emergence of new religious movements,[122] but language and religion are generally regarded as the more objective signifiers of group difference. More difficult is the identification of ethnic minorities.[123] José Bengoa explains:

[I]t is often not easy to make ethnic differentiations between human groups ... In anthropology, ethnic values come somewhere between purely racial and entirely cultural values, between the physical, genetic features of human populations and characteristics derived from cultural activity, history and the imaginative and constructive behaviour of human beings. Ethnic values, then, comprise a set of customs, traditions, cultural expressions and collective history that forms a network of links conferring a special identity on a particular human group. Usually those values are accompanied by a specific language and religion. Not infrequently there are also physical features, even if these are not merely racial.[124]

An ethnic group is a group of persons, 'predominantly of common descent, who think of themselves as collectively possessing a separate identity based ... on shared cultural characteristics, usually language

---

[119] See Thornberry, *International law and the rights of minorities*, pp. 161–3.

[120] See, for example, albeit in a different context, *Prosecutor* v. *Akayesu*, International Criminal Tribunal for Rwanda, judgment, 2 September 1998, Case No. ICTR-96-4-T, 37 ILM (1998) 1399, para. 515.

[121] See, for example, Article 1(a)(ii) of the European Charter for Regional or Minority Languages, adopted at Strasbourg, 5 November 1992, in force 1 March 1998, ETS No. 148.

[122] Human Rights Committee, General Comment No. 22, 'The right to freedom of thought, conscience and religion (Article 18)', adopted 30 July 1993, reprinted in 'Compilation of General Comments and General Recommendations', p. 155, para. 2.

[123] Cf. *Prosecutor* v. *Akayesu*, para. 513: 'An ethnic group is generally defined as a group whose members share a common language or culture.'

[124] José Bengoa, 'Existence and recognition of minorities', UN Doc. E/CN.4/Sub.2/AC.5/ 2000/WP.2, 3 April 2000, para. 42.

or religion'.[125] Persons belonging to ethnic, religious or linguistic minorities may share some distinctive physical features, but it is the cultural differences which are relevant in distinguishing the members of one ethnic group from another.[126] Rodolfo Stavenhagen explains the idea of culture:

[T]he *sum total of the material and spiritual activities and products of a given social group which distinguishes it from other similar groups*. Thus understood, culture is also seen as a coherent self-contained *system of values, and symbols as well as a set of practices* that a specific cultural group reproduces over time and which provides individuals with the required signposts and meanings for behaviour and social relationships in everyday life.[127]

In the context of Article 27, ethnicity is understood in terms of cultural difference, given the syntax of the provision, 'which literally relates enjoyment of culture to the ethnic group'.[128] The Human Rights Committee has observed that 'culture manifests itself in many forms, including a particular way of life associated with the use of land resources, especially in the case of indigenous peoples'.[129] The concept of culture includes,[130] but is not restricted to, traditional

---

[125] Vernon Van Dyke, 'The individual, the state and ethnic communities in political theory', in Will Kymlicka (ed.), *The rights of minority cultures* (Oxford: Oxford University Press, 1995), p. 31, at p. 32. See also Eyassu Gayim, *The concept of minority in international law: a critical study of the vital elements* (Rovaniemi: University of Lapland Press, 2001), p. 42.

[126] See Perry Keller, 'Re-thinking ethnic and cultural rights in Europe' (1998) 18 *Oxford Journal of Legal Studies* 29, 36. See also Shaheen Mozaffar and James Scarritt, 'Why territorial autonomy is not a viable option for managing ethnic conflict in African plural societies', in William Safran and Ramón Máiz (eds.), *Identity and territorial autonomy in plural societies* (London: Frank Cass, 2000), p. 230, at p. 232.

[127] Rodolfo Stavenhagen, 'Cultural rights: a social science perspective', in Halina Niec (ed.), *Cultural rights and wrongs* (Paris: UNESCO Publishing, 1998), p. 1, at p. 5 (emphasis in original). Culture can also refer to 'culture as capital', the accumulated material heritage of mankind or particular groups, exemplified by monument and artefacts, or 'culture as creativity', the process and products of artistic and scientific creation: Stavenhagen, *ibid.* See also Keller, 'Re-thinking ethnic and cultural rights in Europe', 36.

[128] Thornberry, *International law and the rights of minorities*, p. 161. Article 27 of the International Covenant on Civil and Political Rights: 'persons belonging to [*ethnic, religious* or *linguistic*] minorities shall not be denied the right, in community with the other members of their group, to enjoy their own *culture*, to profess and practise their own religion, or to use their own language' (emphasis added).

[129] Human Rights Committee, General Comment No. 23, 'Rights of minorities (Article 27)', para. 7.

[130] '[M]inorities or indigenous groups have a right to the protection of traditional activities such as hunting, fishing or, as in the instant case, reindeer

cultures.[131] Culture, according to Jeremy Waldron, is 'an enduring array of social practices, substituting as a way of life for a whole people'.[132] Differences of language,[133] and religion,[134] are the primary indicia of culture difference.

Self-consciousness

Article 27 of the International Covenant on Civil and Political Rights provides a right of cultural security for minority groups. The provision recognises the rights of persons belonging to minorities to enjoy their own culture, to profess and practise their own religion, and/or to use their own language (or at least that the rights 'shall not be denied'). For a group to be recognised as a minority, (some of) its members must manifest a desire for the continued existence of the group as a distinct cultural entity. The group must 'show, if only implicitly, a sense of solidarity, directed towards preserving their culture, traditions, religion or language' (Capotorti).[135]

husbandry': *Länsman et al.* v. *Finland (No. 1)*, Communication No. 511/1992, UN Doc. CCPR/C/52/D/511/1992, 8 November 1994, para. 9.5.

[131] Forms of traditional culture include language, literature, music, dance, games, mythology, rituals, customs, handicrafts, architecture and other arts: see UNESCO Recommendation on the Safeguarding of Traditional Culture and Folklore, adopted by the General Conference of the United Nations Educational, Scientific and Cultural Organization, 15 November 1989, para. A. See also UNESCO Convention for the Safeguarding of the Intangible Cultural Heritage, adopted by the General Conference of the United Nations Educational, Scientific and Cultural Organization, 17 October 2003.

[132] Jeremy Waldron, 'Cultural identity and civic responsibility', in Will Kymlicka and Wayne Norman (eds.), *Citizenship in diverse societies* (Oxford: Oxford University Press, 2000), p. 155, at p. 160.

[133] Thornberry, *International law and the rights of minorities*, p. 163. See also Donald Horowitz, *Ethnic groups in conflict* (Berkeley: University of California Press, 1985), p. 219; and Will Kymlicka, 'Western political theory and ethnic relations in Eastern Europe', in Will Kymlicka and Magda Opalski (eds.), *Can liberal pluralism be exported? Western political theory and ethnic relations in Eastern Europe* (Oxford: Oxford University Press, 2001), p. 13, at p. 18.

[134] Marta Reynal-Querol, 'Ethnicity, political systems, and civil wars' (2002) 46 *Journal of Conflict Resolution* 29, 32. See also Geoff Gilbert, 'Religious minorities and their rights: a problem of approach' (1997) 5 *International Journal on Minority and Group Rights* 97, 99. GA Res. 36/55, adopted 25 November 1981, 'Declaration on the Elimination of All Forms of Intolerance and of Discrimination Based on Religion or Belief', preamble: 'religion or belief, for anyone who professes either, is one of the fundamental elements in his conception of life.'

[135] Deschênes refers to a group 'having a sense of solidarity with one another, motivated, if only implicitly, by a collective will to survive and whose aim to achieve equality with the majority in fact and in law'. See also Philip Vuciri Ramaga, 'The group concept in minority protection' (1993) 15 *Human Rights Quarterly* 575, 583.

Article 27 does not prohibit, or exclude the possibility of, the voluntary assimilation of members of minority groups into the dominant/majority culture.[136] Groups of individuals whose ambition is to assimilate into a dominant culture are not minorities for the purposes of Article 27. Assimilation is a process by which individuals who are not members of a dominant/majority group adopt its values, beliefs and practices. Forced assimilation, the banning of the linguistic, religious and cultural practices of minority groups, is proscribed in the international instruments concerning minorities.[137] International law does not prohibit policies of integration,[138] provided that they do not have the effect of denying the right of persons belonging to minorities to enjoy their own culture, to profess and practise their own religion, or to use their own language. The aim of a process of integration is to create a social culture to which all members of the State can share an attachment, because it reflects, at least in part, their cultural values, beliefs and practices (including, potentially, a tolerance of cultural difference).

Towards a definition

In its General Comment on Article 27, the Human Rights Committee concluded that the existence of an ethnic, religious or linguistic minority 'requires to be established by objective criteria'.[139] The preceding analysis suggests the following criteria should apply: (1) the relevant group must not exceed 50 per cent of the total population; (2) persons belonging to the group should speak a language, practice a religion and/or

---

[136] See also Articles 2(2) and 3(2) of GA Res. 47/135, adopted 18 December 1992, 'Declaration on the Rights of Persons belonging to National or Ethnic, Religious and Linguistic Minorities'. See, for example, John Danley, 'Liberalism, aboriginal rights, and cultural minorities' (1991) 20 *Journal of Philosophy and Public Affairs* 168, 180.

[137] See, for example, Article 1(1) of GA Res. 47/135, adopted 18 December 1992, 'Declaration on the Rights of Persons belonging to National or Ethnic, Religious and Linguistic Minorities': 'States shall protect the existence and the national or ethnic, cultural, religious and linguistic identity of minorities within their respective territories.' Forced assimilation is difficult to reconcile with the individual human rights to freedom of expression (Article 19(2) of the International Covenant on Civil and Political Rights), and religion (Article 18(1), *ibid.*), and the right to moral autonomy recognised in the international human rights instruments.

[138] Integration is a 'reciprocal process whereby the dominant group and the ethnic-cultural groups adopt certain elements of each other's culture, without disappearance of all cultural differences': Albert Musschenga, 'Intrinsic value as a reason for the preservation of minority cultures' (1998) 1 *Ethical Theory and Moral Practice* 201, 202.

[139] Human Rights Committee, General Comment No. 23, 'Rights of minorities (Article 27)', para. 5.2. Cf. Geoff Gilbert, 'Religious minorities and their rights: a problem of approach' (1997) 5 *International Journal on Minority and Group Rights* 97, 102.

enjoy a culture distinct from the language, religion and/or culture of the dominant/majority population; (3) the cultural values, beliefs and practices of the group (including those manifested in the language or the religion of the group) should together comprise a 'way of life' for the members of the group; and (4) the members of the group should recognise their distinctiveness from other persons in the State, and evidence a desire to maintain these differences.

It is not possible to create a typology of minority groups with fixed characteristics. Minorities are imagined communities. Membership is a matter of mutual recognition, secured by the possession of general characteristics.[140] Minorities exist, for the purposes of international law, because they fall within the scope of application of Article 27 of the International Covenant on Civil and Political Rights.[141] Claims under Article 27 do not arise in the abstract.[142] The concern should not be to identify ethnic, religious or linguistic 'minorities' to which the relevant rights may be accorded, but to evaluate complaints that the actions (or inactions) of the State have the effect of denying a particular individual the right to enjoy their own culture, to profess and practise their own religion, or to use their own language. In *Diergaardt* v. *Namibia*, members of the Rehoboth Baster Community complained that the confiscation of collectively owned property robbed the group of the basis of its economic livelihood, endangering its traditional existence as a collective of mainly cattle-raising farmers (which was the basis of its cultural, social and ethnic identity).[143] The Human Rights Committee concluded that the relationship between the authors' way of life and the lands in question was not one 'that would have given rise to a distinctive culture'.[144] There was no violation of Article 27.[145] The members of the Rehoboth Baster Community could not show that they enjoyed 'a distinct culture which is intimately bound up with or dependent on the use

---

[140] See Avishai Margalit and Joseph Raz, 'National self-determination', in Will Kymlicka (ed.), *The rights of minority cultures* (Oxford: Oxford University Press, 1995), p. 79, at pp. 81–5.

[141] See Thornberry, *International law and the rights of minorities*, p. 156.

[142] The Human Rights Committee has determined that the 'right to enjoy one's culture cannot be determined *in abstracto* but has to be placed in context': *Länsman et al.* v. *Finland (No. 1)*, Communication No. 511/1992, UN Doc. CCPR/C/52/D/511/1992, 8 November 1994, para. 9.3. See also *Mahuika et al.* v. *New Zealand*, Communication No. 547/1993, UN Doc. CCPR/C/70/D/547/1993, 15 November 2000, para. 9.4.

[143] *Diergaardt et al.* v. *Namibia*, Communication No. 760/1997, UN Doc. CCPR/C/69/D/760/1996, 25 July 2000, para. 3.1.

[144] *Ibid.*, para. 10.6.   [145] *Ibid.*

of these particular lands'. The claim was essentially an economic one rather than a cultural claim.[146] No determination was required as to whether the Rehoboth Baster Community constituted a minority for the purposes of Article 27.

'Persons belonging to minorities ...'

Article 27 of the International Covenant on Civil and Political Rights confers rights on individuals.[147] The International Covenant does not recognise 'minorities' as a subject of international law,[148] capable of possessing international rights, and having the capacity to maintain its rights by bringing international claims.[149] Literally, the right is one of individual participation: persons belonging to minorities shall not be denied the right, in community with others, to enjoy their own culture, to profess and practise their own religion, or to use their own language.[150] A right of individual participation is recognised in Article 27, but it is of secondary importance to the cultural survival of the group. The position is confirmed in the Human Rights Committee's Opinions in *Lovelace* v. *Canada*, and *Kitok* v. *Sweden*.

[146] *Diergaardt et al.* v. *Namibia*, Concurring Individual Opinion by Elizabeth Evatt and Cecilia Medina Quiroga. Economic activities may come within the ambit of Article 27, 'if they are an essential element of the culture of a community': *Mahuika et al.* v. *New Zealand*, Communication No. 547/1993, UN Doc. CCPR/C/70/D/547/1993, 15 November 2000, para. 9.3.

[147] Human Rights Committee, General Comment No. 23, 'Rights of minorities (Article 27)', para. 3.1.

[148] Cf. Conference on Yugoslavia Arbitration Commission: Opinions on Questions Arising from the Dissolution of Yugoslavia, 31 ILM (1992) 1488, Opinion No. 2, para. 4(i): 'the Serbian population in Bosnia-Herzegovina and Croatia *is entitled to all the* rights concerned to minorities and ethnic groups under international law' (emphasis added).

[149] Ian Brownlie, *Principle of public international law* (5th edn, Oxford: Oxford University Press, 1998), p. 56. Cf. Article 1(1) of the International Covenant on Civil and Political Rights (Part I), which recognises the right of 'peoples' to self-determination. In *Chief Bernard Ominayak and the Lubicon Lake Band* v. *Canada*, the Human Rights Committee made the following point: 'While all peoples have the right of self-determination, ... the question whether the Lubicon Lake Band constitutes a "people" is not an issue for the Committee ... The Optional Protocol provides a procedure under which individuals can claim that their individual rights have been violated. These rights are set out in ... Articles 6 to 27, inclusive. *There is, however, no objection to a group of individuals, who claim to be similarly affected, collectively to submit a communication about alleged breaches of their rights*': *Chief Bernard Ominayak and the Lubicon Lake Band* v. *Canada*, Communication No. 167/1984, UN Doc. CCPR/C/38/D/167/1984, 10 May 1990, para. 32.1 (emphasis added).

[150] Article 27 of the International Covenant on Civil and Political Rights.

Following her marriage to a non-Indian, Sandra Lovelace lost her status as a Maliseet Indian, and was denied the right to live on the Tobique Reserve. This was particularly significant, given the loss of the 'cultural benefits of living in an Indian community, the emotional ties to home, family, friends and neighbours, and the loss of identity'.[151] Article 27 recognises a right for persons belonging to minorities to enjoy their own culture in community with other members of their group. The provision does not contain a justification clause. The Human Rights Committee concluded that it was not possible to regard all interferences in the exercise of rights protected by Article 27 as a violation of the provision.[152] Restrictions on the right of participation in the minority culture are permitted, but only when such restrictions enjoy 'both a reasonable and objective justification and [are] consistent with the other provisions of the Covenant, read as a whole'.[153] In *Lovelace*, the Committee accepted that it was necessary to define the category of persons entitled to live on the reserve, for the purpose of 'protection of its resources and preservation of the identity of its people'.[154] The particular decision to deny Sandra Lovelace the right of residence was not, though, 'reasonable, or necessary to preserve the identity of the tribe'. The restriction constituted a violation of Article 27.[155]

In *Kitok* v. *Sweden*, the author, a member of the Sami minority, complained that he was prevented from engaging in reindeer herding, an activity central to Sami culture. Relevant legislation divided the Sami population into reindeer-herding and non-reindeer-herding Sami. The right to engage in reindeer herding was restricted to those Sami who were members of a Sami village. These Sami, numbering some 2,500, enjoyed additional rights, for example as regards hunting and fishing. The remaining Sami, the great majority of the estimated 15,000 to

---

[151] *Lovelace* v. *Canada*, Communication No. 24/1977, UN Doc. CCPR/C/13/D/24/1977, 30 July 1981, para. 13.1. Sandra Lovelace was 'born and registered' a Maliseet Indian, but lost her rights 'and status as an Indian' under the Indian Act when she married a non-Indian (para. 1). The Human Rights Committee concluded that she was 'ethnically a Maliseet Indian', and, as she had only been absent from her home reserve for a few years during the existence of her marriage, she was entitled to be regarded as belonging to this minority and to claim the benefits of Article 27 of the Covenant (para. 14).

[152] *Ibid.*, para. 15.

[153] *Ibid.*, para. 16. See also on this point *Mahuika et al.* v. *New Zealand*, Communication No. 547/1993, UN Doc. CCPR/C/70/D/547/1993, 15 November 2000, para. 9.6.

[154] *Ibid.*, para. 15.   [155] *Ibid.*, para. 17.

20,000 Sami population, and including the author, enjoyed no special rights. Sweden admitted that this latter group 'found it more difficult to maintain their Sami identity and many of them are today assimilated into Swedish society'.[156] The relevant legislation was introduced in order to secure the viability of reindeer herding as an economic activity, and thus to secure the preservation and well being of the Sami minority. In the opinion of the Human Rights Committee, 'these objectives and measures [were] reasonable and consistent with Article 27 of the Covenant'.[157] The Committee concluded:

In resolving this problem, in which there is an apparent conflict between the legislation, which seems to protect the rights of the minority as a whole, and its application to a single member of that minority, the Committee has been guided by the *ratio decidendi* in [*Lovelace* v. *Canada*], namely, that *a restriction upon the right of an individual member of a minority must be shown to have a reasonable and objective justification and to be necessary for the continued viability and welfare of the minority as a whole*. After a careful review of all the elements involved in this case, the Committee is of the view that there is no violation of Article 27 by the State party. In this context, the Committee notes that Mr Kitok is permitted, albeit not as of right, to graze and farm his reindeer, to hunt and to fish.[158]

An Opinion that seemingly validates a State policy that has the potential to exclude four out of every five members of a group from one of its defining cultural activities must be subject to some criticism. The Opinion makes clear, however, the prior importance of the protection of the minority culture. Where a restriction on the right of individual participation is necessary for the continued viability and welfare of the minority group as a whole, the right of the group (or more accurately the other members of the group) to cultural security 'trumps' the individual right of participation.[159] Whilst the rights protected under Article 27 are individual rights, they depend in turn on the ability of the minority group to maintain its culture, language or

---

[156] *Kitok* v. *Sweden*, Communication No. 197/1985, UN Doc. CCPR/C/33/D/197/1985, 10 August 1988, para. 4.2. In *Kitok*, the Human Rights Committee expressed 'grave doubts' as to whether certain provisions of Swedish legislation, and their application to Ivan Kitok, were compatible with Article 27 of the Covenant. The legislation defined a 'member of a Sami community' as, essentially, those persons entitled to engage in reindeer husbandry (para. 9.6). The Committee observed that 'a person who is ethnically a Sami can be held not to be a Sami for the purposes of the Act', and expressed its concern regarding 'the ignoring of objective ethnic criteria in determining membership of a minority' (para. 9.7).

[157] *Ibid.*, para. 9.5.   [158] *Ibid.*, para. 9.8 (emphasis added).

[159] See also Article 5(1) of the International Covenant on Civil and Political Rights.

religion.[160] The primary aim of Article 27 is to ensure 'the survival and continued development of the cultural, religious and social identity of the minorities concerned'.[161]

The right to cultural security

The intentional physical destruction of a national, ethnical, racial or religious group is an act of genocide.[162] In 1948, the UN General Assembly adopted a Convention on the Prevention and Punishment of the Crime of Genocide. Genocide occurs when any of the following acts are committed, with the intent to destroy, a national, ethnical, racial or religious group, in whole or in part: (a) killing members of the group; (b) causing serious bodily or mental harm to members of the group; (c) deliberately inflicting conditions of life calculated to bring about its physical destruction; (d) imposing measures intended to prevent births within the group; and (e) forcibly transferring children of the group to another group.[163]

A proposal to include cultural genocide in the Genocide Convention was rejected.[164] The Genocide Convention is not concerned with the

---

[160] Human Rights Committee, General Comment No. 23, 'Rights of minorities (Article 27)', para. 6.2.

[161] *Ibid.*, para. 9. As explained by Birame Ndiaye, member of the Human Rights Committee: 'The rationale of Article 27 is the preservation of the three minorities referred to, and not the protection of the rights enunciated therein, merely for the sake of protection': *Ballantyne and Davidson, and McIntyre* v. *Canada*, Communication Nos. 359/1989 and 385/1989, UN Doc. CCPR/C/47/D/359/1989, 5 May 1993, Individual Opinion by Birame Ndiaye (dissenting).

[162] In 1946, the General Assembly described genocide as the 'denial of the right to existence of human groups, as homicide is the denial of the right to live of human beings': GA Res. 96 (I), adopted 11 December 1946, 'The Crime of Genocide'. See also Raphael Lemkin, *Axis rule in occupied Europe* (Washington, DC: Carnegie Endowment for International Peace, 1944), and Raphael Lemkin, 'Genocide as a crime under international law' (1947) 41 *American Journal of International Law* 145.

[163] Article II of the Convention on the Prevention and Punishment of the Crime of Genocide, adopted by General Assembly Resolution 260 A (III), 9 December 1948, in force 12 January 1951.

[164] The proposal defined 'cultural genocide' as 'any deliberate act committed with the intent to destroy the language, religion or culture of a national, racial or religious group on grounds of national or racial origin or religious belief such as: (1) Prohibiting the use of the language of the group in daily intercourse or in schools, or the printing and circulation of publication in the language of the group; (2) Destroying, or preventing the use of, libraries, museums, schools, historical monuments, places of worship or other cultural institutions and objects of the groups': Economic and Social Council, *ad hoc* committee, Summary Record of Meetings 175–225, UN ESCOR,

destruction of the distinct values, traditions, identities, languages, or places or objects of cultural importance which differentiate one ethno-cultural group from another.[165] Nor is cultural genocide listed as a crime in the Rome Statute of the International Criminal Court.[166]

Article 27 of the International Covenant on Civil and Political Rights recognises a legal prohibition on acts of cultural genocide. The proscription on the use of a minority language in public and private, or the destruction of the libraries, museums, schools, historical monuments, places of worship and other cultural institutions of ethnic, religious or linguistic minorities will violate Article 27: persons belonging to minorities have the right 'to enjoy their own culture, to profess and practise their own religion, or to use their own language'.[167] The scope of protection afforded by Article 27 extends beyond the prohibition on cultural genocide. The provision recognises a right which 'shall not be denied'. States parties are required to establish an effective legal regime for the protection of minority cultures. The protection should extend to both the acts of the State party, and those of other persons within the State.[168]

In *Chief Bernard Ominayak and the Lubicon Lake Band v Canada*, the Human Rights Committee concluded that the State had not taken the appropriate measures required to protect the culture of the group, and determined a violation of Article 27. Members of the Band have continuously inhabited, hunted, trapped and fished in an area now in

---

3 Year, 7 Session, Supplement No. 6, at 6, UN Doc. E/3/SR. 175–225 (1948), referred to in Johannes Morsink, 'Cultural genocide, the Universal Declaration, and minority rights' (1999) 21 *Human Rights Quarterly* 1009, 1023.

[165] See James Crawford, 'The rights of peoples: "peoples" or "governments"?', in James Crawford (ed.), *The rights of peoples* (Oxford: Clarendon Press, 1988), p. 55, at pp. 59–60; see also Benedict Kingsbury, 'Reconciling five competing conceptual structures of indigenous peoples' claims in international and comparative law', in Philip Alston (ed.), *Peoples' rights* (Oxford: Oxford University Press, 2001), p. 69, at p. 73.

[166] Rome Statute of the International Criminal Court, adopted 17 July 1998, in force 1 July 2002, 37 ILM (1998) 999. A number of provisions concern minorities: the list of 'crimes against humanity' includes 'forced pregnancy' (Article 7(1)(g)), defined as the unlawful confinement of a woman forcibly made pregnant, with the intent, inter alia, of affecting the ethnic composition of any population (Article 7(2)(f)); the persecution of any identifiable group or collectivity on political, racial, national, ethnic, cultural or religious grounds (Article 7(1)(h)); and the 'crime of apartheid' (Article 7(1)(j)). 'War crimes' include the intentional directing of attacks against buildings dedicated, inter alia, to religion, and historic monuments, provided they are not military objectives (Article 8(2)(b)(ix)). See also Article 8(2)(e)(iv).

[167] Article 27 of the International Covenant on Civil and Political Rights.

[168] Human Rights Committee, General Comment No. 23, 'Rights of minorities (Article 27)', para. 6.1.

northern Alberta since time immemorial. They speak Cree as their primary language, and maintain their traditional culture, religion, political structure and subsistence economy.[169] In a complaint to the Human Rights Committee, the Band argued that the Canadian Government had allowed the provincial government of Alberta to expropriate the territory of the Lubicon Lake Band for the benefit of private corporate interests, for example in issuing leases for oil and gas exploration. This resulted in the destruction of the Band's traditional hunting and trapping territory, and consequently of its 'way of life'.[170] In its Opinion, the Human Rights Committee concluded: 'Historical inequities, to which the State party refers, and certain more recent developments threaten the way of life and culture of the Lubicon Lake Band, and constitute a violation of Article 27 so long as they continue.'[171] The Committee accepted the State party's proposals to rectify the situation, inter alia, by the establishment of a reserve for the Lubicon Lake Band, the provision of mineral rights, community facilities, an economic self-sufficiency package and cash compensation.[172]

The Human Rights Committee's Opinion in *Lubicon Lake Band* v. *Canada* is the only one in which it has determined a violation of the right to cultural security provided by Article 27, as opposed to the right of individual participation, and it may be significant that Canada had accepted 'that the Lubicon Lake Band has suffered a historical inequity and that they are entitled to a reserve and related entitlements'.[173] In other Opinions, the Committee has failed to determine a violation of the Covenant, although it has affirmed the absolute nature of the rights protected by Article 27. The negative formulation of the provision ('shall not be denied') is significant. No 'margin of appreciation' is recognised, and the State may not seek to balance the cultural security of the group against the interests of the wider community.

Not all interferences in the 'way of life' of the persons belonging to a minority group will constitute a violation of the cultural rights recognised in Article 27. In *Länsman* v. *Finland (No. 1)*, the authors complained that the proposed quarrying of stone on the flank of Etelä-Riutusvaara, a mountain with spiritual significance to Sami culture, and its transportation through reindeer-herding territory, would violate their rights under Article 27. The Human Rights Committee accepted that it was

---

[169] *Chief Bernard Ominayak and the Lubicon Lake Band* v. *Canada*, Communication No. 167/1984, UN Doc. CCPR/C/38/D/167/1984, 10 May 1990, para. 2.2.
[170] See *ibid.*, para. 29.1.   [171] *Ibid.*, para. 33.   [172] *Ibid.*, para. 33.   [173] *Ibid.*, para. 24.1.

'undisputed that the authors are members of a minority within the meaning of Article 27 and as such have the right to enjoy their own culture; it is further undisputed that reindeer husbandry is an essential element of their culture'.[174] In the opinion of the Committee:

Article 27 requires that a member of a minority shall not be denied his right to enjoy his culture. Thus, measures whose impact amount to a denial of the right will not be compatible with the obligations under Article 27. However, measures that have a certain limited impact on the way of life of persons belonging to a minority will not necessarily amount to a denial of the right under Article 27.[175]

The relevant question was whether the impact of the quarrying on Mount Riutusvaara was 'so substantial that it does effectively deny to the authors the right to enjoy their cultural rights in that region'.[176] The Committee concluded the quarrying which had already taken place did not constitute a denial of the authors' right to enjoy their own culture, noting that reindeer herding in the area did not appear to have been adversely affected by the quarrying of stone that had occurred.[177] With regard to the authors' concerns about future activities, the Committee was of the opinion that 'economic activities must, in order to comply with Article 27, be carried out in [such] a way that the authors [may] continue to benefit from reindeer husbandry'.[178]

In *Länsman v. Finland (No. 2)* the Human Rights Committee again concluded that proposed logging activities did not 'appear to threaten the survival of reindeer husbandry'.[179] The authors had challenged the plans of the Finnish Central Forestry Board to approve the logging, and the construction of a number of roads in the area occupied by the Muotkatunturi Herdsmen's Committee. According to the Committee, the question was whether the logging (existing and proposed) was 'of such proportions as to deny the authors the right to enjoy their culture in that area'.[180] The Committee was unable to conclude that it was.[181]

---

[174] *Länsman et al. v. Finland (No. 1)*, Communication No. 511/1992, UN Doc. CCPR/C/52/D/511/1992, 8 November 1994, para. 9.2.

[175] *Ibid.*, para. 9.4.   [176] *Ibid.*, para. 9.5.   [177] *Ibid.*, para. 9.6.   [178] *Ibid.*, para. 9.8.

[179] *Länsman et al. v. Finland (No. 2)*, Communication No. 671/1995, UN Doc. CCPR/C/58/D/671/1995, 22 November 1996, para. 10.6.

[180] *Ibid.*, para. 10.4.

[181] *Ibid.*, para. 10.5. As far as future logging activities were concerned, the Human Rights Committee observed that the proposals did not appear to threaten the survival of reindeer husbandry: *ibid.*, para. 10.6. See on this point, *Länsman et al. (No. 3) v. Finland*, Communication No. 1023/2001, UN Doc. CCPR/C/83/D/1023/2001, 15 April 2005.

In its Opinion, the Committee noted that 'different activities in themselves may not constitute a violation of this Article, [but that] such activities, taken together, may erode the rights of Sami people to enjoy their own culture'.[182]

Measures deliberately aimed at the destruction of the distinctive culture of a minority group constitute acts of cultural genocide. They are prohibited by Article 27 (both as a treaty obligation, and in its formulation reflecting a rule of general international law). In other cases, the culture of the group (including the use of language and the practice of religion) may be threatened by the legitimate activities of the State, or private actors. Not all interferences in the enjoyment of cultural rights constitute a violation of Article 27. The relevant question is whether the interference(s) deny persons belonging to minorities the right to enjoy their own culture, to profess and practise their own religion, or to use their own language. In many cases, there will be a legitimate difference of opinion between the State party and the members of the minority group on this question.

Positive measures

Despite the negative formulation of Article 27 ('shall not be denied'), the Human Rights Committee has concluded that 'positive measures by States may also be necessary to protect the identity of a minority and the rights of its members to enjoy and develop their culture and language and to practise their religion, in community with the other members of the group'.[183] Where positive measures are selectively applied to the members of one or more minority groups, they constitute a 'preference', based on ethnicity, language and/or religion.[184] They do not constitute acts of discrimination, prohibited by the International Covenant on Civil and Political Rights.[185] The principle of

---

[182] *Ibid.*, para. 10.7. See also *Äärelä and Näkkäläjärvi* v. *Finland*, Communication No. 779/ 1997, UN Doc. CCPR/C/73/D/779/1997, 7 November 2001, para. 7.6.

[183] Human Rights Committee, General Comment No. 23, 'Rights of minorities (Article 27)', para. 6.2. See also Dominic McGoldrick, 'Canadian Indians, cultural rights and the Human Rights Committee' (1991) 40 *International and Comparative Law Quarterly* 658, 668.

[184] See Human Rights Committee, General Comment No. 18, 'Non-discrimination', adopted 10 November 1989, reprinted in 'Compilation of General Comments and General Recommendations', p. 146, para. 7.

[185] Policies of 'affirmative action' may be introduced in order to diminish or eliminate the conditions which cause or help to perpetuate discrimination prohibited by the

non-discrimination does not require identical treatment in every instance.[186] Positive measures designed to facilitate the rights of members of ethnic, religious or linguistic minorities to enjoy their own culture, to profess and practise their own religion, or to use their own language constitute a legitimate differentiation under the Covenant, provided that they are 'aimed at correcting conditions which prevent or impair the enjoyment of the rights guaranteed under Article 27', and 'provided that they are based on reasonable and objective criteria'.[187]

Measures that are not based on reasonable and objective criteria will violate the non-discrimination provision contained in Article 26. This position was confirmed in the Human Rights Committee's Opinion in *Waldman* v. *Canada*. The author was the father of two school-age children, and a member of the Jewish faith. In the province of Ontario, Roman Catholic schools received public funding.[188] Other religious schools were required to fund themselves through private sources, including by charging tuition fees. There was no evidence that the different treatment, between the Roman Catholic faith and the Jewish faith, was based on reasonable and objective criteria. The Committee determined a violation of Article 26.[189]

Positive measures may include the recognition of exemption rights: 'individually exercised negative liberties granted to members of a religious or cultural group whose practices are such that a generally

---

International Covenant: Human Rights Committee, General Comment No. 18, 'Non-discrimination', para. 10.

[186] *Ibid.*, para. 8.

[187] Human Rights Committee, General Comment No. 23, 'Rights of minorities (Article 27)', para. 6.2. The position is confirmed in Article 8(3) of GA Res. 47/135, adopted 18 December 1992, 'Declaration on the Rights of Persons belonging to National or Ethnic, Religious and Linguistic Minorities'.

[188] The system of public funding for Catholic schools originated with Canada's 1867 Constitution. There was a concern that the Protestant majority might exercise its power over education to take away the rights of the Roman Catholic minority. The solution was to guarantee the rights of Catholics to denominational education: *Waldman* v. *Canada*, Communication No. 694/1996, UN Doc. CCPR/C/67/D/694/1996, 5 November 1999, para. 2.3. The Human Rights Committee concluded that the factors that might have been relevant in the nineteenth century could not justify different treatment for different groups in the present day: *ibid.*, para. 10.4.

[189] *Ibid.*, para. 10.6. In a Concurring Individual Opinion, Martin Scheinin made the following point: 'In order to avoid discrimination in funding religious (or linguistic) education for some but not all minorities States may legitimately base themselves on whether there is a constant [and sufficient] demand for such education': *Waldman* v. *Canada*, Individual Opinion by Member Martin Scheinin (concurring), para. 5.

and ostensibly neutral law would be a distinctive burden on them'.[190] They allow individual members of minority groups to exercise 'self-government' on questions of cultural practice: persons belonging to minorities may decide to follow the practices of the majority or minority (there is no duty, for example, on persons belonging to the Sikh minority in the United Kingdom to refrain from wearing motorcycle helmets).

It is not possible to exempt all cultural practices from the application of general laws. The reasoning is well illustrated in *Employment Division, Ore Department of Human Resources* v. *Smith*,[191] before the US Supreme Court. The respondents had been denied unemployment compensation under a state law disqualifying employees discharged for work-related misconduct. They had been dismissed for ingesting peyote, a prohibited narcotic, for sacramental purposes at a ceremony of their Native American Church. The Supreme Court refused to recognise a general right of exemption where an individual objected to laws on religious grounds. The Court noted that objections might arise, inter alia, to the payment of taxes, social welfare legislation, child labour laws, animal cruelty laws, environmental protection laws and laws providing for racial equality.[192] The Supreme Court concluded that the circumstances in which a religious practice might be exempted from the application of general laws could not be discerned by the Courts, but could be recognised by democratic legislatures. The Court accepted that 'leaving accommodation to the political process will place at a relative disadvantage those religious practices that are not widely engaged in; but that unavoidable consequence of democratic government must be preferred to a system in which each conscience is a law unto itself or in which judges weigh the social importance of all laws against the centrality of all religious beliefs'.[193]

International human rights law does not recognise a general right for individuals to be exempted from the application of laws that conflict

---

[190] Jacob Levi, *The multiculturalism of fear* (Oxford: Oxford University Press, 2000), p. 128. Examples in the United States include the use of peyote for religious purposes by American Indians, mandatory schooling laws for Amish children, and various hunting, fishing and land-use regulations for certain indigenous peoples: *ibid.*, 128–9.

[191] *Employment Division, Ore Department of Human Resources* v. *Smith*, 494 US 872 (1990).

[192] *Ibid.*, 889.

[193] *Ibid.*, 890. See Lawrence Rosen, 'The right to be different: indigenous peoples and the quest for a unified theory' (1997) 107 *Yale Law Journal* 227, 228.

with their own cultural or religious values, beliefs and practices.[194] In *Singh Bhinder* v. *Canada*, before the Human Rights Committee, the applicant, a Sikh who wore a turban in his daily life, refused to wear safety headgear at work. For this reason he was dismissed from his employment as a maintenance electrician. The author claimed that his right to manifest his religious beliefs had been restricted by the enforcement of the hard hat regulation.[195] The State party argued that the right to freedom of religion did not impose any duty of 'reasonable accommodation', and did not include an obligation to grant waivers to members of religious groups which would enable them to practise their religion.[196] The Opinion of the Human Rights Committee accepted that the application of the relevant legislation operated in such a way as to discriminate against persons of the Sikh religion,[197] but concluded that it was 'reasonable and directed towards objective purposes that are compatible with the Covenant [i.e. the prevention of injury]'.[198] There was no violation of the International Covenant.[199]

Whilst the International Covenant does not recognise a general right to the exemption of religious and cultural practices from general law, it does not insist on the uniform application of general regulations. In *Riley et al.* v. *Canada*, the authors complained about a regulation which permitted Khalsa Sikh officers to substitute turbans for the traditional wide brimmed 'mountie' stetson and forage cap of the Royal Canadian Mounted Police.[200] The authors complained that the exemption violated their rights to equal protection and equal benefit of the law.[201] The Human Rights Committee declared the communication inadmissible,[202] as the authors had failed to show how the enjoyment of their rights under the Covenant had been affected by allowing Khalsa Sikh officers to wear religious symbols. They could not be considered to be 'victims' within the meaning of Article 1 of the Optional Protocol.[203] The Opinion may be read narrowly, given that the authors were retired and not serving members of the Royal Canadian Mounted Police.[204] The

---

[194] See, for example, *Chapman* v. *UK*, Reports of Judgments and Decisions 2001-I, para. 96: 'the fact of being a member of a minority with a traditional lifestyle different from that of the majority of a society does not confer an immunity from general laws intended to safeguard assets common to the whole society such as the environment.'

[195] *Singh Bhinder* v. *Canada*, Communication No. 208/1986, UN Doc. CCPR/C/37/D/208/1986, 28 October 1989, para. 3.

[196] *Ibid.*, para. 4.5.   [197] *Ibid.*, para. 6.1.   [198] *Ibid.*, para. 6.2.   [199] *Ibid.*, para. 6.3.

[200] *Riley et al.* v. *Canada*, Communication No. 1048/2002, UN Doc. CCPR/C/74/D/1048/2002, 15 April 2002, para. 2.1.

[201] *Ibid.*, para. 3.5.   [202] *Ibid.*, para. 5.   [203] *Ibid.*, para. 4.2.   [204] See *ibid.*, para. 2.2.

Opinion should be read as confirming the possibility that States parties may exempt the members of minority groups from the application of general laws. The principle of non-discrimination does not require identical treatment in every instance.[205] Positive measures designed to facilitate the rights of members of ethnic, religious or linguistic minorities to enjoy their own culture, to profess and practise their own religion, or to use their own language constitute a legitimate basis for differential treatment under the International Covenant on Civil and Political Rights.[206]

In relation to 'positive measures', the Human Rights Committee has accepted the possibility of limiting participation in a particular economic activity to certain members of a minority group;[207] restrictions on the rights of residence in particular territories to persons belonging to minorities;[208] and the setting aside of land for a reserve, within which the minority group may 'maintain its culture, control its way of life and achieve economic self-sufficiency'.[209] The Committee has not made any systematic attempt to delimit the positive measures that may be permitted or required under Article 27. Nor would it be possible for it to do so. The following illustrate some of the more common demands of minority groups: the exemption of the group's practices from State regulation; the recognition of minority religions in public life, for example by recognising significant religious dates as public holidays; public recognition of minority languages, by for example adopting the minority language as an official or working language of the State, or by allowing members of the minority to communicate with public officials in the minority language, or providing street signs and other public information in the minority language; State support, often financial, for minority cultural activities; the teaching of, and in, the minority language in State schools; and the provision of State funding for the establishment and maintenance of minority schools. The political

---

[205] See Human Rights Committee, General Comment No. 18, 'Non-discrimination', adopted 10 November 1989, reprinted in 'Compilation of General Comments and General Recommendations', p. 146, para. 8.

[206] Human Rights Committee, General Comment No. 23, 'Rights of minorities (Article 27)', para. 6.2.

[207] *Kitok* v. *Sweden*, Communication No. 197/1985, UN Doc. CCPR/C/33/D/197/1985, 10 August 1988.

[208] *Lovelace* v. *Canada*, Communication No. 24/1977, UN Doc. CCPR/C/13/D/24/1977, 30 July 1981.

[209] *Chief Bernard Ominayak and the Lubicon Lake Band* v. *Canada*, Communication No. 167/1984, UN Doc. CCPR/C/38/D/167/1984, 10 May 1990, para. 29.10.

demands of persons belonging to ethnic, religious or linguistic minorities are as diverse as the groups themselves, and the plurality of identities within those groups. They can only be evaluated in the context of the particular circumstances extant in a State party at a particular time.

The UN Declaration on Minorities

On 18 December 1992, the UN General Assembly adopted, by consensus, a 'Declaration on the Rights of Persons belonging to National or Ethnic, Religious and Linguistic Minorities'.[210] Certain of its provisions reflect general international law, providing a more detailed elaboration of the rights of persons belonging to minorities. The Declaration was '[i]nspired' by Article 27 of the International Covenant on Civil and Political Rights.[211] The scope of application of Article 27 concerns persons belonging to ethnic, religious or linguistic minorities. The UN Declaration on Minorities additionally refers to persons belonging to 'national minorities'. This reference does extend the scope of application of the Declaration beyond the groups protected by Article 27.[212]

The Declaration recognises an obligation on States to 'ensure that persons belonging to minorities may exercise fully and effectively all their human rights and fundamental freedoms without any discrimination and in full equality before the law'.[213] Persons belonging to

---

[210] GA Res. 47/135, adopted 18 December 1992, 'Declaration on the Rights of Persons belonging to National or Ethnic, Religious and Linguistic Minorities'.

[211] Preamble, *ibid.*

[212] Asbjørn Eide, 'Commentary to the Declaration on the Rights of Persons Belonging to National or Ethnic, Religious and Linguistic Minorities', UN Doc. E/CN.4/Sub.2/AC.5/2001/2, 2 April 2001, para. 6. The Commentary was prepared by the Chairperson of the Working Group on Minorities of the Sub-Commission on the Promotion and Protection of Human Rights. It is intended to serve as a guide to GA Res. 47/135, adopted 18 December 1992, 'Declaration on the Rights of Persons belonging to National or Ethnic, Religious and Linguistic Minorities': Eide, 'Commentary', para. 2. The term 'national' does not restrict the personal scope of application of the Declaration in comparison to Article 27: it is not synonymous with 'citizen'. Reference to 'national' concerns 'personal rather than legal characteristics': Patrick Thornberry, 'The UN Declaration on the Rights of Persons Belonging to National or Ethnic, Religious and Linguistic Minorities: background, analysis, observations and an update', in Alan Philips and Alan Rosas (eds.), *Universal minority rights* (Turku/Åbo: Institute for Human Rights, Åbo Akademi University, 1995), p. 13, at p. 30.

[213] Article 4(1) of the UN Declaration on Minorities.

minorities have the right to participate effectively in cultural, religious, social, economic and public life;[214] they have the right to establish and maintain their own associations;[215] and to establish and maintain contacts with other members of their group and with persons belonging to other minorities, as well as contacts across frontiers with citizens of other States to whom they are related by national or ethnic, religious or linguistic ties.[216]

The Declaration recognises that persons belonging to minorities 'have the right to enjoy their own culture, to profess and practise their own religion, and to use their own language, in private and in public, freely and without interference or any form of discrimination' (note the positive formulation, in contrast to Article 27).[217] States are required to 'encourage conditions' for the promotion of the ethnic, cultural, religious and linguistic identity of minorities within their respective territories.[218] They are obliged to take positive measures 'to create favourable conditions to enable persons belonging to minorities to express their characteristics and to develop their culture, language, religion, traditions and customs', except 'where specific practices are in violation of national law and contrary to international standards'.[219] The words 'contrary to international standards' should be read as meaning contrary to international human rights standards.[220] The cultural or religious practices of all groups that violate human rights law should be prohibited.[221] The exercise of the rights in the UN Declaration 'shall not prejudice the enjoyment by all persons of universally recognized human rights and fundamental freedoms'.[222] Reference to 'national law' is, according to Asbjørn Eide, intended 'to respect the margin of appreciation which any State must have regarding which practices it wants to prohibit, taking into account the particular conditions prevailing in that country. As long as the prohibitions are based on reasonable and objective grounds, they

---

[214] Article 2(2), *ibid*. See also Article 4(5), *ibid*.: 'States should consider appropriate measures so that persons belonging to minorities may participate fully in the economic progress and development in their country'.

[215] Article 2(4), *ibid*.   [216] Article 2(5), *ibid*.   [217] Article 2(1), *ibid*.   [218] Article 1(1), *ibid*.

[219] Article 4(2), *ibid*. Measures taken by States to ensure the effective enjoyment of the rights of persons belonging to minorities shall not prima facie be considered contrary to the principle of equality: Article 8(3), *ibid*.

[220] Eide, 'Commentary to the Declaration on the Rights of Persons Belonging to National or Ethnic, Religious and Linguistic Minorities', para. 57.

[221] *Ibid*.   [222] Article 8(2) of the UN Declaration on Minorities.

must be respected.'[223] Practices that are permitted in one State may be legitimately proscribed in another.

The Declaration recognises the right of persons belonging to minorities to enjoy their own culture, to profess and practise their own religion and to use their own language.[224] States are required to 'protect' the existence of the national or ethnic, cultural, religious or linguistic identity of minorities on their territories, and to 'encourage conditions for the promotion of that identity'.[225] Few details as to the necessary positive measures are provided. The notable exception is Article 4(3): 'States should take appropriate measures so that, wherever possible, persons belonging to minorities may have adequate opportunities to learn their mother tongue or to have instruction in their mother tongue'. The provision is both exhortatory and conditional.[226] Policies concerning national or ethnic, religious and linguistic minorities will emerge through the mechanisms and institutions of public/political decision-making – in accordance with the principles recognised in the Declaration.

The protection of national minorities in Europe

A more detailed scheme concerning national minorities has emerged in Europe, which has been the traditional focus of the minorities question. The term 'national minority' is associated with the minority protection regime introduced in Europe by the League of Nations in the post-First World War Versailles settlement.[227] The League of Nations scheme did not refer, however, to national minorities, but to minorities. The Polish Minorities Treaty refers to the 'Polish nation',[228] and to 'racial, religious or linguistic minorities'.[229] The Polish nation enjoyed the right of national self-determination, whilst 'Polish nationals belonging to racial,

---

[223] Eide, 'Commentary to the Declaration on the Rights of Persons Belonging to National or Ethnic, Religious and Linguistic Minorities', para. 58. See Patrick Thornberry, *Indigenous peoples and international law* (Manchester: Manchester University Press, 2002), pp. 424–6.

[224] Article 2(1) of the UN Declaration on Minorities.   [225] Article 1(1), *ibid.*

[226] See Eide, 'Commentary to the Declaration on the Rights of Persons Belonging to National or Ethnic, Religious and Linguistic Minorities', para. 60.

[227] See, for example, Perry Keller, 'Re-thinking ethnic and cultural rights in Europe' (1998) 18 *Oxford Journal of Legal Studies* 29, 32.

[228] Preamble, Treaty of Peace Between the United States of America, the British Empire, France, Italy, and Japan and Poland, 28 June 1919.

[229] See Articles 8, 9, and 12, *ibid.*

religious or linguistic minorities' enjoyed certain 'minority' rights.[230] The term 'national', in relation to 'minority', was omitted to avoid any association with collective rights.[231]

In contemporary instruments concerning the protection of minorities, the term 'national minority' was introduced in the UN Declaration on National or Ethnic, Religious and Linguistic Minorities.[232] The Declaration does not make any distinction in the allocation of rights to persons belonging to ethnic, religious, linguistic and national minorities, although Asbjørn Eide recognises that it is possible to argue that the different categories of minorities might enjoy different rights: persons belonging to religious minorities enjoying only the minority rights to profess and practise their religion; those belonging to linguistic minorities those minority rights relating to education and the use of the minority language; and persons belonging to ethnic minorities those minority rights relating to the preservation and development of other aspects of their culture. The category of national minority 'would then have still stronger rights relating not only to their culture but to the preservation and development of their national identity'.[233]

The scope of application of contemporary European instruments concerns 'persons belonging to national minorities'. The principal instruments are the Framework Convention for the Protection of National Minorities, adopted by the Council of Europe, and the Copenhagen Document, adopted by the participating States of the Organization for Security and Co-operation in Europe.[234] The following sections consider the contemporary protection of the rights of persons belonging to national minorities in Europe. Particular attention is paid to the extent to which the regime is able to provide a more detailed

---

[230] See Nathaniel Berman, '"But the alternative is despair": European nationalism and the modernist renewal of international law' (1993) 106 *Harvard Law Review* 1792, 1824.

[231] Nathaniel Berman, 'The international law of nationalism: group identity and legal history', in David Wippman (ed.), *International law and ethnic conflict* (Ithaca: Cornell University Press, 1998), p. 25, at p. 41.

[232] GA Res. 47/135, adopted 18 December 1992, 'Declaration on the Rights of Persons belonging to National or Ethnic, Religious and Linguistic Minorities'. Cf. the scope of application of Article 27 of the International Covenant on Civil and Political Rights, which refers to 'ethnic, religious or linguistic'.

[233] Eide, 'Commentary to the Declaration on the Rights of Persons Belonging to National or Ethnic, Religious and Linguistic Minorities', para. 7.

[234] The symbiotic nature of the regimes is recognised in the OSCE Budapest Summit Declaration on Genuine Partnership in a New Era, 34 ILM (1995) 764, Part VIII, 'The Human Dimension', para. 22, and in the preamble to the Framework Convention for the Protection of National Minorities.

elaboration of the necessary measures required for the protection and promotion of national minority identity.

Framework Convention for the Protection of National Minorities

The Council of Europe is an international organisation with forty-five member States, which aims to 'achieve a greater unity between its members for the purpose of safeguarding and realising the ideals and principles which are their common heritage'.[235] Central to its work is the protection of human rights. The principal instrument of the Council of Europe is the Convention for the Protection of Human Rights and Fundamental Freedoms (1950) (ECHR).[236] The European Convention on Human Rights prohibits discrimination in the enjoyment of the rights in the Convention, inter alia, on the ground of 'association with a national minority' (the term is not defined),[237] but does not contain a self-standing provision concerning the protection of national minorities (cf. Article 27 of the International Covenant on Civil and Political Rights).[238] A proposal to adopt an 'additional protocol on the rights of national minorities' was rejected by the member States of the Council of Europe,[239] who decided instead to adopt a Framework Convention for the Protection of National Minorities.[240]

The monitoring of States parties' compliance with their commitments under the Framework Convention is the responsibility of the Committee of Ministers of the Council of Europe.[241] States parties are obliged to transmit periodic reports providing information on the

---

[235] Article 1(a) of the Statute of the Council of Europe, adopted London, 5 May 1949, in force 3 August 1949, ETS No. 1.

[236] Convention for the Protection of Human Rights and Fundamental Freedoms (as amended), adopted at Rome, 4 November 1950, in force 3 September 1953, ETS No. 5.

[237] Article 14 of the European Convention on Human Rights. See also Article 1 of Protocol No. 12 to the Convention for the Protection of Human Rights and Fundamental Freedoms, adopted at Rome, 4 November 2000, in force 1 April 2005, ETS No. 177.

[238] The European Court of Human Rights has concluded that the vulnerable position of gypsies as a minority requires that 'some special consideration should be given to their needs and their different lifestyle ... To this extent there is thus a positive obligation imposed on the Contracting States by virtue of Article 8 ['right to respect for his private and family life'] to facilitate the gypsy way of life'. *Chapman* v. *UK*, Reports of Judgments and Decisions 2001-I, para. 96. Also, *Connors* v. *UK*, Judgment, 27 May 2004, para. 82.

[239] Parliamentary Assembly, Recommendation 1201, adopted 1 February 1993, 'Additional protocol on the rights of national minorities to the European Convention on Human Rights (1950)'.

[240] Framework Convention for the Protection of National Minorities, adopted at Strasbourg, 1 February 1995, in force 1 February 1998, ETS No. 157.

[241] Article 24(1), *ibid.*

legislative and other measures taken to give effect to the principles set out in the Framework Convention.[242] In evaluating these reports, the Committee of Ministers is assisted by an Advisory Committee on the Framework Convention,[243] which prepares an Opinion on the measures taken by the State party.[244] These Opinions provide an important contribution to the understanding of the commitments of States parties under the Framework Convention.[245] Having received the Opinion, and a comment from the relevant State party, the Committee of Ministers adopts, where appropriate, a Resolution in respect of the State Party concerned.

National minorities

The beneficiaries of the provisions of the Framework Convention are 'persons belonging to national minorities'.[246] No definition of the term 'national minority' is provided,[247] as it proved impossible to arrive at one capable of mustering the support of all Council of Europe member States.[248] In the absence of a definition in the text, the Advisory

---

[242] Article 25(1), *ibid.* See also Article 25(2), *ibid.*   [243] Article 26(1), *ibid.*

[244] See Rules of Procedure of the Advisory Committee on the Framework Convention for the Protection of National Minorities, adopted by the Advisory Committee on 29 October 1998, Council of Europe Doc. ACFC/INF(1998)002.

[245] See generally 'Collection of Opinions of the Advisory Committee on the Framework Convention for the Protection of National Minorities', ACFC/I/Secr(2003)001 rev.2. The resolutions of the Council of Ministers generally follow the Opinions of the Advisory Committee on the Framework Convention, but are couched in more opaque and diplomatic language, and do not assist greatly in the elaboration of States parties' commitments.

[246] Two dominant understandings of the term 'national minority' appear in the literature: (1) a feeling of association with a 'nation'; and (2) a restriction of the term 'minority' to include only those individuals who are citizens of the State: Eyassu Gayim, *The concept of minority in international law: a critical study of the vital elements* (Rovaniemi: University of Lapland Press, 2001), p. 74 and references cited.

[247] Cf. Article 1 of the Parliamentary Assembly, Recommendation 1201, adopted 1 February 1993, 'Additional Protocol on the Rights of National Minorities to the European Convention on Human Rights (1950)': 'For the purposes of [the European Convention on Human Rights (1950)] the expression "national minority" refers to a group of persons in a state who: (a) reside on the territory of that state and are citizens thereof; (b) maintain longstanding, firm and lasting ties with that state; (c) display distinctive ethnic, cultural, religious or linguistic characteristics; (d) are sufficiently representative, although smaller in number than the rest of the population of that state or of a region of that state; (e) are motivated by a concern to preserve together that which constitutes their common identity, including their culture, their traditions, their religion or their language.'

[248] Explanatory Report on the Framework Convention for the Protection of National Minorities, Council of Europe Doc. H(94)10, Strasbourg, November 1994, para. 12.

Committee has accepted that States parties enjoy a certain 'margin of appreciation' in defining the scope of application of the Framework Convention, 'in order to take the specific circumstances prevailing in their country into account'. This margin of appreciation must be exercised in accordance with the general principles of international law and those recognised in the Framework Convention, and 'should not be a source of arbitrary or unjustified distinctions'.[249]

In the identification of 'national minorities', the starting point is the self-identification by the group, or at least some of its members,[250] that the group is a national minority (or that the group is entitled to the benefit of the provisions in the Framework Convention).[251] In the opinion of the Advisory Committee, the possibility of relying on the protection of the Framework Convention 'should be offered only as an option and it should be applied only to the extent this is accepted by the persons concerned'.[252] There should be no attempt to impose an ethno cultural identity on any person, or group of persons.[253]

The Advisory Committee has rejected the idea that there can be a strict taxonomy of the ethno-cultural groups recognised in inter national legal instruments. In its Opinion on Denmark, the Committee noted that the Danish Government took the view that, because of the existence of territorial self-government arrangements, the populations of Greenland and the Far-Oer Islands did not fall within the scope of application of the Framework Convention. Additionally, the Government noted that these persons 'do not consider themselves as national minorities, because they are entitled to a different form of protection as *an indigenous people* or *a people*'.[254] The Advisory Committee did not share the view that persons constituting an indigenous people or people could not at the same time benefit from the protection afforded to persons constituting national minorities: 'The fact that a group of persons may be entitled to a different form of

---

[249] See inter alia, Opinion on Albania, ACFC/INF/OPI(2003)004, para. 18.

[250] Where there is a dispute amongst the members of a group as to whether the group is, in fact, a national minority, the Advisory Committee has concluded that members of the group may rely on the provisions of the Framework Convention: Opinion on Finland, ACFC/INF/OPI(2001)002, para. 16.

[251] Article 3 of the Framework Convention for the Protection of National Minorities, provides: 'Every person belonging to a national minority shall have the right freely to choose to be treated or not to be treated as such.'

[252] Opinion on Russian Federation, ACFC/INF/OPI(2003)005, para. 25.

[253] Opinion on Ukraine, ACFC/INF/OPI(2002)010, para. 21.

[254] Opinion on Denmark, ACFC/INF/OPI(2001)005, para. 16 (emphasis in original).

protection, cannot by itself justify their exclusion from other forms of protection.'[255] The Advisory Committee concluded that the *a priori* exclusion of Greenlanders and Far-Oese persons was not compatible with the Framework Convention.[256] Persons belonging to ethno-cultural groups which fall within the scope of application of the Framework Convention may enjoy the protection of the measures provided in the Framework Convention, if they so choose, notwithstanding their designation under domestic law,[257] or the fact that the group enjoys the protection of other international instruments, concerning, for example, the rights of indigenous peoples or peoples.[258]

The Framework Convention refers repeatedly to the issue of ethnic, cultural, religious and linguistic identity. The preamble notes that a pluralist and genuinely democratic society should 'not only respect the ethnic, cultural, linguistic and religious identity of each person belonging to a national minority, but also create appropriate conditions enabling them to express, preserve and develop this identity'.[259] Article 3 confirms that it is for each person belonging to a national minority to have the right to choose to be treated, or not treated, as such.[260] The Explanatory Report on the Framework Convention notes that the choice to associate is 'inseparably linked to objective criteria relevant to the person's identity'.[261] Article 5(1) refers to the essential elements of the identity of persons belonging to national minorities, 'namely their religion, language, traditions and cultural heritage'.[262] The

---

[255] *Ibid.*, para. 17. The Advisory Committee further noted that, whilst the Greenlanders and Far-Oese persons might enjoy the effective protection of their identity (language, education, culture etc.) within the respective home rule areas, no such protection would exist outside of those areas, notably in mainland Denmark: *ibid.*

[256] *Ibid.*, para. 18.

[257] The Advisory Committee on the Framework Convention has confirmed that the Framework Convention does not require that States parties, in their domestic legislation, use the term 'national minority' to describe the relevant group: Opinion on Russian Federation, ACFC/INF/OPI(2003)005, para. 26.

[258] On the rights of indigenous peoples and peoples, see chapter 2.

[259] Preamble to the Framework Convention for the Protection of National Minorities.

[260] Article 3(1), *ibid.*

[261] Explanatory Report on the Framework Convention for the Protection of National Minorities, para 35.

[262] Article 5(1) of the Framework Convention for the Protection of National Minorities. The provision does not prohibit voluntary assimilation: Explanatory Report on the Framework Convention for the Protection of National Minorities, para. 45. Article 5(2) of the Framework Convention for the Protection of National Minorities prohibits policies and practices aimed at forced assimilation: the destruction of different ethno-cultural identities.

provision lists the essential elements of the identity of a national minority, but should not be read as implying 'that all ethnic, cultural, linguistic or religious differences necessarily lead to the creation of national minorities'.[263] National minorities are 'minorities' for the purposes of Article 27 of the International Covenant on Civil and Political Rights,[264] but not all ethnic, religious or linguistic minorities are national minorities.

The term 'national minority' is sometimes associated with those groups that have enjoyed a 'historic presence' in the State.[265] Will Kymlicka, for example, uses the term to refer to 'groups that formed complete and functioning societies on their historic homeland prior to being incorporated into a larger State'.[266] A number of obligations in the Framework Convention apply only in respect of 'areas inhabited by persons belonging to national minorities traditionally or in substantial numbers',[267] and 'areas traditionally inhabited by substantial numbers of persons belonging to a national minority'.[268] The majority of provisions are not restricted in their territorial scope of application. Reference to areas inhabited by persons belonging to national minorities traditionally and/or in substantial numbers in some, but not all, provisions of the Framework Convention implies both that persons belonging to national minorities may live in areas outside of the territories traditionally inhabited by the group,[269] and that there may be national minority groups which do not have a territorial 'homeland'.

---

[263] Explanatory Report on the Framework Convention for the Protection of National Minorities, para. 43.

[264] See Human Rights Committee, Concluding Observations on Serbia and Montenegro, UN Doc. CCPR/CO/81/SEMO, 12 August 2004, para. 23: 'The State party should ensure that all members of ethnic, religious and linguistic minorities, whether or not their communities are recognized as national minorities, enjoy effective protection against discrimination and are able to enjoy their own culture, to practise and profess their own religion, and use their own language, in accordance with Article 27 of the Covenant.'

[265] See Patrick Thornberry, 'The UN Declaration on the Rights of Persons Belonging to National or Ethnic, Religious and Linguistic Minorities', p. 34.

[266] Will Kymlicka, 'Western political theory and ethnic relations in Eastern Europe', in Will Kymlicka and Magda Opalski (eds.), *Can liberal pluralism be exported? Western political theory and ethnic relations in Eastern Europe* (Oxford: Oxford University Press, 2001), p. 13, at p. 23.

[267] See Articles 10(2) and 14(2) of the Framework Convention for the Protection of National Minorities.

[268] Article 11(3), *ibid.* See also Article 16.

[269] Distinct ethno-cultural groups emerge where patterns of cultural behaviour are reproduced from generation to generation, given the historical geographical stability

In its Opinion on Denmark, the Advisory Committee concluded that 'given the historic presence of Roma [a non-territorial group] in Denmark ... persons belonging to the Roma community cannot *a priori* be excluded from the personal scope of application of the Framework Convention'.[270] National minorities are not, necessarily, sub-State nations.[271]

Other writers have associated the term 'national minority' with groups that constitute a 'minority in one country but which formed the majority in the mother country'.[272] On this understanding it should have been possible to identify the beneficiaries of the rights recognised in the Framework Convention. This was not the case. It is also worthy of note that the Framework Convention recognises the right of persons belonging to national minorities to establish and maintain free and peaceful contacts across frontiers 'in particular' with 'those with whom they share an ethnic, cultural, linguistic or religious identity, or a common cultural heritage'.[273] The right is not restricted to persons belonging to national minorities who share an ethnic, cultural, linguistic or religious identity with the majority/titular population of a neighbouring State. In its Opinion on Albania, the Advisory Committee noted that the State party described the Roma and Aromanians/Vlachs as 'linguistic

---

of the group: Perry Keller, 'Re-thinking ethnic and cultural rights in Europe' (1998) 18 *Oxford Journal of Legal Studies* 29, 36.

[270] Opinion on Denmark, ACFC/INF/OPI(2001)005, para. 22. See also the declarations by Germany (Opinion on Germany, ACFC/INF/OPI(2002)008, para. 12) and Sweden (Opinion on Sweden, ACFC/INF/OPI(2003)006, para. 16). The full list of declarations is available at http://conventions.coe.int/treaty/Commun/ListeDeclarations.asp?NT = 157&CLNT = ENG (last visited 21 January 2005).

[271] Cf. Keller, 'Re-thinking ethnic and cultural rights in Europe', 32: Europe may be considered as being composed of 'larger and smaller building block nations whose problems stem from the fact that linguistic and cultural boundaries are not consistent with those of the nation states of Europe'. According to Josef Kunz, the legal regime for the protection of minorities was the 'strict and logical corollary of the principle of self-determination of nations': Josef Kunz, 'The present status of international law for the protection of minorities' (1954) 48 *American Journal of International Law* 282, 282.

[272] The idea that 'national minorities' are those groups which constitute a 'minority in one country but which formed the majority in the mother country', often following changes in international boundaries, has found some support in the UN Working Group on Minorities: José Bengoa, 'Existence and recognition of minorities', UN Doc. E/CN.4/Sub.2/AC.5/2000/WP.2, 3 April 2000, at footnote 5. See also Geoff Gilbert, 'Minority rights under the Council of Europe', in Peter Cumper and Steven Wheatley (eds.), *Minority rights in the 'new' Europe* (The Hague: Kluwer Law International, 1999), p. 53, at p. 53. The Declaration by Denmark, which designates the German minority in South Jutland, accords with the 'kin-State' definition of national minorities: Opinion on Denmark, ACFC/INF/OPI(2001)005, para. 12.

[273] Article 17(1) of the Framework Convention for the Protection of National Minorities.

minorities' rather than 'national minorities', on the basis that these groups 'do not have a kin-state'. The Advisory Committee encouraged the Government 'to re-examine the question of the designation of the Roma and Aromanians/Vlachs as linguistic minorities, as opposed to national minorities'.[274]

Upon signing the Framework Convention, a number of States parties issued declarations on its scope of application.[275] Some of these simply identify the relevant beneficiaries of the provisions, i.e. the States parties' national minority groups. According to the definition by Denmark, 'the Framework Convention shall apply to the German minority in South Jutland'.[276] The declaration by Germany provides that the provisions of the Framework Convention will apply in respect of 'the Danes of German citizenship and the members of the Sorbian people with German citizenship [and] members of the ethnic groups traditionally resident in Germany, the Frisians of German citizenship and the Sinti and Roma of German citizenship'.[277] Sweden declared that the national minorities in Sweden are Sami, Swedish Finns, Tornedalers, Roma and Jews.[278]

The declarations by Austria, Estonia and Switzerland consider that the term national minority applies to those ethnic, religious or linguistic groups that can point to long-standing, firm and lasting ties with the relevant State party, and whose members are citizens of the State. The declaration by Austria defined national minorities as 'those groups which come within the scope of application of the Law on Ethnic Groups ... and which live and traditionally have had their home in parts of the territory of the Republic of Austria and which are composed of Austrian citizens with non-German mother tongues and with their own ethnic cultures'.[279] Estonia referred to the following criteria: citizens of Estonia who reside on the territory of Estonia; maintain long-standing, firm and lasting ties with Estonia; are distinct from Estonians on the basis of their ethnic, cultural, religious or linguistic

---

[274] Opinion on Albania, ACFC/INF/OPI(2003)004, para. 20.
[275] On the legal status of the declarations of States parties to the Framework Convention, see Maria Telalian, 'European Framework Convention for the Protection of National Minorities and its personal scope of application', in Gudmundur Alfredsson and Maria Stavropoulou (eds.), Justice pending: indigenous peoples and other good causes (The Hague: Kluwer Law International, 2002), p. 117, at pp. 127–32.
[276] Opinion on Denmark, ACFC/INF/OPI(2001)005, para. 12.
[277] Opinion on Germany, ACFC/INF/OPI(2002)008, para. 12.
[278] Opinion on Sweden, ACFC/INF/OPI(2003)006, para. 16.
[279] Opinion on Austria, ACFC/INF/OPI(2002)009, para. 12.

characteristics; and are motivated by a concern to preserve together their cultural traditions, their religion or their language, which constitute the basis of their common identity.[280] The declaration by Switzerland defined national minorities as 'groups of individuals numerically inferior to the rest of the population of the country or of a canton, whose members are Swiss nationals, have long-standing, firm and lasting ties with Switzerland and are guided by the will to safeguard together what constitutes their common identity, in particular their culture, their traditions, their religion or their language'.[281]

Citizenship may not, by itself, constitute the basis for excluding a group of persons from the scope of application of the Framework Convention.[282] The exclusion of persons who would otherwise fall under its scope of application on the basis that they are not citizens is incompatible with the objects and purposes of the Framework Convention. The Advisory Committee has called on Estonia to 're-examine its approach reflected in the declaration in consultation with those concerned and consider the inclusion of additional persons belonging to minorities, in particular non-citizens, in the application of the Framework Convention'.[283]

In its Opinion on Albania, the Advisory Committee noted the 'historic presence of Egyptians in Albania and the desire of persons belonging to this group to identify themselves as persons belonging to a national minority, and ... their ethnic background, history, traditions and cultural heritage'.[284] The Committee concluded that the *a priori* exclusion of the Egyptian minority in Albania from the personal scope of application of the Framework Convention 'was not compatible with the Framework Convention'.[285] The Committee has also concluded that 'the historic presence of Roma in Denmark [means that] persons belonging to the Roma community cannot *a priori* be excluded from the

---

[280] Opinion on Estonia, ACFC/INF/OPI(2002)005, para. 13.

[281] Opinion on Switzerland, ACFC/INF/OPI(2003)007, para. 16.

[282] On the requirement of citizenship, see also the declarations by Germany (Opinion on Germany, ACFC/INF/OPI(2002)008, para. 12) and Poland (Opinion on Poland, ACFC/INF/OP/I(2004)005, para. 15).

[283] Opinion on Estonia, ACFC/INF/OPI(2002)005, para. 18. Cf. declaration by the Russian Federation 'attempts to exclude from [its] scope ... persons who permanently reside in the territory of States Parties ... and [who] previously had a citizenship but have been arbitrarily deprived of it. [This] contradicts the purpose of the Framework Convention': Opinion on Russian Federation, ACFC/INF/OPI(2003)005, footnote at para. 20.

[284] Opinion on Albania, ACFC/INF/OPI(2003)004, para. 22.   [285] *Ibid.*

personal scope of application of the Framework Convention';[286] that the 'historic presence of the Csangos in Romania [means that] the Romanian authorities should favourably consider the extension of the Framework Convention to [such] persons';[287] and agreed with the Italian Government that the Framework Convention 'must be applied to [certain] historical linguistic minorities … [and that it was] of the opinion that, especially in view of their attested historical presence in Italy, the Roma should also be entitled to the protection afforded by the Framework Convention'.[288]

Ethnic, cultural, religious or linguistic communities that have enjoyed a historic presence in a State party may not be denied their right to recognition as national minorities under the Framework Convention. The converse does not apply: States parties are not obliged to exclude persons belonging to 'new' minorities from its personal scope of application. The Advisory Committee has commended open and inclusive approaches to the scope of application of the Framework Convention.[289] In its Opinion on the United Kingdom, the Committee strongly welcomed 'the inclusive approach' of the United Kingdom in its interpretation of the term national minority as 'a group of persons defined by colour, race, nationality (including citizenship) or ethnic or national origin'.[290]

In the absence of an agreed definition of the term 'national minority', States parties enjoy a certain margin of appreciation in determining the scope of application of the Framework Convention. That margin of appreciation is limited by the 'ordinary meaning to be given to the terms of the [Framework Convention] in their context and in the light of its object and purpose'.[291] The declarations of the States parties and the Opinions of the Advisory Committee, taken with the fact that the Framework Convention concerns only national minorities, and not ethnic, religious or linguistic minorities, permits (but does not require) States parties to exclude persons belonging to 'new' minorities (those created through the process of mass migration since the Second World War) from the scope of application of the Framework

---

[286] Opinion on Denmark, ACFC/INF/OPI(2001)005, para. 22.
[287] Opinion on Romania, ACFC/INF/OPI(2002)001, para. 18.
[288] Opinion on Italy, ACFC/INF/OPI(2002)007, para. 16.
[289] See, for example, Opinion on Lithuania, ACFC/INF/OPI(2003)008, para. 19; and Opinion on Russian Federation, ACFC/INF/OPI(2003)005, para. 21.
[290] Opinion on United Kingdom, ACFC/INF/OPI(2002)006, para. 14.
[291] Article 31(1) of the Vienna Convention on the Law of Treaties.

Convention.[292] Citizenship is one factor that may be taken into account in determining whether a person is a member of an 'old' or 'new' minority, but it is not a conclusive factor.

The 'rights' of persons belonging to national minorities

The Framework Convention does not create any rights for persons belonging to national minorities, but recognises a number of obligations incumbent on States parties.[293] A number of the provisions confirm the application of individual human rights provisions to persons belonging to national minorities. States parties are, for example, required to recognise the right of persons belonging to a national minority to manifest their religion and to establish religious institutions,[294] and to use the minority language, in private and in public.[295] The Framework Convention further obliges States parties to guarantee to persons belonging to national minorities the right to equal treatment, and the right to different treatment. Article 4(1) requires State parties to guarantee to persons belonging to national minorities 'the right of equality before the law and of equal protection of the law'.[296] Any discrimination based on belonging to a national minority shall be prohibited.[297] Article 5(1) obliges States parties to 'undertake to promote the conditions necessary for persons belonging to national minorities to

---

[292] Article 27 of the International Covenant on Civil and Political Rights appears to exclude the possibility of recognising new minorities: 'In those States in which ethnic, religious or linguistic minorities exist …' Cf. Human Rights Committee, General Comment No. 23, 'Rights of minorities (Article 27)', para. 5.2.

[293] According to the European Court of Human Rights, the Framework Convention 'sets out general principles and goals but signatory states were unable to agree on means or implementation': *Chapman* v. *UK*, Reports of Judgments and Decisions 2001-I, para. 94.

[294] Article 8 of the Framework Convention for the Protection of National Minorities. See also the rights to freedom of peaceful assembly, association, expression and freedom of thought, conscience and religion: Article 7, *ibid*. See also Articles 19 and 23.

[295] Article 10(1), *ibid*.

[296] Article 4(1), *ibid*. Where necessary, State parties shall adopt 'adequate measures', in order to promote, in all areas of economic, social, political and cultural life, full and effective equality between persons belonging to a national minority and those belonging to the majority: Article 4(2) of the Framework Convention for the Protection of National Minorities. These measures are not to be considered an act of discrimination: Article 4(3), *ibid*.

[297] Article 4(1), *ibid*. Cf. Article 14 of the European Convention on Human Rights. See also Article 1 of Protocol No. 12 to the Convention for the Protection of Human Rights and Fundamental Freedoms, adopted at Rome, 4 November 2000, in force 1 April 2005, ETS No. 177.

maintain and develop their culture and to preserve the essential elements of their identity, namely their religion, language, traditions and cultural heritage'.[298]

In contrast to international legal instruments concerning 'minorities',[299] the Framework Convention contains a number of detailed commitments. States parties are required to recognise the rights of persons belonging to national minorities to hold opinions and to receive and impart information and ideas in the minority language;[300] to the official recognition of their name in the minority language;[301] to display signs, inscriptions and other information of a private nature visible to the public in the minority language;[302] to set up and to manage their own private educational and training establishments;[303] to learn the minority language;[304] and to maintain contacts across frontiers with persons lawfully staying in other States, in particular those with whom they share an ethnic, cultural, linguistic or religious identity, or a common cultural heritage.[305]

Other obligations in the Framework Convention are vaguely formulated and struck through with conditional clauses. Article 10(2) provides: 'In areas inhabited by persons belonging to national minorities traditionally or in substantial numbers, if those persons so request and where such a request corresponds to a real need, the Parties shall endeavour to ensure, as far as possible, the conditions which would make it possible to use the minority language in relations between those persons and the administrative authorities.'[306] No definitions of

---

[298] Article 5(1) of the Framework Convention for the Protection of National Minorities.
[299] See Article 27 of the International Covenant on Civil and Political Rights, and GA Res. 47/135, adopted 18 December 1992, 'Declaration on the Rights of Persons belonging to National or Ethnic, Religious and Linguistic Minorities'.
[300] Article 9(1) of the Framework Convention for the Protection of National Minorities.
[301] Article 11(1), *ibid*.   [302] Article 11(2), *ibid*.
[303] Article 13(1), *ibid*. Recognition of the right of persons belonging to national minorities to set up and to manage their own private educational and training establishments does not entail any financial obligations for States parties: Article 13(2), *ibid*. The Framework Convention does not exclude the possibility of State funding: Explanatory Report on the Framework Convention for the Protection of National Minorities, para. 73.
[304] Article 14(1), *ibid*. Where persons belonging to national minorities are taught the minority language, or taught in the minority language, this shall be implemented without prejudice to the learning of the official language or the teaching in the official language (Article 14(2), *ibid*.), given that 'knowledge of the official language is a factor of social cohesion and integration': Explanatory Report on the Framework Convention for the Protection of National Minorities, para. 78.
[305] Article 17(1), *ibid*.   [306] Article 10(2), *ibid*.

the relevant terms are provided. States parties are deliberately provided with a wide margin of appreciation in the implementation of the provision.[307] Article 14(2) provides: 'In areas inhabited by persons belonging to national minorities traditionally or in substantial numbers, if there is sufficient demand, the Parties shall endeavour to ensure, as far as possible and within the framework of their education systems, that persons belonging to those minorities have adequate opportunities for being taught the minority language or for receiving instruction in this language.'[308] No definitions of the terms 'traditionally or in substantial numbers', 'sufficient demand' or 'adequate opportunities' are provided in the text, or in the Explanatory Report. In recognition of the possible financial, administrative and technical difficulties associated with the provision of education in and of minority languages, Article 14(2) is worded flexibly, leaving States parties a wide measure of discretion as to its implementation.[309]

The thirty-seven States parties to the Framework Convention have accepted that the protection of national minorities and the rights and freedoms of persons belonging to national minorities 'forms an integral part of the international protection of human rights, and as such falls within the scope of international co-operation'.[310] They have accepted important, if limited, obligations in respect of the recognition of certain rights for persons belonging to national minorities, although the Advisory Committee has made few determinations that a particular law, regulation or practice is 'not compatible' with the provisions of the Framework Convention.[311] Commitments in respect of the

---

[307] Explanatory Report on the Framework Convention for the Protection of National Minorities, para. 64.

[308] Article 14(2) of the Framework Convention for the Protection of National Minorities.

[309] Explanatory Report on the Framework Convention for the Protection of National Minorities, para. 75.

[310] Article 1 of the Framework Convention for the Protection of National Minorities.

[311] See, for example, in relation to Article 9 (access to the media without discrimination): Opinion on Azerbaijan, ACFC/INF/OPI(2004)001, para. 108; Opinion on Russian Federation, ACFC/INF/OPI(2003)005, para. 76; Opinion on Ukraine, ACFC/INF/OPI(2002)010, paras. 43 and 97; Article 11(1) (right to recognition of names in the minority language): Opinion on Azerbaijan, ACFC/INF/OPI(2004)001, para. 111; Article 11(2) (right to display signs in the minority language): Opinion on Estonia, ACFC/INF/OPI(2002)005, para. 43; Opinion on Lithuania, ACFC/INF/OPI(2003)008, para. 58; Article 12(3) (equal access to education): Opinion on Albania, ACFC/INF/OPI(2003)004, para. 59; Opinion on Czech Republic, ACFC/INF/OPI(2002)002, para. 61; Opinion on Hungary, ACFC/INF/OPI(2001)004, para. 41; Opinion on Serbia and Montenegro, ACFC/INF/OPI(2004)002, para. 89; and Opinion on Slovakia, ACFC/INF/OPI(2001)001, para. 39 (all concerning the treatment of Roma children in schools).

right to the use of a minority language with the administrative authorities, the provision of education in the minority language, and the display of public information in the minority language are recognised,[312] but the circumstances in which they are to be implemented are not clear. Other demands of national minority groups, for example for the establishment of local self-government regimes, are not directly addressed in the Framework Convention. Article 15 provides only that the States parties 'shall create the conditions necessary for the effective participation of persons belonging to national minorities … in public affairs, in particular those affecting them'.[313] No right to autonomy or territorial self-government is provided.[314]

Organization for Security and Co-operation in Europe

The Organization for Security and Co-operation in Europe (OSCE) is a regional security organisation with fifty-five participating States.[315] The OSCE has a broad concept of security, which includes issues relating to human rights and democracy.[316] OSCE commitments are politically, not legally, binding, although they do establish standards of behaviour which the participating States are committed to upholding.[317] Initially, the OSCE process, begun with the signing of the (Helsinki) Final Act of

[312] See Article 11(3): 'In areas traditionally inhabited by substantial numbers of persons belonging to a national minority, the Parties shall endeavour, in the framework of their legal system, including, where appropriate, agreements with other States, and taking into account their specific conditions, to display traditional local names, street names and other topographical indications intended for the public also in the minority language when there is a sufficient demand for such indications.'

[313] Article 15 of the Framework Convention for the Protection of National Minorities.

[314] Cf. Parliamentary Assembly, Recommendation 1201, adopted 1 February 1993, 'Additional protocol on the rights of national minorities to the European Convention on Human Rights (1950)', Article 11: 'In the regions where they are in a majority the persons belonging to a national minority shall have the right to have at their disposal appropriate local or autonomous authorities or to have a special status, matching the specific historical and territorial situation and in accordance with the domestic legislation of the state.' See Venice Commission, 'Opinion on the Interpretation of Article 11 of the Draft Protocol to the European Convention on Human Rights Appended to Recommendation 1201 of the Parliamentary Assembly, Council of Europe Doc. CDL-INF(1996)004, 22 March 1996.

[315] The OSCE was previously the Conference on Security and Co-operation in Europe (CSCE). This work refers to the organisation throughout as the Organization for Security and Co-operation in Europe (OSCE).

[316] See generally *OSCE Human Dimension Commitments: A Reference Guide* (Warsaw: OSCE Office for Democratic Institutions and Human Rights, 2001).

[317] These political commitments may 'harden' into legal norms. See, for example, *Sidiropoulos and Others* v. *Greece*, Reports of Judgments and Decisions 1998-IV, para. 44.

the Conference on Security and Co-operation in Europe (1975) (CSCE), was not concerned with the position of persons belonging to national minorities, beyond the issue of non-discrimination.[318] In the 1990s, ethnic conflicts and ethnic tensions in Central and Eastern Europe raised the issue of national minorities to the top of the CSCE/OSCE's agenda, where it has remained.[319]

The participating States of the OSCE have been willing to adopt detailed and far-reaching commitments in respect of their national minorities, including the recognition of certain *rights* for persons belonging to national minorities. Additionally, they have established the post of High Commissioner on National Minorities.[320] The High Commissioner is 'an instrument of conflict prevention',[321] whose formal role is to provide 'early warning' and, as appropriate, 'early action', in respect of tensions involving national minority issues which have the potential to develop into conflict.[322] Informally, the role of the High Commissioner is to assist in the resolution of disputes between the central authorities in participating States and their national minorities.[323] The High Commissioner has focused primarily on situations involving persons belonging to a national minority who share an ethnic, cultural, religious or linguistic identity with the majority/titular population of a neighbouring State, a situation which constitutes a potential source of inter-, as well as intra-, State tension.[324]

---

[318] Final Act of the Conference on Security and Co-operation in Europe (1975) 14 ILM (1975) 1293, principle VII, para. 4: 'The participating States on whose territory national minorities exist will respect the right of persons belonging to such minorities to equality before the law, will afford them the full opportunity for the actual enjoyment of human rights and fundamental freedoms and will, in this manner, protect their legitimate interests in this sphere.'

[319] See, for example, the OSCE Charter for European Security, adopted Istanbul, November 1999, 39 ILM (2000) 255, para. 30; also 'OSCE Strategy to Address Threats to Security and Stability in the Twenty-First Century', OSCE Doc. MC.DOC/1/03, adopted Maastricht, 2 December 2003, para. 38.

[320] Declaration and Decisions from Helsinki Summit (1992), 31 ILM (1992) 1385, Chapter II, para. 1. See OSCE Charter for European Security, Istanbul, November 1999, 39 ILM (2000) 255, para. 30: 'We commend the essential work of the High Commissioner on National Minorities. We reaffirm that we will increase our efforts to implement the recommendations of the High Commissioner on National Minorities.'

[321] Declaration and Decisions from Helsinki Summit (1992), para. II(2).

[322] *Ibid.*, para. II(3).

[323] See Arie Bloed, 'The OSCE and the issue of national minorities', in Alan Philips and Alan Rosas (eds.), *Universal minority rights* (Turku/Åbo: Institute for Human Rights, Åbo Akademi University, 1995), p. 113, at pp. 116–19.

[324] See 'Introduction', *Lund Recommendations on the Effective Participation of National Minorities in Public Life* (The Hague: Foundation on Inter-Ethnic Relations, 1999). See John Packer,

None of the relevant CSCE/OSCE instruments defines the term 'national minority'. The first OSCE High Commissioner on National Minorities remarked that the existence of a minority was 'a question of fact and not of definition … I would dare to say that I know a minority when I see one.'[325] According to the High Commissioner, a national minority is a group with a linguistic, ethnic or cultural identity which distinguishes it from the majority, and which 'not only seeks to maintain its identity but also tries to give stronger expression to that identity'.[326] The 1990 Copenhagen Document refers to the right of persons belonging to national minorities to express, preserve and develop their 'ethnic, cultural, linguistic or religious identity'.[327] National minorities are ethnic, cultural, religious or linguistic minorities, although, as noted in the Report of the CSCE Meeting of Experts on National Minorities, 'not all ethnic, cultural, linguistic or religious differences necessarily lead to the creation of national minorities'.[328]

The OSCE Copenhagen Document contains important commitments in respect of human rights, democratic government and the rights of persons belonging to national minorities. The participating States recognised the right of persons belonging to national minorities 'to express, preserve and develop their ethnic, cultural, linguistic or religious identity and to maintain and develop their culture in all its aspects, free of any attempts at assimilation against their will'.[329] Persons belonging to national minorities have the right to use freely their mother tongue in private as well as in public,[330] and to establish and maintain educational institutions, and to seek voluntary financial and other contributions as well as public assistance.[331] Participating

---

'The origin and nature of the Lund Recommendations on the Effective Participation of National Minorities in Public Life' (2000) 11 *Helsinki Monitor* 29. The text of the Recommendations appears as an annex to the Article. See also www.osce.org/hcnm/documents/recommendations/lund/index.php3 (last visited 10 January 2005).

[325] Max van der Stoel, OSCE, High Commissioner on National Minorities, keynote address at the opening of the OSCE Minorities Seminar in Warsaw in 1994: www.osce.org/hcnm/mandate/ (last visited 10 January 2005).

[326] *Ibid.*

[327] OSCE Document of the Copenhagen Meeting of the Conference on the Human Dimension ('Copenhagen Document'), 29 ILM (1990) 1318, para. 32. Participating States committed themselves to protect the 'ethnic, cultural, linguistic and religious identity of national minorities on their territory': Copenhagen Document, para. 33. See also Report of the CSCE Meeting of Experts on National Minorities (1991), 30 ILM (1991) 1692, Part III.

[328] Report of the CSCE Meeting of Experts on National Minorities, Part II.

[329] Copenhagen Document, para. 32. [330] *Ibid.*, para. 32.1. [331] *Ibid.*, para. 32.2.

States further committed themselves to 'endeavour to ensure' that persons belonging to national minorities, notwithstanding the need to learn the official language(s), have adequate opportunities for instruction of their mother tongue or in their mother tongue, as well as, wherever possible and necessary, for its use before public authorities, in conformity with applicable national legislation.[332]

The Copenhagen Document recognises both the negative and the positive aspects of the right to cultural security: participating States are to 'protect the ethnic, cultural, linguistic and religious identity of national minorities on their territory and create conditions for the promotion of that identity'.[333] The commitments do not extend to the introduction of territorial self-government for national minorities, although the OSCE participating States have recognised the value of 'autonomous administrations corresponding to the specific historical and territorial circumstances of national minorities' as one mechanism by which the identity of national minorities may be protected and promoted.[334]

Conclusion

Ethno-cultural groups are imagined communities. It is not possible to provide a typology of national or ethnic, religious and linguistic minorities and accord the relevant group the appropriate 'minority rights'. The international instruments concerning minorities (and, in Europe, national minorities) do not define the beneficiaries of the rights of minorities, and the consequential rights of minorities. They are concerned with the protection of the practice(s) of culture by cultural minorities. The legal regime recognises both a negative and a positive aspect of the right to cultural security. Persons belonging to minorities 'shall not be denied the right, in community with the other members of their group, to enjoy their own culture, to profess and practise their own religion, or to use their own language'.[335] Moreover, States are required

---

[332] *Ibid.*, para. 34.   [333] *Ibid.*, para. 33.

[334] *Ibid.*, para. 35. See also OSCE Charter for European Security, Istanbul, November 1999, 39 ILM 255 (2000), para. 19; Report of the CSCE Meeting of Experts on National Minorities, Part IV; and Recommendations 15 and 19, Lund Recommendations on the Effective Participation of National Minorities in Public Life. See also Proposals of the European Centre for Minority Issues Seminar, 'Towards Effective Participation of Minorities', UN Doc. E/CN.4/Sub.2/AC.5/1999/WP.4, 5 May 1999, para. 10.

[335] Article 27 of the International Covenant on Civil and Political Rights. See also Article 2(1) of GA Res. 47/135, adopted 18 December 1992, 'Declaration on the Rights of Persons belonging to National or Ethnic, Religious and Linguistic Minorities'.

to take positive measures to protect the minorities within their respective territories, and to encourage conditions for the promotion of their identity.[336] They must introduce legislative and other measures 'to create favourable conditions to enable persons belonging to minorities to express their characteristics and to develop their culture, language, religion, traditions and customs, except where specific practices are in violation of national law and contrary to international standards'.[337] The principle of cultural security is accepted by the international community, but few positive commitments are recognised. States' policies concerning minorities will emerge through domestic decision-making procedures – in accordance with the principle of the right of cultural security for persons belonging to minorities. In the absence of the recognition of detailed substantive rights for persons belonging to minorities, the right of political participation in relevant decision-making processes is central to the protection of culture, and in determining the 'rights' of minorities. This issue is examined in chapter 3.

---

[336] Article 1(1) of GA Res. 47/135, 'Declaration on Minorities'.
[337] See Article 4(2), *ibid.*

2 The self-determination of peoples

International law recognises a right of cultural security for national, ethnic, cultural, religious and linguistic minorities. The decentralisation of power to local communities increases the possibilities that minority groups may participate effectively in decision-making processes, concerning, for example, language and education policy.[1] For a number of ethno-cultural groups, the desire for political self-government forms part of the collective identity of the group.[2] Members of the group consider that 'the political and the national unit should be congruent',[3] and that borders should be drawn, and institutions arranged, 'to allow the group political freedom from

---

[1] Asbjørn Eide, 'Commentary to the Declaration on the Rights of Persons Belonging to National or Ethnic, Religious and Linguistic Minorities', UN Doc. E/CN.4/Sub.2/AC.5/2001/2, 2 April 2001, para. 46. See also Benedict Kingsbury, ' "Indigenous peoples" in international law: a constructivist approach to the controversy' (1998) 92 *American Journal of International Law* 414, 450–3. Cf. Robert Dahl, *On democracy* (New Haven and London: Yale University Press, 1998), at p. 110.

[2] See Ghia Nodia, 'Nationalism and democracy', in Larry Diamond and Marc Plattner (eds.), *Nationalism, ethnic conflict and democracy* (Baltimore: Johns Hopkins University Press, 1994), p. 3, at pp. 11–12. In 2003, there were twenty-two armed self-determination conflicts, and a further seventy-six territorially concentrated groups seeking greater self-determination by political means: David Quinn and Ted Robert Gurr, 'Self-determination movements and their outcomes', in Monty Marshall and Ted Robert Gurr, *Peace and conflict 2003* (College Park, MD: University of Maryland, Center for International Development and Conflict Management, 2003), p. 26.

[3] Ernest Gellner, *Nations and nationalism* (Oxford: Blackwell, 1983), p. 1. See also Allen Buchanan, 'Towards a theory of secession' (1991) 101 *Ethics* 322, 328; and S. James Anaya, 'The capacity of international law to advance ethnic or nationality rights claims' (1990) 75 *Iowa Law Review* 837, 838.

domination by other groups'.[4] In other words, each 'nation' should have its own State, if it so desires.[5]

Ethno-cultural groups demanding territorial self-government consider themselves, in the nomenclature of international law, 'peoples' (or 'nations') rather than 'minorities'.[6] Reference is made to the right of peoples to self-determination.[7] The rights of persons belonging to minorities and the rights of peoples are related, but distinct.[8] The rights of minorities do not include the right to self-government, either in the form of separation or secession (sovereign self-determination),[9] or territorial autonomy within the State (less-than-sovereign self-determination).[10]

This chapter examines the right of peoples to self-determination.[11] In particular, it considers the implications of the recognition of a right of

---

[4] Jacob Levi, *The multiculturalism of fear* (Oxford: Oxford University Press, 2000), p. 137. See also Michael Hechter, *Containing nationalism* (Oxford: Oxford University Press, 2000), p. 6.

[5] Buchanan, 'Towards a theory of secession', 328. Particular problems arise where two Nations claim the same territory. See Gellner, *Nations and nationalism*, p. 2; and Thomas Franck, *The empowered self: law and society in the age of individualism* (Oxford: Oxford University Press, 2001), p. 23.

[6] See David Copp, 'International law and morality in the theory of secession' (1998) 2 *Journal of Ethics* 219, 227.

[7] Gerry Simpson, 'The diffusion of sovereignty' (1996) 32 *Stamford Journal of International Law* 255, 274–5.

[8] Human Rights Committee, General Comment No. 23, 'Rights of minorities (Article 27)', adopted 8 April 1994, reprinted in 'Compilation of General Comments and General Recommendations adopted by human rights treaty bodies', UN Doc. HRI/GEN/1/Rev.7, 12 May 2004 (hereafter 'Compilation of General Comments and General Recommendations'), p. 158, para. 3.1. See also Rosalyn Higgins, 'Postmodern tribalism and the right to secession', in Catherine Brölmann et al. (eds.), *Peoples and minorities in international law* (Dordrecht: Martinus Nijhoff, 1993), p. 29, at p. 32.

[9] Human Rights Committee, General Comment No. 23, 'Rights of minorities (Article 27)', para. 3.2: the enjoyment of the rights of persons belonging to minorities in Article 27 of the International Covenant on Civil and Political Rights 'does not prejudice the sovereignty and territorial integrity of a State party'. See also Article 8(4) of GA Res. 47/135, adopted 18 December 1992, 'Declaration on the Rights of Persons belonging to National or Ethnic, Religious and Linguistic Minorities'; and Article 21 of the Framework Convention for the Protection of National Minorities, adopted at Strasbourg, 1 February 1995, in force 1 February 1998, ETS No. 157.

[10] No right of autonomy can be read into Article 27 of the International Covenant on Civil and Political Rights, adopted by GA Res. 2200A (XXI), 16 December 1966, in force 23 March 1976; or GA Res. 47/135, adopted 18 December 1992, 'Declaration on the Rights of Persons belonging to National or Ethnic, Religious and Linguistic Minorities'; or the Framework Convention on National Minorities.

[11] See Philip Alston (ed.), *Peoples' rights* (Oxford: Oxford University Press, 2001); S. James Anaya, *Indigenous peoples in international law* (Oxford: Oxford University Press, 1996); Catherine Brölmann et al. (eds.), *Peoples and minorities in international law* (Dordrecht:

self-determination for peoples within the State. The following section considers the evolution of the principle of equal rights and self-determination of peoples, recognised in the Charter of the United Nations. The right of self-determination 'beyond colonialism' is then considered. Two aspects of the right of peoples to self-determination may be discerned: first, a limited and exceptional right of external self-determination (i.e. the right to determine the international status of the territory) for peoples excluded from political life, and for the 'constituent peoples' of an ethnic-federation in the process of dissolution; and, secondly, a right of internal self-determination (territorial self-government) for indigenous peoples and peoples.

Decolonisation

Demands for separation, secession or territorial self-government by ethno-cultural groups rely on a 'reinterpretation of the principle of the self-determination of nations'.[12] In the aftermath of the First World War, the political map of Europe was reconfigured in accordance with the principle of national self-determination of peoples.[13] Where politically feasible, and consistent with the allies' strategic interests,

---

Martinus Nijhoff, 1993); Antonio Cassese, *Self-determination of peoples: a legal reappraisal* (Cambridge: Cambridge University Press, 1995); James Crawford (ed.), *The rights of peoples* (Oxford: Clarendon Press, 1988); Héctor Gros Espiell, *The right to self-determination: implementation of United Nations resolutions* (New York: United Nations, 1980); Eyassu Gayim, *The principle of self-determination: a study of its historical and contemporary legal evolution* (Oslo: Norwegian Institute of Human Rights, 1990); Hurst Hannum, *Autonomy, sovereignty, and self-determination: the accommodation of conflicting rights* (Philadelphia: University of Pennsylvania Press, 1990); Karen Knop, *Diversity and self-determination in international law* (Cambridge: Cambridge University Press, 2002); Robert McCorquodale (ed.), *Self-determination in international law* (Aldershot: Ashgate/Dartmouth, 2000); Thomas Musgrave, *Self-determination and minorities* (Oxford: Oxford University Press, 2000); Rein Müllerson, *International law, rights and politics: developments in Eastern Europe and the CIS* (London: Routledge, 1994); Michla Pomerance, *Self-determination in law and practice* (The Hague: Martinus Nijhoff, 1982); A. Rigo Sureda, *The evolution of the right of self-determination: a study of United Nations practice* (Leiden: Sijthoff, 1973); Stephen Tierney (ed.), *Accommodating national identity: new approaches in international and domestic law* (The Hague: Kluwer Law International, 2000); Christian Tomuschat (ed.), *Modern law of self-determination* (Dordrecht: Martinus Nijhoff, 1993); and U. O. Umozurike, *Self-determination in international law* (Hamden, CT: Archon Books, 1972).

[12] Donald Horowitz, 'The cracked foundations of the right to secede' (2003) 14 *Journal of Democracy* 5, 5.

[13] Josef Kunz, 'The present status of international law for the protection of minorities' (1954) 48 *American Journal of International Law* 282, 282.

boundaries were drawn to coincide with ethno-cultural identity.[14] Ethnically homogenous 'Nation' States were created following the collapse of the multi-national Hapsburg, Ottoman, Russian and German Empires:[15] Romania as a State for Romanians, for example.[16] The process was foreshadowed in President Woodrow Wilson's 'Fourteen Points' address to Congress in 1918, in which he called for the establishment of a State of Poland, 'which should include the territories inhabited by indisputably Polish populations'.[17] The application of the national self-determination principle sought, on objective criteria, to identify 'Nations',[18] and to recognise their sovereign and independent existence. The Treaty of Versailles provided for the holding of a number of plebiscites, 'but these were limited to the determination of the future of certain hotly disputed border regions'.[19]

No legal right of national self-determination was recognised in the Covenant of the League of Nations, or in general international law.[20] Outside of Europe, in respect of those 'colonies and territories' taken from Germany and the Ottoman Empire, and 'inhabited by peoples not

[14] David Wippman, 'Introduction: ethnic claims and international law', in David Wippman (ed.), *International law and ethnic conflict* (Ithaca: Cornell University Press, 1998), p. 1, at pp. 8–9.

[15] Nathaniel Berman, ' "But the alternative is despair": European nationalism and the modernist renewal of international law' (1993) 106 *Harvard Law Review* 1792, 1794.

[16] Donald Horowitz, 'The cracked foundations of the right to secede', 6. The multi-nation States of Czechoslovakia and Yugoslavia were also created: *ibid*.

[17] Point XIII of Woodrow Wilson, 'An address to a Joint Session of Congress' (The Fourteen Points Address)', 8 January 1918, reprinted in Arthur S. Link *et al.* (ed.), *The Papers of Woodrow Wilson* (Princeton, NJ: Princeton University Press, 1966–94), vol. 45, p. 534. See generally Michla Pomerance, 'The United States and self-determination: perspectives on the Wilsonian conception' (1976) 70 *American Journal of International Law* 1; and Guyora Binder, 'The case for self-determination' (1993) 29 *Stanford Journal of International Law* 223, 228.

[18] Objective factors are those elements not 'chosen' in a literal sense by the individuals or groups concerned, such as religion, race, language, a common history, and a national territory, while subjective factors refer to manifestations of the political will of the people: Berman, 'But the alternative is despair', 1812. See also Nathaniel Berman, 'Sovereignty in abeyance: self-determination and international law' (1988) 7 *Wisconsin International Law Journal* 51, 91.

[19] Berman, 'But the alternative is despair', 1859–60. The Versailles Treaty, 225 CTS 188, 203 (1919), provided for plebiscites in Schleswig (Article 109), several border districts between East Prussia and Poland (Articles 94 and 96), the Saar (Article 49), and Upper Silesia (Article 88), and a 'public expression of opinion' in Eupen and Malmedy (Article 34). See Berman, *ibid*.

[20] See 'The Aaland Island Question: Report of the Committee of Jurists' (1920) 3 *League of Nations Official Journal, Special Supplement* 5, referred to in Brad Roth, *Governmental illegitimacy in international law* (Oxford: Oxford University Press, 2000), p. 206.

yet able to stand by themselves under the strenuous conditions of the modern world', the League of Nations Covenant recognised that 'there should be applied the principle that the well-being and development of such peoples form a sacred trust of civilisation'.[21] The principle was given effect by entrusting the 'tutelage of such peoples' to 'advanced nations',[22] who exercised authority over the territories on behalf of the League of Nations, on terms agreed by the Council of the League.[23] The Covenant recognised that the inhabitants of these territories had the 'potentiality for independent existence'.[24] The ultimate objective of the sacred trust, according to the International Court of Justice in 1971, was 'the self-determination and independence of the peoples concerned'.[25]

According to its Charter, one of the purposes of the United Nations is to 'develop friendly relations among nations based on respect for the principle of equal rights and self-determination of peoples'.[26] The expression 'equal rights and self-determination of peoples' is not defined, nor do the *travaux préparatoires* explain what the phrase was intended to mean.[27] No right of peoples to self-determination is

---

[21] Article 22 of the League of Nations Covenant (1919). The territories were further divided: communities that could provisionally be recognised as independent nations, 'subject to the rendering of administrative advice and assistance by a Mandatory until such time as they are able to stand alone'; other peoples, who were at such a stage that the Mandatory 'must be responsible for the administration of the territory'; and territories which 'can be best administered under the laws of the Mandatory as integral portions of its territory': *ibid*.

[22] *Ibid*.

[23] See Thomas Musgrave, *Self-determination and minorities* (Oxford: Oxford University Press, 2000), p. 31.

[24] *Legal Consequences for States of the Continued Presence of South Africa in Namibia (South West Africa) Notwithstanding Security Council Resolution 276 (1970)*, ICJ Reports (1971), p. 16, 49 ILR 2, para. 46.

[25] *Ibid*., para. 53. The concept of the sacred trust was 'confirmed and expanded to all "territories whose peoples have not yet attained a full measure of self-government" [by Article 73 of the UN Charter]': *ibid*., para. 52.

[26] Article 1(2) of the Charter of the United Nations, adopted 26 June 1945, in force 24 October 1945. The UN is required to promote universal respect for human rights and fundamental freedoms for all, without distinction as to race, sex, language or religion, with a view to the creation of conditions of stability and well-being which are necessary for 'peaceful and friendly relations among nations based on respect for the principle of equal rights and self-determination of peoples': Article 55, *ibid*.

[27] Musgrave, *Self-determination and minorities*, p. 64. The inclusion of a reference to the 'equal rights and self-determination of peoples' in Articles 1(2) and 55 of the UN Charter followed from a proposal by the Soviet Union. The reason for its inclusion is not explained in the *travaux préparatoires*, although the Soviet Foreign Minister Molotov was clear that it was related to the ability of dependent countries being enabled 'as soon as possible to take the path of national independence': Musgrave, *ibid*.

recognised in the Charter, although the principle underpins Chapters XI and XII of the Charter. Chapter XII authorised the United Nations to establish, under its authority, an international trusteeship system for the administration and supervision of such 'trust territories' as may be placed under the system by individual agreement.[28] The terms of trusteeship were agreed by the States directly concerned.[29] One of the objectives of the system was to promote the political, economic, social and educational advancement of the inhabitants of territories, and their 'progressive development towards self-government or independence as may be appropriate to the particular circumstances of each territory and its peoples and the freely expressed wishes of the peoples concerned'.[30] All eleven trust territories achieved self-determination through independence, or free association with an independent state.[31]

Chapter XI of the Charter concerns those colonial territories not placed under the authority of the United Nations.[32] Article 73 obliges member States with responsibilities for the administration of 'territories whose peoples have not yet attained a full measure of self-government' to recognise the principle that the interests of the inhabitants of these territories are paramount, and to accept as a 'sacred trust' the obligation to promote to the utmost 'the well-being of the inhabitants of these territories'.[33] Reference to territories whose peoples have not 'yet' attained a full measure of self-government implies that the ultimate objective of the Charter is self-government for the populations of non-self-governing territories.

States responsible for the administration of non-self-governing territories are required to 'ensure, with due respect for the culture of the peoples concerned, their political, economic, social, and

[28] Article 75 of the UN Charter. See Francis Sayre, 'Legal problems arising from the United Nations trusteeship system' (1948) 42 *American Journal of International Law* 263. The international trusteeship system applied to: (a) territories held under League of Nations mandate; (b) territories detached from enemy states as a result of the Second World War; and (c) territories voluntarily placed under the system by states responsible for their administration: Article 77(1) of the UN Charter. Cf. Article 77(2), *ibid.*
[29] Article 79, *ibid.*   [30] Article 76(b), *ibid.*
[31] British Togoland, Somaliland, French Togoland, French Cameroons, British Cameroons, Tanganyika, Ruanda-Urundi, Western Samoa, Nauru, New Guinea and the Trust Territory of the Pacific Islands.
[32] Chapter XI concerns territories 'known to be of the colonial type': Principle I of GA Res. 1541 (XV), adopted 15 December 1960, 'Principles which should guide Members in determining whether or not an obligation exists to transmit the information called for under Article 73e of the Charter'.
[33] Article 73, *chapeau*, of the UN Charter.

educational advancement',[34] to 'develop self-government, to take due account of the political aspirations of the peoples, and to assist them in the progressive development of their free political institutions'.[35] As Michla Pomerance notes, upon these meagre and tentative foundations, 'the United Nations proceeded to construct an edifice of practice in which, increasingly, full "external" self-determination ... was viewed as an imperative and immediate goal for all peoples "under colonial or alien domination"'.[36] On 14 December 1960, the UN General Assembly adopted Resolution 1514 (XV), 'Declaration on the Granting of Independence to Colonial Countries and Peoples'. The resolution determined that the 'process of liberation is irresistible and irreversible', and proclaimed the necessity of 'bringing to a speedy and unconditional end colonialism in all its forms and manifestations'.[37] Resolution 1514 (XV) transformed the principle of equal rights and self-determination of peoples into a legal right: 'All peoples have the right to self-determination; by virtue of that right they freely determine their political status and freely pursue their economic, social and cultural development.'[38] Paragraph 5 provides:

Immediate steps shall be taken, in Trust and Non-Self-Governing Territories or all other territories which have yet to attain independence, *to transfer all powers to the peoples of those territories,* without any conditions or reservations, *in accordance with their freely expressed will and desire,* without any distinction as to race, creed or colour, in order to enable them to enjoy complete independence and freedom.[39]

There is some doubt as to whether at the time of its adoption Resolution 1514 (XV) represented an accurate statement of international law,[40] although in 1975 the International Court of Justice

---

[34] Article 73(a), *ibid.*   [35] Article 73(b), *ibid.*

[36] Michla Pomerance, *Self-determination in law and practice* (The Hague: Martinus Nijhoff, 1982), p. 10.

[37] GA Res. 1514 (XV), adopted 14 December 1960, 'Declaration on the granting of independence to colonial countries and peoples', preamble.

[38] Para. 2, *ibid.*   [39] Para. 5, *ibid.* (emphasis added).

[40] Helen Quane, 'The United Nations and the evolving right to self-determination' (1998) 47 *International and Comparative Law Quarterly* 537, 551. GA Res. 1514 (XV) was adopted by eighty-nine votes to nil, with nine abstentions – all of the colonial powers. Rosalyn Higgins observes that there were no opposing States, and that the number of abstentions was very low: the 'resolution must be taken to represent the wishes and beliefs of the full membership of the United Nations': Rosalyn Higgins, *The development of international law through the political organs of the United Nations* (London: Oxford University Press, 1963), p. 101. See also SC Res. 183 (1963), para. 4, which reaffirms the interpretation of self-determination laid down in GA Res. 1514 (XV) as follows: 'All peoples have the right to self-determination.'

concluded that the resolution 'provided the basis for the process of decolonization'.[41] Any doubt was removed with the adoption, by consensus, of General Assembly Resolution 2625 (XXV), 'Declaration on Principles of International Law Concerning Friendly Relations and Co-operation among States in Accordance with the Charter of the United Nations'.[42] Resolution 2625 (XXV) confirms that, by virtue of the principle of equal rights and self-determination of peoples enshrined in the Charter, 'all peoples have the right freely to determine, without external interference, their political status'. The implementation of the principle requires the bringing about of 'a speedy end of colonialism, having due regard to the freely expressed will of the peoples concerned'.[43] The populations of non-self-governing territories were recognised as enjoying the right to determine the international status of the territory, irrespective of the attitude of the colonial power.[44] In the vast majority of cases, the progress to self-government or independence was consensual, and the UN General Assembly did not advocate or support a right of secession for non-self-governing territories, except where self-determination was opposed by the colonial power.[45] Where the colonial power did resist the transfer of power to the people of a non-self-governing territory, 'the colonial administration was for all intents and purposes stripped of *de jure* recognition in the international system, and left only with the *de facto* recognition accorded illegitimate regimes'.[46]

---

[41] *Western Sahara Case*, ICJ Reports (1975), p. 12, 59 ILR 13, para. 57. See also *ibid.*, para. 55.

[42] Guyora Binder, 'The case for self-determination' (1993) 29 *Stanford Journal of International Law* 223, 236.

[43] GA Res. 2625 (XXV), adopted 24 October 1970, 'Declaration on Principles of International Law Concerning Friendly Relations and Co-operation among States in Accordance with the Charter of the United Nations'. GA Res. 2625 (XXV) further provides that the 'subjection of peoples to alien subjugation, domination and exploitation constitutes a violation of the principle [of equal rights and self-determination of peoples], as well as a denial of fundamental human rights, and is contrary to the Charter'. GA Res. 2625 (XXV) may be regarded as an authoritative interpretation of the Charter: Ian Brownlie, *Principle of public international law* (5th edn, Oxford: Oxford University Press, 1998), p. 15.

[44] Alain Pellet, 'Legal opinion on certain questions of international law raised by the Reference', reprinted in Anne Bayefsky, *Self-determination in international law: Quebec and lessons learned* (The Hague: Kluwer Law International, 2000), p. 85, at p. 94.

[45] James Crawford, 'State practice and international law in relation to unilateral secession': 'Expert Opinion Accompanying the Attorney General of Canada's Factum, *Reference re Secession of Quebec* [1998] 2 SCR 217, reprinted in Bayefsky, *Self-determination in international law*, p. 31, para. 12.

[46] Roth, *Governmental illegitimacy in international law*, p. 211.

Independence is not the objective of the principle of equal rights and self-determination of peoples when applied to non-self-governing territories. The objective is the determination of the international status of the territory, in accordance with the freely expressed will of the peoples concerned.[47] According to Principle VI of Resolution 1541 (XV), a non-self-governing territory may be said to have reached a full measure of self-government by: '(a) Emergence as a sovereign and independent State; (b) Free association with an independent State; or (c) Integration with an independent State.'[48] Free association should be the result of a free and voluntary choice 'expressed through informed and democratic processes'.[49] The integration of a non-self-governing territory with an independent State should be the result of 'the freely expressed wishes of the territory's peoples[,] ... their wishes having been expressed through informed and democratic processes, impartially conducted and based on universal adult suffrage'.[50] No particular mechanism is provided for a people opting for independence, which is recognised as the default choice. According to Judge Dillard, in his Separate Opinion in the *Western Sahara Case*, the right of peoples to self-determination is satisfied 'by a free choice not by a particular consequence of that choice or a particular method of exercising it'.[51] In the case, the International Court of Justice defined the principle of self-determination as 'the need to pay regard to the freely expressed will of peoples'.[52]

In 1962, the General Assembly confirmed that Southern Rhodesia was a non-self-governing territory.[53] The General Assembly called on the

---

[47] See, for example, SC Res. 217 (1965), para. 3, which reaffirmed GA Res. 1514 (XV), and condemned the 'usurpation of power by a racist settler minority in Southern Rhodesia and regards the declaration of independence by it as having no legal validity'.

[48] Principle VI of GA Res. 1541 (XV). Cf. GA Res. 2625 (XXV): 'The establishment of a sovereign and independent State, the free association or integration with an independent State *or the emergence into any other political status freely determined by a people* constitute modes of implementing the right of self-determination by that people' (emphasis added).

[49] Principle VII of GA Res. 1541 (XV).   [50] Principle IX(b), *ibid*.

[51] *Western Sahara Case*, ICJ Reports (1975), p. 12, 59 ILR 13, Separate Opinion of Judge Dillard, 59 ILR 133, 140. The cardinal restraint which the legal right of self-determination imposes, is that 'it is for the people to determine the destiny of the territory and not the territory the destiny of the people': *ibid*., p. 139.

[52] *Western Sahara Case*, ICJ Reports (1975), p. 12, 59 ILR 13, para. 59. The validity of the principle of self-determination is not affected by the fact that in certain cases the General Assembly has dispensed with the requirement of consulting with the inhabitants of a given territory: *ibid*., para. 59.

[53] GA Res. 1747 (XVI), adopted 27 June 1962, 'The Question of Southern Rhodesia', para. 1.

United Kingdom, the colonial power, to put in place a constitution which would ensure the 'rights of the majority of the people, on the basis of "one man, one vote", in conformity with the principles of the Charter of the United Nations and ... resolution 1514 (XV)'.[54] In 1978, the Security Council declared that the termination of the 'illegal' regime, and restoration of legality in Southern Rhodesia would allow 'for a peaceful and democratic transition to genuine majority rule and independence'.[55] The democratic transition required the holding of free and fair elections on the basis of universal adult suffrage.[56] The principle of equal rights and self-determination of peoples recognises the right of the majority in a non-self-governing territory to determine its international status through democratic processes.[57]

The colonised 'peoples'

The UN Charter obliges member States with responsibilities for the administration of non-self-governing territories to transmit to the Secretary-General 'statistical and other information of a technical nature relating to economic, social, and educational conditions in the territories for which they are respectively responsible'.[58] On 15 December 1960, the General Assembly adopted Resolution 1541 (XV), 'Principles Which Should Guide Members in Determining Whether or Not an Obligation Exists to Transmit the Information Called for under Article 73e of the Charter'.[59] Resolution 1541 (XV) provides that the obligation to transmit information exists, prima facie, in respect of a territory 'which is geographically separate and is distinct ethnically and/or culturally from the country administering it'.[60] Where the relationship between metropolitan territory and the geographically separate territory 'arbitrarily places the latter in a position or status of

---

[54] *Ibid.*, para. 2(a). See also GA Res. 1760 (XVII), adopted 31 October 1962, 'Question of Southern Rhodesia'.

[55] SC Res. 423 (1978), para. 3.   [56] *Ibid.*, para. 4.

[57] In Fiji, the UK proposed the use of communal rolls for the Indian and Fijian populations. This was rejected by the General Assembly which insisted that independence should be attained only on the basis of the 'one man, one vote' principle: Pomerance, *Self-determination in law and practice*, p. 21.

[58] Article 73(e) of the UN Charter. See Higgins, *The development of international law through the political organs of the United Nations*, pp. 113–16.

[59] According to the International Court of Justice, GA Res. 1541 (XV) complements, 'in certain of its aspects', GA Res. 1514 (XV): *Western Sahara Case*, ICJ Reports (1975), p. 12, 59 ILR 13, para. 57.

[60] Principle IV of GA Res. 1541 (XV). The obligation continues until such time as the relevant territory has obtained 'a full measure of self-government': Principle II, *ibid.*

subordination', the presumption of non-self-governing status is supported.[61]

Resolution 1541 (XV) adopts a 'salt water' test in determining the existence of a colonial situation. The resolution refers to a 'geographically separate' territory. It follows that geographically contiguous territories are excluded from the definition.[62] The illegitimacy of colonialism does not depend on misrule, or the fact of rule by 'Others': the mere fact of 'ethnic distinctiveness cannot by itself explain why colonialism is worse than cases in which minorities are subject to majority rule'.[63] The UN documents on decolonisation recognise the illegitimacy of any 'political-economic relationship between a dominant Western nation and a subservient non-Western people'.[64] An argument that the principle of equal rights and self-determination of peoples should be applied to populations within the metropolitan territory (the 'Belgian Thesis') did not prevail.[65] The General Assembly resolutions on 'colonised' peoples may not be applied to 'peoples' within the metropolitan territory of sovereign and independent States. The resolutions make a clear distinction between colonial-type territories and the metropolitan territory: the territory of a colony or other non-self-governing territory has, 'under the Charter, a status separate and distinct from the territory of the State administering it'.[66] According to Resolution 1514 (XV): 'Any attempt aimed at the partial or total disruption of the national unity and the territorial integrity of a country is incompatible with the purposes and principles of the Charter of the United Nations'.[67]

Following the First World War, the principle of national self-determination was applied to 'politically shapeless ethnic communities'.

---

[61] Principle V, *ibid.*

[62] James Crawford, *The creation of states in international law* (Oxford: Clarendon Press, 1979), p. 359.

[63] Lea Brilmayer, 'Secession and self-determination: a territorial interpretation' (1991) 16 *Yale Journal of International Law* 177, 196.

[64] Ved Nanda, 'Self-determination in international law: the tragic tale of two cities – Islamabad (West Pakistan), and Dacca (East Pakistan)' (1972) 66 *American Journal of International Law* 321, 321, at footnote 1.

[65] Patrick Thornberry, *International law and the rights of minorities* (Oxford: Clarendon Press, 1991), pp. 16–17. Article 73 of the UN Charter refers to 'territories whose peoples have not yet attained a full measure of self-government'. Cf. Article 74 of the UN Charter.

[66] GA Res. 2625 (XXV).

[67] See GA Res. 1514 (XV), para. 6. See also the preamble to GA Res. 1654 (XVI), adopted 27 November 1961, 'The situation with regard to the implementation of the Declaration on the granting of independence to colonial countries and peoples'.

In the UN era, 'the inhabitants, however haphazardly assembled by the colonial Power, [took] over the pre-existing political units as independent states'.[68] Questions of territorial size, geographical isolation and limited resources were not permitted to delay the implementation of the right of peoples to self-determination recognised in Resolution 1514 (XV).[69] The principle of self-determination was transformed from a tool for State-making, to 'a corrective to the historical injustice of alien subjugation'.[70] The 'peoples' of non-self-governing territories were defined by their relationship to the political unit, and not by any racial, ethnic, cultural, religious or linguistic characteristics. Exceptions to the territorial approach concerned: the reunification of pre-colonial entities, such as Morocco and Somalia; the voluntary union of two separate colonies; and circumstances where the inhabitants were opposed to maintaining a unitary political entity, for example in India and Ruanda-Urundi.[71] Thomas Musgrave identifies the adoption of Resolution 1514 (XV) as the point when the UN became increasingly unwilling to permit any partition of non-self-governing territories 'no matter how different or incompatible their constituent ethnic or religious groups might be'.[72] In the process of decolonisation, no attempt was made to distinguish between different peoples within a non-self-governing *territory*.[73]

The territorial approach was confirmed by the application of the principle of *uti possidetis*: the requirement for the recognition of existing administrative borders, unless the relevant parties or another

---

[68] Rupert Emerson, 'Self-determination' (1971) 65 *American Journal of International Law* 459, 463. See also S. James Anaya, *Indigenous peoples in international law* (Oxford: Oxford University Press, 1996), p. 78.

[69] GA Res. 2621 (XXV), adopted 12 October 1970, 'Programme of Action for the Full Implementation of the Declaration on the Granting of Independence to Colonial Countries and Peoples', para. 9. See also GA Res. 35/118, adopted 11 December 1980, 'Plan of Action for the Full Implementation of the Declaration on the Granting of Independence to Colonial Countries and Peoples', Annex, para. 17. See Michla Pomerance, *Self-determination in law and practice* (The Hague: Martinus Nijhoff, 1982), p. 19.

[70] Diane Orentlicher, 'Separation anxiety: international responses to ethno-separatist claims' (1998) 23 *Yale Journal of International Law* 1, 43.

[71] Quane, 'The United Nations and the evolving right to self-determination', 552.

[72] Musgrave, *Self-determination and minorities*, p. 159. See also Michla Pomerance, *Self-determination in law and practice*, p. 19; and Thomas Franck, 'Postmodern tribalism and the right to secession', in Catherine Brölmann *et al.* (eds.), *Peoples and minorities in international law* (Dordrecht: Martinus Nijhoff, 1993), p. 3, at pp. 7–8.

[73] James Crawford, 'State practice and international law in relation to secession' (1998) 69 *British Year Book of International Law* 85, 91.

decision-maker, such as the United Nations, determines otherwise.[74] The regime on self-determination that emerged in the United Nations era concerned 'juridically defined groups associated with territorial units', not 'social collectivities'.[75] Hurst Hannum explains:

> In the context of post-1945 decolonization ... the primary, and often sole, definition of 'peoples' was that of non-European inhabitants of former colonies, without further regard for ethnicity, language, religion, or other objective characteristics of such colonized peoples (apart from the fact of colonization itself). Territory, not 'nationhood,' was the determining factor.[76]

The territorial interpretation of 'peoples' was confirmed in the Human Rights Committee Opinion in *Gillot et al.* v. *France*. French citizens, resident in New Caledonia, a French non-self-governing territory,[77] complained that they had been excluded from referendums concerning the institutional development of New Caledonia, and the possibility that the territory might accede to independence.[78] The Human Rights Committee concluded that, whilst it does not have the competence under the Optional Protocol to consider a communication alleging a violation of the right to self-determination, 'it may interpret Article 1, when this is relevant, in determining whether rights protected in parts II and III of the Covenant have been violated [and] in this case, it may take Article 1 into account in interpretation of Article 25 of the Covenant'.[79] Article 25 of the International Covenant on Civil and Political Rights concerns the rights of political participation: the rights of citizens to take part in the conduct of public affairs, and to vote and to be elected at genuine periodic elections.

---

[74] Steven Ratner, 'Drawing a better line: *uti possidetis* and the borders of new states' (1996) 90 *American Journal of International Law* 590, 598.

[75] Benedict Kingsbury, ' "Indigenous peoples" in international law: a constructivist approach to the controversy' (1998) 92 *American Journal of International Law* 414, 438.

[76] Hurst Hannum, *Autonomy, sovereignty, and self-determination: the accommodation of conflicting rights* (Philadelphia: University of Pennsylvania Press, 1990), p. 36.

[77] See GA Res. 41/41, adopted 2 December 1986, 'Implementation of the Declaration on the Granting of Independence to Colonial Countries and Peoples', para. 1.

[78] The State party accepted that the referendums formed 'part of a process of self-determination by the people of this territory, even if they do not all have the direct purpose of determining the question of the territory's accession to full sovereignty': *Gillot et al.* v. *France*, Communication No. 932/2000, UN Doc. CCPR/C/75/D/932/2000, 26 July 2002, para. 8.3.

[79] *Ibid.*, para. 13.4. The Committee was not, however, 'expressing a view on the definition of the concept of "peoples" ' (para. 13.16), although it concluded that the restrictive criteria applied for participation in self-determination referendums could 'be justified only in relation to Article 1 of the Covenant' (*ibid.*).

Inclusion on the electoral roll for the initial referendum, held in November 1998, was conditional on ten years' residence in the territory, on the date of the ballot. For future referendums, inclusion requires that the elector was permitted to participate in the first referendum, or that they are able to prove specific links with the territory of New Caledonia (birth, family ties, etc.), or that they will have been living in the territory for twenty years on the date of the referendum in question.[80] According to France, 'it is natural to consider that persons "concerned" in votes held in the context of a self-determination process are those who prove that they have particular ties to the territory whose fate is in question, ties which legitimize their participation in the vote'.[81] In establishing 'ties to the territory', the State party relied on 'objective' criteria, and not on issues of 'ethnic origin or political choices'.[82] The Human Rights Committee agreed that 'it would not be unreasonable to limit participation in local referendums to persons "concerned" by the future of New Caledonia who have proven, sufficiently strong ties to that territory'.[83] The Committee concluded that the criteria applied by France did not establish different rights for different ethnic groups or groups distinguished by their national extraction.[84] The Committee accepted that the restriction on the right to vote in the decolonisation process was not disproportionate, as it permitted the 'participation of residents who, over and above their ethnic origin or political affiliation, have helped, and continue to help, build New Caledonia through their sufficiently strong ties to the territory'.[85]

'Self-determination beyond colonialism'[86]

The term 'peoples' is applied in the Charter of the United Nations to the populations of non-self-governing territories,[87] and the populations of

---

[80] Ibid., para. 8.5.   [81] Ibid., para. 8.14.

[82] Ibid., para. 8.16. Those ties could be evaluated in terms of length of residence in the territory; possession of customary civil status; the existence of moral and material interests in the territory, combined with the birth of the person concerned or his parents in the territory: ibid., para. 8.15.

[83] Ibid.   [84] Ibid., para. 13.11.   [85] Ibid., para. 14.7.

[86] 'There is a substantial body of doctrine and practice on "self-determination beyond colonialism" ': Legal Consequences of the Construction of a Wall in the Occupied Palestinian Territory, International Court of Justice, Advisory Opinion, 9 July 2004, 43 ILM (2004) 1009, Separate Opinion of Judge Higgins, para. 29.

[87] Article 73 of the UN Charter.

trust territories.[88] Additionally, the preamble begins 'We the peoples of the United Nations'. It concludes with 'our respective Governments … do hereby establish an international organization to be known as the United Nations'.[89] The term 'peoples' in the Charter refers additionally to 'peoples organised as States'.[90] A violation of the right to self-determination occurs when the State is subject to alien domination or foreign occupation.[91] The UN General Assembly has declared its firm opposition to acts of foreign military intervention, aggression and occupation, 'since these have resulted in the suppression of the right of peoples to self-determination'.[92] The application of the right of self-determination to the people of the State as a whole is 'essentially a negative matter'. All that is required is that 'there not be external interference which impairs the ability of the state freely to make its own choices'.[93] The relationship between the rights of peoples to

---

[88] Article 76(b), *ibid*. The term is also applied to the 'people of [a] strategic area' designated as such under an international trusteeship agreement: Article 83(2), *ibid*.

[89] Preamble to the UN Charter. The term 'nations' in the UN Charter refers to States, to the original signatories of the Charter which were not States (Byelorussia, Ukraine, the Philippines and British India), and to colonies, mandates and protectorates: Quane, 'The United Nations and the evolving right to self-determination', 545. See also Higgins, *The development of international law through the political organs of the United Nations*, pp. 15–17. According to the UN Secretariat, the word 'nation' in the Charter includes colonies, mandates, protectorates and quasi-states as well as states; the word 'people' is used in connection with self-determination: (1945) 18 UNCIO 657, referred to in Musgrave, *Self-determination and minorities*, p. 155. GA Res. 55/2, adopted 8 September 2000, 'Millennium Declaration', para. 3, refers to 'nations and peoples'.

[90] Quane, 'The United Nations and the evolving right to self-determination', 540. Principle VIII of GA Res. 1541 (XV) provides that the integration of a colonial territory into the metropolitan State 'should be on the basis of complete equality between the *peoples* of the erstwhile Non-Self-Governing Territory *and those* of the independent country with which it is integrated' (emphasis added). The clause subsequently refers to the 'peoples of both territories'.

[91] See GA Res. 2625 (XXV), and Vienna Declaration and Programme of Action (1993), ILM 32 (1993) 1661, para. I(2).

[92] GA Res. 58/161, adopted 22 December 2003, 'Universal realization of the right of peoples to self-determination', para. 2. See also GA Res. 54/155, adopted 29 February 2000, and GA Res. 55/85, adopted 28 February 2001. The General Assembly has affirmed on a number of occasions that the military occupation of a State by one or more outside powers is a violation of the right of the people of the State to self-determination. See, for example, GA Res. 34/22, adopted 14 November 1979, 'The situation in Kampuchea', and GA Res. 35/37, adopted 20 November 1980, 'The situation in Afghanistan and its implications for international peace and security'.

[93] Rupert Emerson, 'Self-determination' (1971) 65 *American Journal of International Law* 459, 466. See Principle VIII of the Conference on Security and Co-operation in Europe, (Helsinki) Final Act (1975), 14 ILM (1975) 1292. The Helsinki Final Act does not recognise any right of self-determination for groups within the State: Patrick Thornberry,

self-determination and the practice of democracy (internal self-government) is examined in chapter 3.

The contemporary position in international law on the right of peoples to self-determination is expressed in Article 1, common to the International Covenants: 'All peoples have the right of self-determination. By virtue of that right they freely determine their political status and freely pursue their economic, social and cultural development.'[94] The formulation reflects the position under general international law.[95] In *Legal Consequences of the Construction of a Wall in the Occupied Palestinian Territory*, the International Court of Justice recognised that the 'principle' of self-determination of peoples, 'enshrined in the United Nations Charter, and reaffirmed by the General Assembly in Resolution 2625 (XXV) and common Article 1 ... was recognised in international law as a "right" of peoples to self-determination: a right *erga omnes*'.[96]

The term 'people' is not defined in the International Covenants, although Article 1(3) confirms that the term includes the peoples of trust and non-self-governing territories.[97] According to the Human Rights Committee, the scope of application of Article 1 is not restricted

'Self-determination, minorities, human rights: a review of international instruments' (1989) 38 *International and Comparative Law Quarterly* 867, 886.

[94] Article 1(1), common to the International Covenant on Economic, Social and Cultural Rights and the International Covenant on Civil and Political Rights, adopted by GA Res. 2200A (XXI), 16 December 1966, in force 23 March 1976. Proposals to include a right of self-determination in GA Res. 217 (III) A, adopted 10 December 1948, 'Universal Declaration of Human Rights', were rejected, although when it became clear that the right to self-determination would be included in the International Covenants, Western and colonial States sought to extend its application beyond the colonial context: Musgrave, *Self-determination and minorities*, pp. 67–8.

[95] See GA Res. 2625 (XXV), adopted 24 October 1970, 'Declaration on Principles of International Law Concerning Friendly Relations and Co-operation among States in Accordance with the Charter of the United Nations'; Vienna Declaration and Programme of Action (1993), 32 ILM (1993) 1661, para. I(2); Principle VIII of the Conference on Security and Co-operation in Europe, (Helsinki) Final Act (1975), 14 ILM (1975) 1292; and Article 20(1) of the African Charter on Human and Peoples' Rights, adopted at Nairobi, 27 June 1981, in force 21 October 1986, 21 ILM (1982) 58.

[96] *Legal Consequences of the Construction of a Wall in the Occupied Palestinian Territory*, International Court of Justice, Advisory Opinion, 9 July 2004, 43 ILM (2004) 1009, para. 88.

[97] Article 1(3), common to the International Covenant on Economic, Social and Cultural Rights and the International Covenant on Civil and Political Rights: 'The States Parties to the present Covenant, *including those having responsibility for the administration of Non-Self-Governing and Trust Territories*, shall promote the realization of the right of self-determination, and shall respect that right, in conformity with the provisions of the Charter of the United Nations' (emphasis added).

to 'colonised peoples'.[98] Nor is the term restricted to peoples under alien subjugation, domination and exploitation. India, which declared in 1979 that Article 1 of the International Covenant on Civil and Political Rights applied only to 'peoples under foreign domination',[99] has since repudiated this limited interpretation.[100] The Human Rights Committee has confirmed that the term 'peoples' includes the populations of sovereign and independent States. With regard to Article 1(1), the Human Rights Committee has requested States parties to describe the constitutional and political processes which in practice allow the exercise of the right of peoples to self-determination,[101] and complained that 'many [States parties] completely ignore Article 1, provide inadequate information in regard to it or confine themselves to a reference to election laws'.[102]

The Optional Protocol to the International Covenant provides a procedure under which individuals can claim that their human rights have been violated.[103] These rights are set out in Part III of the Covenant, Articles 6 to 27, inclusive. Individual communications may not be brought in respect of the collective right of peoples to self-determination:[104] 'the question whether the community to which the authors belong is a "people" is not an issue for the [Human Rights

---

[98] Human Rights Committee, Concluding Observations on Azerbaijan, UN Doc. A/49/40, 3 August 1994, para. 296. See also Patrick Thornberry, 'Self-determination, minorities, human rights: a review of international instruments' (1989) 38 *International and Comparative Law Quarterly* 867, 878. Cf. Fourth Periodic Report (Sweden), UN Doc. CCPR/C/95/Add.4, 10 November 1994, para. 1; and Second Periodic Report (Algeria), UN Doc. CCPR/C/101/Add.1, 18 May 1998, para. 79.

[99] The declaration was vigorously opposed by a number of States: see, Musgrave, *Self-determination and minorities*, pp. 92–8.

[100] Third Periodic Report (India), UN Doc. CCPR/C/76/Add.6, 17 July 1996, para. 32. Cf. Third Periodic Report (Sri Lanka), UN Doc. CCPR/C/70/Add.6, 27 September 1994, para. 2: '[Article 1 of the International Covenant on Civil and Political Rights applies] only to people under alien and foreign domination and these words do not apply to sovereign independent states or to a section of a people or nation'. See also Fourth Periodic Report (Sri Lanka), UN Doc. CCPR/C/LKA/2002/4, 18 October 2002, paras. 2–4.

[101] Human Rights Committee, General Comment No. 12, 'Article 1 (right to self-determination)', adopted 13 March 1984, reprinted in 'Compilation of General Comments and General Recommendations', p. 134, para. 4.

[102] *Ibid.*, para. 3.

[103] Article 1 of the Optional Protocol to the International Covenant on Civil and Political Rights, adopted by GA Res. 2200A (XXI), 16 December 1966, in force 23 March 1976.

[104] See inter alia, *Chief Bernard Ominayak and the Lubicon Lake Band* v. *Canada*, Communication No. 167/1984, UN Doc. CCPR/C/38/D/167/1984, 10 May 1990, para. 32.1. See also *E. P. et al.* v. *Colombia*, Communication No. 318/1988, UN Doc. CCPR/C/39/D/318/1988, 15 August 1990, para. 8.2.

Committee] to address under the Optional Protocol to the Covenant.'[105] With the exception of indigenous peoples (below), the Human Rights Committee has not made a definitive determination that the term 'peoples' may include groups within the State, although in its Concluding Observations on Yugoslavia, the Committee referred to 'all the peoples' within the territory of the former Yugoslavia.[106] Additionally, the Committee on Economic, Social and Cultural Rights has referred to 'the culture of individuals, minorities, peoples and communities',[107] and 'the affected peoples of that State'.[108]

A number of States' reports, submitted under Article 40 of the International Covenant on Civil and Political Rights, consider the position of certain territories in the section concerning Article 1 (right of peoples to self-determination): the report by Sudan is of the opinion that 'the peoples of the Sudan are now possessed of a Government representing the whole people belonging to the territory without distinction of any kind';[109] the report by Finland notes that the 'right of self-governance of the [Aaland] Islands is, for historical reasons, based on the need of the Swedish speaking population on the Islands to maintain their Swedish culture and other traditions';[110] Spain provides information concerning the 'State of Autonomies';[111] and the report by the United Kingdom refers to the 'substantial devolution of powers to Scotland and Wales', and the possibility of devolution to Northern Ireland.[112]

In *Reference re Secession of Quebec*, the Canadian Supreme Court concluded that it was 'clear that "a people" may include only a portion of the

---

[105] *Diergaardt et al.* v. *Namibia*, Communication No. 760/1997, UN Doc. CCPR/C/69/D/760/1996, 25 July 2000, para. 10.3.

[106] Human Rights Committee, Concluding Observations on Yugoslavia, UN Doc. CCPR/C/79/Add.16, 28 December 1992, para. 1.

[107] Committee on Economic, Social and Cultural Rights, General Comment No. 14, 'The right to the highest attainable standard of health (Article 12)', reprinted in 'Compilation of General Comments and General Recommendations', p. 86, para. 12(c).

[108] Committee on Economic, Social and Cultural Rights, General Comment No. 8, 'The relationship between economic sanctions and respect for economic, social and cultural rights', reprinted in 'Compilation of General Comments and General Recommendations', p. 51, para. 7.

[109] Second Periodic Report (Sudan), UN Doc. CCPR/C/75/Add.2, 13 March 1997, para. 22.

[110] Fifth Periodic Report (Finland), UN Doc. CCPR/C/FIN/2003/5, 24 July 2003, para. 86.

[111] Fourth Period Report (Spain), UN Doc. CCPR/C/95/Add.1, 5 August 1994, para. 3.

[112] Fifth Periodic Report (United Kingdom of Great Britain and Northern Ireland), UN Doc. CCPR/C/UK/99/5, 11 December 2000, para. 11. See also Second Period Report (Uzbekistan), UN Doc. CCPR/C/UZB/2004/2, 3 August 2004, para. 14.

population of an existing state'.[113] The Court noted that the 'Quebec population certainly shares many of the characteristics (such as a common language and culture) that would be considered in determining whether a specific group is a "people" as do other groups within Quebec and/or Canada', including, by implication, the aboriginal population.[114]

The African Charter on Human and Peoples' Rights does not distinguish between 'Human and Peoples' Rights'.[115] Articles 19 to 24 concern the rights of peoples.[116] No definition of the term 'people' is provided. The preamble refers to 'the African peoples', and 'the peoples of Africa'. Article 20(2) refers to 'Colonized or oppressed peoples'. A number of provisions may be read as applying (only) to the populations of sovereign and independent States: 'All peoples shall be equal ... Nothing shall justify the domination of a people by another';[117] '[all peoples] shall freely determine their political status and shall pursue their economic and social development according to the policy they have freely chosen';[118] and 'All peoples shall freely dispose of their wealth and natural resources.'[119] In contrast, Article 21(2) provides that: 'In case of spoliation the dispossessed people shall have the right to the lawful recovery of its property as well as to an adequate compensation.'[120] The act of spoliation concerns the plundering of land and/or property, given the reference to dispossessed peoples. It cannot be read as referring to the populations of sovereign and independent States. 'Peoples', in the context of the African Charter on Human and Peoples' Rights, may include groups within the State. The African Commission on Human and Peoples' Rights has confirmed this interpretation in *Social and Economic Rights Action Center and the Center for Economic and Social Rights v. Nigeria*, where it refers to the 'Ogoni People' of Nigeria.[121]

---

[113] *Reference re Secession of Quebec* [1998] 2 SCR 217, para. 123.   [114] *Ibid.*, para. 125.

[115] Part I of Chapter I of the African Charter on Human and Peoples' Rights.

[116] See generally Rachel Murray and Steven Wheatley, 'Groups and the African Charter on Human and Peoples' Rights' (2003) 25 *Human Rights Quarterly* 213, 226–35.

[117] Article 19 of the African Charter on Human and Peoples' Rights.

[118] Article 20(1), *ibid.*

[119] Article 21(1), *ibid.* See also Article 24: 'All peoples shall have the right to a general satisfactory environment favorable to their development.' See Murray and Wheatley, 'Groups and the African Charter on Human and Peoples' Rights', 231–2.

[120] Article 21 of the African Charter on Human and Peoples' Rights.

[121] *Social and Economic Rights Action Center and the Center for Economic and Social Rights v. Nigeria*, Communication No. 155/96, in Fifteenth Activity Report of the African Commission on Human and Peoples' Rights 2001–2002, ACHPR/RPT.15, paras. 1 and 62. See generally Fons Coomans, 'The *Ogoni* case before the African Commission on Human and Peoples' Rights' (2003) 52 *International and Comparative Law Quarterly* 749.

There is an increasing recognition that the term 'people' in international law may be applied to groups of persons within the State. The conclusion of a meeting of international experts was that the term 'people' defined a group of persons, who regard themselves as a people, and who enjoy 'some or all' of the following characteristics: (i) common historical tradition; (ii) racial or ethnic identity; (iii) cultural homogeneity; (iv) linguistic unity; (v) religious or ideological affinity; (vi) territorial connection; or (vii) common economic life.[122] The South African Constitution provides that the right of the South African people as a whole to self-determination does not preclude the 'recognition of the notion of the right of self-determination of any community sharing a common cultural and language heritage, within a territorial entity in the Republic'.[123] The 1994 Ethiopian Constitution recognises that: 'Every Nation, Nationality and People in Ethiopia has an unconditional right to self-determination, including the right to secession.'[124] A 'Nation, Nationality or People' is defined as a group of people who have or share a large measure of a common culture or similar customs, mutual intelligibility of language, belief in a common or related identities, a common psychological make-up, and who inhabit an identifiable, predominantly contiguous territory.[125]

The consequences of recognising a group within the State as a 'people', with a right to self-determination, are not clear. It might, for example, require the reconfiguration of constitutional structures to accommodate the 'multi-nation' character of the State.[126] The General Framework Agreement for Peace in Bosnia-Herzegovina (Dayton Peace Agreement) refers to the 'Bosniacs, Croats, and Serbs, as constituent

---

[122] 'Final Report and Recommendations of an International Meeting of Experts on the Further Study of the Concept of the Right of People for UNESCO' (1990), SNS-89/ CONF.602/7), referred to in Patrick Thornberry, 'The democratic or internal aspect of self-determination', in Christian Tomuschat (ed.), *Modern law of self-determination* (Dordrecht: Martinus Nijhoff, 1993), p. 101, pp. 124–5. See also Guyora Binder, 'The case for self-determination' (1993) 29 *Stanford Journal of International Law* 223, 226; and Musgrave, *Self-determination and minorities*, chapter 1. Cf. Quane, 'The United Nations and the evolving right to self-determination', 571.

[123] Section 235 of the South African Constitution (1996).

[124] Article 39(1) of the Constitution of Ethiopia (1994).   [125] Article 39(5), *ibid.*

[126] The right of peoples to self-determination enjoys a core of reasonable certainty: 'the right of a community which has a distinct character to have this character reflected in the institutions of government under which it lives': Ian Brownlie, 'The rights of peoples in modern international law', in James Crawford (ed.), *The rights of peoples* (Oxford: Clarendon Press, 1988), p. 1, at p. 5.

peoples [along with others]'.[127] Representatives of the Bosniac, Croat and Serb communities share political power. The 1991 Constitution of the Former Yugoslav Republic of Macedonia identified the Slavic Macedonians as the only constituent nation of the Macedonian State.[128] This led to tensions with the ethnic-Albanian minority, who demanded designation as a 'constituent people'.[129] The 'Framework Agreement' which resolved the crisis considers only that the 'multi-ethnic character of Macedonia's society must be preserved and reflected in public life'.[130]

Alternately, the recognition of a right of self-determination for peoples within the State might provide a legal basis for secession.[131] Certain of the States that emerged following the collapse of the Soviet Empire considered that they had done so through a process of secessionist self-determination.[132] In its report under Article 40 of the International Covenant on Civil and Political Rights, Armenia put forward the argument that the right of peoples to self-determination affords every historical community, or 'nation', the right to its own State: 'International law defines a nation as a historical community of people which has emerged as a result of the formation of a common territory, economic links, literature, language and cultural particularities.'[133]

---

[127] Preamble, Annex 4, 'Constitution of Bosnia and Herzegovina', in the General Framework Agreement for Peace in Bosnia-Herzegovina, 35 ILM (1996) 89.

[128] Eiki Berg and Wim van Meurs, 'Borders and orders in Europe: limits of nation- and state-building in Estonia, Macedonia and Moldova' (2002) 18 *Journal of Communist Studies and Transition Politics* 51, 61.

[129] See Farimah Daftary, 'Conflict resolution in FYR Macedonia: power-sharing or "civic approach"' (2001) 12 *Helsinki Monitor* 291, 300.

[130] Para. 1.3 of the Framework Agreement (Macedonia), 13 August 2001, available at www.president.gov.mk/prilozi/dokumenti/180/FRAMEWORK%20AGREEMENT.pdf (last visited 10 January 2005).

[131] See Donald Horowitz, 'The cracked foundations of the right to secede' (2003) 14 *Journal of Democracy* 5, 5. See also Martti Koskenniemi, 'National self-determination today: problems of legal theory and practice' (1994) 43 *International and Comparative Law Quarterly* 241, 261.

[132] See, for example, the Former Yugoslav Republic of Macedonia's reference to the 'historical, cultural, spiritual, and statehood heritage of the Macedonian people and their struggle over centuries for national and social freedom': Initial Report (The Former Yugoslav Republic of Macedonia), UN Doc. CCPR/C/74/Add.4, 18 May 1998, para. 1; and Slovakia's reference to the '1,000-year efforts of the Slovak nation [to achieve] its own self-determination [as an independent state]': Initial Report (Slovakia), UN Doc. CCPR/C/81/Add.9, 13 February 1996, para. 1.

[133] Initial Report (Armenia), UN Doc. CCPR/C/92/Add.2, 30 April 1998, para. 25. Cf. Initial Report (Azerbaijan), UN Doc. E/1990/5/Add.30, 8 March 1994, paras. 12–14.

Finally, the recognition of a right of self-determination may require the introduction of territorial autonomy.[134] Given that 'national identity', as opposed to other forms of ethno-cultural identity, includes a collective desire for self-government,[135] any constitutional arrangement should establish self-government regimes for each constituent 'people' or 'nation'.[136] Failure to do so might provide a legitimate basis for secession.[137] The 1994 Ethiopian Constitution provides that 'All sovereign power resides in the Nations ... of Ethiopia'.[138] Every Nation has the right to self-determination, including the right to secession,[139] and the right to 'a full measure of self-government which includes the right to establish institutions of government in the territory that it inhabits and to equitable representation in state and Federal governments'.[140] The following sections consider the implications of the recognition of a right of self-determination for peoples within the State.

Sovereign self-determination

International law distinguishes between acts of separation and acts of secession. Separation is a process whereby a new sovereign and independent political unit is created with the consent of the existing State.[141] Secession refers to the situation where a new State is established and recognised without the consent of the 'parent'

---

[134] See, for example, Committee on the Elimination of Racial Discrimination, 'Statement on the human rights of the Kurdish people', adopted 10 March 1999, UN Doc. A/54/18, para. 22: 'the Kurdish people, wherever they live, should be able to lead their lives in dignity, to preserve their culture and to enjoy, wherever appropriate, a high degree of autonomy.'

[135] Alan Patten, 'Democratic secession from a multinational state' (2002) 112 *Ethics* 558, 567.

[136] *Ibid.*, 564–5.

[137] Robert Howse and Karen Knop, 'Federalism, secession, and the limits of ethnic accommodation: a Canadian perspective' (1993) 1 *New Europe Law Review* 269, 312.

[138] Article 8(1) of the Constitution of Ethiopia (1994): 'All sovereign power resides in the Nations, Nationalities and Peoples of Ethiopia.' The terms 'Nations' 'Nationalities' and 'Peoples' are coterminous: see, Article 39(5), *ibid.* See generally Kristen Henrard and Stefan Smis, 'Recent experiences in South Africa and Ethiopia to accommodate cultural diversity: a regained interest in the right of self-determination' (2000) 44 *Journal of African Law* 17.

[139] Article 39(1), *ibid.*

[140] Article 39(3), *ibid.* The Ethiopian Constitution reflects narratives of ethnic oppression and liberation. The political reality is one of dominant and centralised control by the current ruling political party, the Tigray People's Liberation Front (TPLF): Alemante Selassie, 'Ethnic federalism: its promises and pitfalls for Africa' (2003) 28 *Yale Journal of International Law* 51, 65.

[141] See Crawford, *The creation of states in international law*, p. 214. Crawford distinguishes between secession and devolution, rather than separation.

State.[142] The international legal status of a State remains unaffected by the separation or secession of part of its territory.[143] State practice indicates that there are few legal limitations on the ability of States to create new States through the grant of territory,[144] although there must be evidence that the establishment of a new sovereign and independent State reflects the political will of the relevant population.

Few State constitutions recognise a right of separation for part of the State.[145] The permanence of State borders is one of the fundamental givens of political life.[146] The exceptions include (in constitutional theory) the 1994 Ethiopian Constitution, which recognises that 'Every Nation, Nationality and People in Ethiopia has an unconditional right to self-determination, including the right to secession'.[147] A procedure for separation is established, requiring a two-thirds majority of the members of the Legislative Council of the Nation, Nationality or People concerned, and the support of a majority of voters in a referendum

---

[142] James Crawford, 'State practice and international law in relation to secession' (1998) 69 *British Year Book of International Law* 85, 85–6.

[143] A member of the United Nations 'does not cease to be a member from the mere fact that its constitution or frontiers have been modified'. The rights and obligations of membership only cease 'with its extinction as a legal person internationally recognized as such'. In contrast, when a new State is created, whether its population and territory have previously been part of a member state of the United Nations, 'this State cannot ... claim the status of Member of the United Nations unless it has been formally admitted as such in conformity with provisions of the Charter': General Assembly's Sixth (Legal) Committee, UN GAOR 6th Commission, 2nd Session, 43rd Meeting, at 38–9 (1947), referred to in Yehuda Blum, 'UN membership of the "new" Yugoslavia: continuity or break?' (1992) 86 *American Journal of International Law* 830, 831; and Lionel Laing, 'Admission of Indian States to the United Nations' (1949) 43 *American Journal of International Law* 144, 149.

[144] Alain Pellet, 'Legal opinion on certain questions of international law raised by the Reference', reprinted in Bayefsky, *Self-determination in international law*, p. 85, at p. 98. The exceptions are an illusory grant of independence; an incomplete grant of independence; grants of independence in violation of the principle of self-determination, i.e. (i) grants to unrepresentative (racist, minority) governments; and (ii) grants disruptive of the territorial integrity of the self-determination unit; grants in furtherance of illegal policies (e.g. South Africa/Transkei); grants to colonial enclaves, and in other cases of pre-emption rights; and grants in derogation from grants of independence: see James Crawford, *The creation of states in international law* (Oxford: Clarendon Press, 1979), pp. 218–28.

[145] Vicki Jackson, 'Comparative constitutional federalism and transnational judicial discourse' (2004) 2 *International Journal of Constitutional Law* 91, at footnote 138.

[146] Michael Hechter, *Containing nationalism* (Oxford: Oxford University Press, 2000), p. 78. See also Ruth Lapidoth, *Autonomy: flexible solutions to ethnic conflicts* (Washington, DC: United States Institute of Peace Press, 1996), p. 202.

[147] Article 39(1) of the Ethiopian Constitution (1994).

on the question of secession.[148] Other examples include the Constitution of Saint Kitts and Nevis which recognises the right of Nevis to separate from the federation following an affirmative vote of two-thirds of the members of the Nevis Assembly, and the approval of two-thirds of votes cast in a referendum on the question of separation;[149] the Constitution of Uzbekistan, which recognises the right of the Republic of Karakalpakstan to withdraw from Uzbekistan on the basis of a nationwide referendum of the people of Karakalpakstan;[150] and the Constitutional Charter of Serbia and Montenegro, which recognises that, after an interim period, both Serbia and Montenegro have the right to initiate the procedure for withdrawal from the State Union following a positive vote by the relevant people in a referendum.[151]

Additionally, a right of separation may be recognised as part of a post-conflict settlement. Examples include the 'Machakos Protocol' on Sudan, which provides that, after an interim period of six years, during which South Sudan will enjoy a large degree of autonomy, a referendum will be held for the 'people of South Sudan to: confirm the unity of the Sudan by voting to adopt the system of government established under the Peace Agreement; or to vote for secession'.[152] The Agreement Reached in the Multi-Party Negotiations recognises the 'legitimacy of whatever choice is freely exercised by a majority of the people of

---

[148] Article 39(4), *ibid*. Ethiopia recognised the right of the people of Eritrea to a referendum on the question of independence. In April 1993, a free and fair referendum was held in Eritrea, supervised by international observers. Over 99 per cent of the voters favoured independence. According to the Eritrea–Ethiopia Boundary Commission, 'On 27 April 1993, Eritrea became independent, and was admitted as a member of the United Nations. On 29 April 1993, Ethiopia recognised Eritrea's sovereignty and independence': Decision Regarding Delimitation of the Border between the State of Eritrea and the Federal Democratic Republic of Ethiopia, 41 ILM (2002) 1057, para. 2.12. Cf. SC Res. 828 (1993), and GA Res. 47/230, adopted 28 May 1993, 'Admission of Eritrea to membership in the United Nations'. See generally Bereket Habte Selassie, 'Self-determination in principle and practice: the Ethiopian–Eritrean experience' (1997) 29 *Columbia Human Rights Law Review* 91, 116; Quane, 'The United Nations and the evolving right to self-determination', 564–5; and Henrard and Smis, 'Recent experiences in South Africa and Ethiopia to accommodate cultural diversity', 40.

[149] Section 113 of the Saint Christopher and Nevis Constitution Order (1983).

[150] Article 74 of the Constitution of Uzbekistan.

[151] Article 60 of the Constitutional Charter of Serbia and Montenegro.

[152] Machakos Protocol, 'Agreed text on the right to self-determination for the peoples of South Sudan', adopted 20 July 20 2002, para. 2.5, available at www.usip.org/library/pa/sudan/sudan_machakos07202002_toc.html (last visited 23 January 2005). See also Protocol on Power Sharing, signed at Naivasha, Kenya, 26 May 2004, www.usip.org/library/pa/sudan/power_sharing_05262004.pdf (last visited 14 June 2005). See SC Res. 1590 (2005).

Northern Ireland with regard to its status, whether they prefer to continue to support the Union with Great Britain or a sovereign united Ireland'.[153] Independence is not an option. The Agreement recognises the right of the 'people of the island of Ireland alone, by agreement between the two parts respectively[,] to exercise their right of self-determination on the basis of consent, freely and concurrently given, North and South, to bring about a united Ireland, if that is their wish, accepting that this right must be achieved and exercised with and subject to the agreement and consent of a majority of the people of Northern Ireland'.[154]

Democratic theory has failed to delimit, with any clarity, the circumstances in which a right of separation or secession should be recognised by democratic governments.[155] According to the 'illegal taking' model, secession is permitted where the territory has been unjustly incorporated into the State.[156] The model is sometimes applied to Estonia, Latvia and Lithuania.[157] The 'pact' model recognises a unilateral right of secession for the constituent territories and/or peoples of ethnic federations.[158] A right of secession exists for those territories and/or peoples which were party to the original agreement by which the State

---

[153] Agreement Reached in the Multi-Party Negotiations, Belfast, 10 April 1998, 37 ILM (1998) 751, 'Constitutional Issues', para. 1(i). See Northern Ireland Act 1998, 39 ILM (2000) 927, section 1(1): '(1) It is hereby declared that Northern Ireland in its entirety remains part of the United Kingdom and shall not cease to be so without the consent of a majority of *the people of Northern Ireland* voting in a poll held for the purposes of this section in accordance with Schedule 1. (2) But if the wish expressed by a majority in such a poll is that Northern Ireland should cease to be part of the United Kingdom and form part of a united Ireland, the Secretary of State shall lay before Parliament such proposals to give effect to that wish as may be agreed between Her Majesty's Government in the United Kingdom and the Government of Ireland' (emphasis added).

[154] Agreement Reached in the Multi-Party Negotiations, 'Constitutional Issues', para. 1(ii).

[155] Allen Buchanan, 'Towards a theory of secession' (1991) 101 *Ethics* 322, 323. See also Diane Orentlicher, 'Separation anxiety: international responses to ethno-separatist claims' (1998) 23 *Yale Journal of International Law* 1, 46.

[156] Buchanan, 'Towards a theory of secession', 329. See also Robert Howse and Karen Knop, 'Federalism, secession, and the limits of ethnic accommodation: a Canadian perspective' (1993) 1 *New Europe Law Review* 269, 292. See, on this point, S. James Anaya, 'The capacity of international law to advance ethnic or nationality rights claims' (1990) 75 *Iowa Law Review* 837, 838.

[157] Cf. Roland Rich, 'Recognition of states: the collapse of Yugoslavia and the Soviet Union' (1993) 4 *European Journal of International Law* 36, 37–8.

[158] An ethnic federation is characterised by the existence of federal units which approximate to ethno-cultural groupings, and which reflect the national, ethnic, cultural, religious or linguistic identities of the dominant/majority group in the constituent entities (see below).

was constituted, when the terms of the constituting pact are breached.[159] According to the 'misconduct' model, where a State fails to recognise and protect the 'universal equal rights of individuals', a right of secession exists for the members of a group who do not enjoy equal rights.[160] Secession is a remedy of last resort, available to the 'collection of individuals whose rights have been systematically violated by the state, and the territory to be carved out is the land inhabited by the affected group'.[161]

The 'plebiscitary' model argues that a right of secession should be recognised where a majority of a territorially concentrated group expresses a desire to establish a sovereign and independent State, through referendums or elections.[162] Majority support for the establishment of a sovereign and independent State provides a right for the territory to secede.[163] The 'plebiscitary' model draws on the contractual model of democracy, and may in principle be applied to a single individual.[164] Any group of citizens that withdraws its consent to the legitimate authority of the State enjoys, on that basis alone, a right of secession.[165] The 'national self-determination' model of secession argues that the right applies only to 'nations': each 'nation' should have its own State, if it so desires.[166] Related to the national self-determination model is the 'failure of recognition' model of

---

[159] Howse and Knop, 'Federalism, secession, and the limits of ethnic accommodation', 301.

[160] *Ibid.*, 304. Secession is justified where policies or economic programmes systematically work to the disadvantage of one group whilst benefiting another, providing the basis for secessionist claims: Buchanan, 'Towards a theory of secession', 330.

[161] Howse and Knop, 'Federalism, secession, and the limits of ethnic accommodation', 304. See also Allen Buchanan, 'Democracy and secession', in Margaret Moore (ed.), *National self-determination and secession* (Oxford: Oxford University Press, 1998), p. 14, at p. 25.

[162] See, for example, Alan Patten, 'Democratic secession from a multinational state' (2002) 112 *Ethics* 558, 561.

[163] See Daniel Philpott, 'In defence of self-determination' (1995) 105 *Ethics* 352, 379. Subsequent to the act of secession, members of territorially concentrated groups within the new State may exercise their right to sovereign self-determination: *ibid.*, 380. Cf. Patten, 'Democratic secession from a multinational state', 578.

[164] Buchanan, 'Democracy and secession', 21. See also Buchanan, 'Towards a theory of secession', 326.

[165] Howse and Knop, 'Federalism, secession, and the limits of ethnic accommodation', 307. See also Philpott, 'In defence of self-determination', 361. The human right to political participation does not provide the citizen with the right to self-determination: *Diergaardt et al.* v. *Namibia*, Communication No. 760/1997, UN Doc. CCPR/C/69/D/760/1996, 6 September 2000, para. 10.8. Cf. Individual opinion by Martin Scheinin (concurring).

[166] See Buchanan, 'Towards a theory of secession', 328.

secession. According to this model, a multi-nation State should be (re)configured so that its multi-national character is both recognised and accommodated.[167] The State should introduce 'meaningful constitutional arrangements that recognize the distinct national identity of the secessionist group'.[168] Given that the group has expressed, as part of its identity, a collective desire for self-government,[169] the constitutional arrangement must establish a self-government regime for the people demanding the right to self-determination.[170] The 'failure of recognition' model considers that a failure to accord rights of self-government justifies, as a remedy of last resort, a right of secession.[171]

Secession in international law

When politicians and political philosophers talk about a 'right of secession', they are concerned to establish a moral right, from which legal consequences should flow.[172] A moral right of secession may create an obligation on the State to grant independence, or for the international community to recognise the secessionist entity as sovereign and independent, irrespective of the attitude of the existing sovereign authorities. This is not the position under international law. For a new State to be established, it must possess the relevant criteria of statehood: (a) a permanent population; (b) a defined territory; (c) government; and (d) a capacity to enter into relations with other States.[173] These criteria are based on the principle of 'effectiveness among territorial units'.[174]

The secessionist territory must demonstrate that it has effective and independent political control. This is a necessary, but not a sufficient

---

[167] James Tully, 'Introduction', in Alain Gagnon and James Tully (eds.), *Multinational democracies* (Cambridge: Cambridge University Press, 2001), p. 1, at p. 3.

[168] Patten, 'Democratic secession from a multinational state', 563.   [169] *Ibid.*, 567.

[170] *Ibid.*, 564–5.

[171] Howse and Knop, 'Federalism, secession, and the limits of ethnic accommodation', 312.

[172] Political philosophers accept that there might be cases where a prima facie case for secession should not lead to the creation of a new sovereign entity. See, for example, Daniel Philpott, 'In defence of self-determination' (1995) 105 *Ethics* 352, 363 and 371.

[173] Article 1 of the Montevideo Convention on the Rights and Duties of States, adopted 26 December 1933: reprinted (1934) 28 (Supplement) *American Journal of International Law* 75.

[174] James Crawford, *The creation of states in international law* (Oxford: Clarendon Press, 1979), p. 36. According to Brad Roth, they collapse into one: 'such population and territory as are found under the effective control of an independent government': Brad Roth, *Governmental illegitimacy in international law* (Oxford: Oxford University Press, 2000), p. 130.

criterion for the establishment of a new sovereign and independent State.[175] Without the consent of the existing State, the international community will not recognise secessionist territories as sovereign and independent States.[176] There are a large number of secessionist territories that have not been recognised as sovereign and independent States.[177] There is no general right of secession in international law.[178] The principle of sovereign equality of States includes the recognition that the territorial integrity of the State is 'inviolable'.[179] Any measure aimed at the disruption of the territorial integrity of a State 'is incompatible with the purposes and principles of the Charter'.[180] States must refrain from any act aimed at the 'disruption of the national unity and territorial integrity of any other State'.[181] This position applies in respect of support for secessionist movements, and the premature

---

[175] Cf. the view of Alain Pellet: 'succession secessions are de facto secessions': Alain Pellet, 'Legal opinion on certain questions of international law raised by the Reference', reprinted in Bayefsky, *Self-determination in international law*, p. 85, at p. 116.

[176] James Crawford, 'The right of self determination in international law: the development and future', in Philip Alston (ed.), *Peoples' rights* (Oxford: Oxford University Press, 2001), p. 7, at p. 55. Cf. James Crawford, 'State practice and international law in relation to unilateral secession', Expert Opinion Accompanying the Attorney General of Canada's Factum, *Reference re Secession of Quebec* [1998] 2 SCR 217, reprinted in Bayefsky, *Self-determination in international law*, p. 31, at paras. 9 and 10.

[177] Examples of secessionist territories that have not been recognised include Tibet (China), Katanga (Congo), Biafra (Nigeria), Kashmir (India), East Punjab (India), the Karen and Shan States (Burma), Turkish Federated State of Cyprus (Cyprus), Tamil Elam (Sri Lanka), South Sudan (Sudan), Somaliland (Somalia), Bougainville (Papua New Guinea), Kurdistan (Iraq/Turkey), Republika Srpska (Bosnia and Herzegovina), Chechnya (Russian Federation), Kosovo (Serbia and Montenegro), Abkhazia (Russian Federation), South Ossetia (Russian Federation), Nagorny-Kharabakh (Azerbaijan) and Democratic Republic of Yemen (Yemen): Crawford, 'State practice and international law in relation to unilateral secession', Expert Opinion, *ibid.*, para. 50.

[178] In *Reference re Secession of Quebec* [1998] 2 SCR 217, the Canadian Supreme Court determined that international law 'contains neither a right of unilateral secession nor the explicit denial of such a right, although such a denial is, to some extent, implicit in the exceptional circumstances required for secession to be permitted under the right of a people to self-determination, e.g., the right of secession that arises in the exceptional situation of an oppressed or colonial people' (para. 112). The right of colonial peoples to exercise their right to self-determination by breaking away from the 'imperial' power was, the Court concluded, 'now undisputed' (para. 132). The other clear case where a right to external self-determination accrues is where a people is subject to alien subjugation, domination or exploitation outside a colonial context (para. 133).

[179] GA Res. 2625 (XXV), adopted 24 October 1970, 'Declaration on Principles of International Law Concerning Friendly Relations and Co-operation among States in Accordance with the Charter of the United Nations'.

[180] *Ibid.*   [181] *Ibid.*

recognition of the secessionist unit.[182] The recognition of a right of peoples to self-determination does not change the general rule. The relevant provision is provided in General Assembly Resolution 2625 (XXV), in the section concerning the principle of equal rights and self-determination of peoples:

Nothing in the foregoing paragraphs shall be construed as authorizing or encouraging any action which would dismember or impair, totally or in part, the territorial integrity or political unity of sovereign and independent States conducting themselves in compliance with the principle of equal rights and self-determination of peoples as described above and thus possessed of a government representing the whole people belonging to the territory without distinction as to race, creed or colour.

In international law, a representative democracy is entitled to determine its own reaction to the expression of one part of the population for secession,[183] even when the call for secession is accompanied by supportive referenda.[184] In *Reference re Secession of Quebec*, the Supreme Court of Canada was asked to consider whether international law provides Quebec the 'right to effect the secession of Quebec from Canada unilaterally?'[185] According to the Supreme Court, the principle of self-determination in international law has evolved 'within a framework of respect for the territorial integrity of existing states'.[186] A State whose government represents the whole of the 'people or peoples resident within its territory, on a basis of equality and without discrimination, and respects the principles of self-determination in its own internal arrangements, is entitled to the protection under international law of its territorial integrity'.[187] No right of secession existed in the

---

[182] A state is a political community, within whatever territorial boundaries, that existing states collectively decide 'ought to be self-governing': Roth, *Governmental illegitimacy in international law*, p. 131. Cf. Conference on Yugoslavia Arbitration Commission: Opinions on Questions Arising from the Dissolution of Yugoslavia, 31 ILM (1992) 1488, Opinion No. 8, para. 2: 'while recognition of a state by other states has only declarative value, such recognition, along with membership of international organizations, bears witness to these states' conviction that the political entity so recognized is a reality and confers on it certain rights and obligations under international law.'

[183] James Crawford, 'State practice and international law in relation to secession' (1998) 69 *British Year Book of International Law* 85, 113.

[184] *Ibid.*, 116.

[185] The Court defined secession as an act by which one section of the State withdraws itself from the political and constitutional authority of the State, 'with a view to achieving statehood for a new territorial unit on the international plane': *Reference re Secession of Quebec* [1998] 2 SCR 217, para. 83.

[186] *Ibid.*, para. 127.   [187] *Ibid.*, para. 130.

context of Canadian representative democracy: 'Quebec could not, despite a clear referendum result, purport to invoke a right of self-determination to dictate the terms of a proposed secession to the other parties to the federation.'[188]

Nor, the Supreme Court of Canada concluded, could the central Government 'be indifferent to a clear expression of a clear majority of Quebecers that they no longer wish to remain in Canada'. The vote would need to be followed by negotiations to address the potential separation of Quebec from Canada: 'There would be no conclusions predetermined by law on any issue. Negotiations would need to address the interests of the other provinces, the federal government, Quebec and indeed the rights of all Canadians both within and outside Quebec, and specifically the rights of minorities'.[189] The clear repudiation by the people of Quebec of the existing constitutional order would confer (moral) legitimacy (only) on demands for secession, and place an obligation on the other provinces and the federal government to acknowledge and respect that expression of democratic will by entering into negotiations.

The 'saving clause'[190]

A reverse reading of the relevant clause in General Assembly Resolution 2625 (XXV), 'Declaration on Principles of International Law Concerning Friendly Relations' (above), limits the right to territorial integrity to those States 'conducting themselves in compliance with the principle of equal rights and self-determination of peoples', and 'thus possessed of a government representing the whole people belonging to the territory without distinction as to race, creed or colour'.[191] Reference to the whole people belonging to the territory 'without distinction as to race, creed or colour' should be read as referring to the population of the territory without distinction on irrelevant identity grounds.[192] The

---

[188] *Ibid.*, para. 151.

[189] *Ibid.* See Obiora Chinedu Okafor, 'Entitlement, process, and legitimacy in the emergent international law of secession' (2002) 9 *International Journal on Minority and Group Rights* 41, 50.

[190] See Robert Rosenstock, 'The Declaration on Friendly Relations' (1971) 65 *American Journal of International Law* 713, 732.

[191] The relevant passage, 'at least signals that the "national unity" of a state is earned by its government, and is not a fait accompli': Steven Ratner, 'Drawing a better line: *uti possidetis* and the borders of new states' (1996) 90 *American Journal of International Law* 590, 611.

[192] The formulation follows GA Res. 1514 (XV), which requires that steps be taken to transfer all powers to the peoples of non-self-governing territories, 'in accordance with their freely expressed will and desire, without any distinction as to race, creed or

position is confirmed in the UN Vienna Declaration and Programme of Action, which repeats the formulation, but ends 'and thus possessed of a Government representing the whole people belonging to the territory without distinction of any kind'.[193] No group of persons may be deliberately and systematically excluded from political life.[194]

The systematic exclusion of one part of the population from public life by a 'racist regime' constitutes a violation of the right of the people of the State to self-determination. In 1965, the General Assembly declared that the perpetuation of minority rule in Southern Rhodesia would be incompatible with the principle of equal rights and self-determination of peoples recognised in the Charter of the United Nations and in General Assembly Resolution 1514 (XV).[195] The Protocol Additional to the Geneva Conventions of 12 August 1949, and relating to the Protection of Victims of International Armed Conflicts (Protocol I), refers to 'peoples' fighting against 'racist regimes in the exercise of their right of self-determination'.[196] Article 19 of the African Charter on Human and Peoples' Rights provides: 'All peoples shall be equal; they shall enjoy the same respect and shall have the same rights. Nothing shall justify the domination of a people by another.' In *Communications filed against the Islamic Republic of Mauritania*, the African Commission noted that: 'At the heart of the abuses alleged in the different communications is the question of the domination of one section of the population by another. The resultant discrimination against Black Mauritanians is, according to the complainants ... the result of a negation of the fundamental principle of the equality of peoples as stipulated in the African Charter and [allegedly] constitutes

---

colour': GA Res. 1514 (XV), para. 5. Cf. Antonio Cassese, *Self-determination of peoples: a legal reappraisal* (Cambridge: Cambridge University Press, 1995), pp. 112–13. See also Jan Klabbers and Rene Lefeber, 'Africa: lost between self-determination and *uti possidetis*', in Catherine Brölmann *et al.* (eds.), *Peoples and minorities in international law* (Dordrecht: Martinus Nijhoff, 1993), p. 37, at p. 47; and Musgrave, *Self-determination and minorities*, p. 188.

[193] Vienna Declaration and Programme of Action (1993), 32 ILM (1993) 1661, para. I(2).

[194] See Article 1(1) of the International Convention on the Elimination of All Forms of Racial Discrimination, adopted by GA Res. 2106 (XX), 21 December 1965, in force 4 January 1969.

[195] GA Res. 2012 (XX), adopted 12 October 1965, 'Question of Southern Rhodesia', para. 2. See also Article II of the International Convention on the Suppression and Punishment of the Crime of Apartheid, adopted by GA Res. 3068 (XXVIII), 30 November 1973, in force 18 July 1976.

[196] Article 1(4) of Protocol Additional to the Geneva Conventions of 12 August 1949, and relating to the Protection of Victims of International Armed Conflicts (Protocol I), adopted 8 June 1977, in force 7 December 1979, 16 ILM (1977) 1391.

a violation of its Article 19.'[197] On the facts available to it, the Commission did not find a violation of the Charter, although it identified and condemned the existence of discriminatory practices against certain sectors of the Mauritanian population.[198]

The self-determination remedy in cases of racist rule is the 'establishment of a non-racial democratic society based on self-determination and majority rule through the full and free exercise of universal adult suffrage by all the people'.[199] Where a minority group is systematically excluded from public life, the remedy is representative government. Where a territorially concentrated group is systematically excluded, secession is a potential remedy of last resort, in cases of serious human rights abuses against members of the group.[200] Support for this reverse reading of the 'saving clause' (Resolution 2625 (XXV)) may be found in the decisions of the Canadian Supreme Court in *Reference re Secession of Quebec* and the African Commission on Human and Peoples' Rights in *Katangese Peoples' Congress* v. *Zaire*, and in the practice of humanitarian intervention, as Diane Orentlicher argues that the establishment of an autonomous 'safe-haven' for the Kurds in Iraq supports the arguments for the recognition of a right of secession as a remedy of last resort for oppressed and permanent minorities.[201]

In *Reference re Secession of Quebec*, the Supreme Court of Canada recognised that there were arguments that the right of peoples to self-determination may provide a right to unilateral secession 'when a

---

[197] *Malawi African Association, Amnesty International, Sarr Diop, Union Interafricaine des Droits de l'Homme et des Peuple and RADDHO, Collectif des Veuves et Ayants-Droits, Association Mauritanienne des Droits de l'Homme* v. *Mauritania*, Communication Nos. 54/ 91, 61/91, 98/93, 164/97 to 196/97 and 210/98, in Thirteenth Activity Report of the African Commission on Human and Peoples' Rights 1999–2000, para. 142. See Murray and Wheatley, 'Groups and the African Charter on Human and Peoples' Rights', 230–1.

[198] *Ibid.*   [199] SC Res. 581 (1986), para. 7. See also SC Res. 554 (1984), para. 4.

[200] There is no requirement for the group to live within administrative boundaries established within the State. See James Crawford, 'The right of self-determination in international law: the development and future', in Philip Alston (ed.), *Peoples' rights* (Oxford: Oxford University Press, 2001), p. 7, at p. 65.

[201] Diane Orentlicher, 'Separation anxiety: international responses to ethno-separatist claims' (1998) 23 *Yale Journal of International Law* 1, 49. See also SC Res. 1244 (1999), preamble, adopted following the NATO military intervention in the Federal Republic of Yugoslavia, which refers to the need to establish the conditions in which 'the people of Kosovo can enjoy substantial autonomy within the Federal Republic of Yugoslavia'. See also UNMIK Regulation 2001/9, on a Constitutional Framework for Provisional Self-Government in Kosovo, 15 May 2001, Article 1.1: 'Kosovo is an entity under interim international administration which, with its people, has unique historical, legal, cultural and linguistic attributes.'

people is blocked from the meaningful exercise of its right to self-determination internally'.[202] The Court concluded that it was 'unclear' as to whether this proposition reflected an established international law standard,[203] and even if it did, that the exceptional circumstances in which a right of secession might be recognised did not exist in Quebec.[204] In *Katangese Peoples' Congress* v. *Zaire*, the African Commission on Human and Peoples' Rights considered a communication which requested, inter alia, that it recognise the independence of Katanga.[205] There were no allegations of human rights abuses, with the exception of the alleged denial of the right of peoples to self-determination provided in Article 20 of the African Charter on Human and Peoples' Rights.[206] The Commission noted that, whilst all peoples have a right to self-determination, there existed 'controversy as to the definition of peoples and the content of the right'.[207] It concluded that the request for independence for Katanga had no merit under the African Charter on Human and Peoples' Rights:

In the absence of concrete evidence of violations of human rights to the point that the territorial integrity of Zaire should be called to question and in the absence of evidence that the people of Katanga are denied the right to participate in Government as guaranteed by Article 13(1) of the African Charter, the Commission holds the view that Katanga is obliged to exercise a variant of

---

[202] *Reference re Secession of Quebec* [1998] 2 SCR 217, para. 134.   [203] *Ibid.*, para. 135.

[204] *Ibid.* The judgment of the Constitutional Court of the Russian Federation on 31 July 1995, 'On the constitutionality of the Presidential Decrees and the Resolutions of the Federal Government concerning the situation in Chechnya', concluded that the 'constitutional goal of preserving the integrity of the Russian State accords with the universally recognised international legal principles concerning the right of nations to self-determination'. No consideration was given to the application of the 'saving clause'. Unofficial translation: Venice Commission, Council of Europe Doc. CDL-INF (96) 1, Strasbourg, 10 January 1996.

[205] *Katangese Peoples' Congress* v. *Zaire*, Communication No. 75/92, in Eighth Annual Activity Report of the African Commission on Human and Peoples' Rights, 1994–1995, ACHPR/RPT/8th, Annex VI, para. 1.

[206] *Ibid.*, para. 2. Article 20(1) of the African Charter on Human and Peoples' Rights: 'All peoples shall have the right to existence. They shall have the unquestionable and inalienable right to self-determination. They shall freely determine their political status and shall pursue their economic and social development according to the policy they have freely chosen.'

[207] *Ibid.*, para. 3. The African Commission noted that self-determination may be exercised in any of the following: 'independence, self-government, local government, federalism, confederalism, unitarism or any other form of relations that accords with the wishes of the people but fully cognizant of other recognized principles such as sovereignty and territorial integrity': *ibid.*, para. 4.

self-determination that is compatible with the sovereignty and territorial integrity of Zaire.[208]

Article 13(1) provides: 'Every citizen shall have the right to participate freely in the government of his country, either directly or through freely chosen representatives in accordance with the provisions of the law.' According to the African Commission, a denial of the rights of political participation when accompanied by serious human rights abuses may 'call into question' the territorial integrity of a State party to the African Charter on Human and Peoples' Rights.

In terms of the practice of States, the only candidate for secession in accordance with the 'saving clause' is the emergence of Bangladesh from Pakistan.[209] The 1970 general elections in Pakistan were won by the Awami League, a political party representing the interests of the population of East Pakistan, on a manifesto which proposed the introduction of extensive autonomy for that territory.[210] Following the Awami League's victory, the military and political elite in West Pakistan postponed the convening of the National Assembly, which would have drafted the Constitution, fearing that any Constitution adopted would reflect the League's demand for autonomy, given its majority in the Assembly.[211] The move led to growing demands for independence in East Pakistan.

---

[208] *Ibid.*, para. 6. The African Commission also rejected secessionist claims for Casamance in southern Senegal, noting that 'the reasons advanced are not unique to the Casamance, but can be invoked with a certain measure of profit by other regions of Senegal'. The Commission concluded that 'neither the position of the separatists, nor that of the State authorities, can be taken in its entirety. For this reason, a frank and constructive dialogue must be instituted between the two parties, from which a solution can emerge, a solution which will assure the cohesion and continuity of the people of the united Senegalese State in a community of interest and destiny': Report on Mission of Good Offices to Senegal of the African Commission on Human and Peoples' Rights (1–7 June 1996), Tenth Activity Report of the African Commission on Human and Peoples' Rights, 1996–1997, ACHPR/RPT/10th, Annex VIII. For a general discussion of the Casamance issue, see Lawrence Woocher, 'The "Casamance Question": an examination of the legitimacy of self-determination in Southern Senegal' (2000) 7 *International Journal on Minority and Group Rights* 341.

[209] James Crawford, 'State practice and international law in relation to secession' (1998) 69 *British Year Book of International Law* 85, 92. Cf. Biafra (Nigeria), which was recognised by only five States: Musgrave, *Self-determination and minorities*, p. 198. The Organization of African Unity's 'Resolution on the Situation in Nigeria' (1967) 'condemned' secession in member States: *ibid.*, 105.

[210] Ved Nanda, 'Self-determination in international law: the tragic tale of two cities – Islamabad (West Pakistan), and Dacca (East Pakistan)' (1972) 66 *American Journal of International Law* 321, 313.

[211] *Ibid.*, 323.

Military conflict began on 25 March 1971 when the Army attacked Dacca in East Pakistan, with significant civilian casualties. The following day, Sheikh Mujibur Rahman, the leader of the Awami League, was charged with treasonous acts, and the Awami League was proscribed.[212]

On 26 March 1971, Sheikh Mujibur Rahman proclaimed the independence of East Pakistan, and a civil war broke out. Observers reported that the military force used against the civilian population of East Pakistan was systematic, serious and widespread.[213] In December 1971, Indian forces intervened, allowing the Awami League to establish de facto control over the territory of East Pakistan.[214] An independent political unit was established with Sheikh Mujibur Rahman as its Prime Minister.[215] Within one month, seven States had recognised a new State of Bangladesh.[216] Within eleven months, forty-seven States had recognised an independent Bangladesh.[217] Bangladesh applied for UN admission in 1972, although it was not admitted until September 1974 – after its recognition by Pakistan.[218] The recognition of Bangladesh as a sovereign and independent State without the consent of the government in Pakistan is exceptional. Five factors are worthy of note: the ethno-cultural differences between the populations of East and West Pakistan; evidence of the neo-colonial exploitation of East Pakistan;[219] the exclusion of persons from East Pakistan from public life;[220] the urgency of the situation, reflected in the serious and widespread human rights abuses imputable to the Government of Pakistan; and the physically separate nature of the respective territories.[221]

The 'saving clause' is initially concerned with 'minorities by force':[222] groups identified, stigmatised and excluded by the dominant/majority

---

[212] Ibid., 322.   [213] Ibid., 323 and 332.

[214] There was little support for the Indian intervention in the United Nations. See GA Res. 2793 (XXVI), adopted 7 December 1971, 'Questions considered by the Security Council at its 1606th, 1607th, and 1608th meetings on 4, 5 and 6 December 1971', para. 1.

[215] Nanda, 'Self-determination in international law', 325.   [216] Ibid., 325.

[217] Quane, 'The United Nations and the evolving right to self-determination', 568.

[218] James Crawford, 'State practice and international law in relation to unilateral secession': Expert Opinion Accompanying the Attorney General of Canada's Factum, *Reference re Secession of Quebec* [1998] 2 SCR 217, reprinted in Bayefsky, *Self-determination in international law*, p. 31, at para. 26. Pakistan's membership of the United Nations was unaffected, despite losing over half of its population.

[219] See Nanda, 'Self-determination in international law', 329–30.

[220] Ibid., 328.   [221] Ibid., 334.

[222] See Thornberry, *International law and the rights of minorities*, pp. 9–10; and John Packer, 'Problems in defining minorities', in Bill Bowring and Deidre Fottrell (eds.), *Minority and group rights in the new millennium* (The Hague: Martinus Nijhoff, 1999), p. 223, at p. 254.

group. An act of secession requires the manifestation of the political will of the group to be self-governing. Peoples enjoy a right to self-determination, racial groups do not. An International Commission of Jurists, set up to investigate the events in East Pakistan, concluded that 'by 1970 the population of East Pakistan constituted a separate "people" '.[223] The Commission accepted that there was no universally agreed definition of a people, but that the members of such a group would have certain characteristics in common, which would act as a bond between them. These might be historical, racial or ethnic, cultural or linguistic, religious or ideological, geographical or territorial. The key factor, the Commission of Jurists determined, was not one of an essential or indispensable characteristic but rather a question of ideological and historical fact – the group becomes a people only 'when it becomes conscious of its own identity and asserts its will to exist'.[224] In this case, the self-determination remedy was exercised by the people of the territory of East Pakistan, a population that included a significant religious minority group (Hindus), an indigenous community, the Adivasis, and a group of 'Biharis', broadly sympathetic to maintaining the unity of the State.[225]

The dissolution of ethnic federations

States conducting themselves in compliance with the principle of equal rights and self-determination of peoples have a right to their territorial integrity. International law recognises the possibility of establishing new sovereign and independent States through an act of separation, but not secession. The distinction between the two lies in the attitude of the 'parent' State. No right of secession is recognised for any 'group', notwithstanding the possibility that ethno-cultural groups may be recognised as peoples.[226] This position applies equally to 'territories' in which the members of an ethno-cultural group constitute the majority,

---

[223] International Commission of Jurists, *The events in East Pakistan, 1971: a legal study* (Geneva: International Commission of Jurists, 1972), p. 47. See Musgrave, *Self-determination and minorities*, pp. 161–2.

[224] *Ibid.*

[225] Minority Rights Group (ed.), *World directory of minorities* (London: Minority Rights Group International, 1997), p. 542.

[226] See Committee on the Elimination of Racial Discrimination, 'General Recommendation XXI on the right to self-determination', adopted 15 March 1996, reprinted in 'Compilation of General Comments and General Recommendations', p. 212, para. 6.

including the constituent units of an ethnic federation:[227] a federal
State in which the constituent units approximate to the distribution
of national, ethnic, cultural, religious or linguistic groupings, and
which reflect the ethno-cultural identity of the majority group in the
constituent entity. International law does not recognise any right of
secession for the territories or peoples that were party to the original
agreement (or subsequent agreements) by which the State was
constituted.[228]

In cases of dissolution, there is no State from which the separatist
entity can seek consent for its separation.[229] In the process of dissolution, the existing State ceases to exist. It is replaced by new sovereign
and independent entities.[230] There is no continuer State. The act of
dissolution may be voluntary or involuntary.[231] In the case of ethnic
federations, the dissolution of the 'parent' State will see the emergence of territories which approximate to the distribution of ethno-
cultural groupings as sovereign and independent 'Nation' States.
Where the constituent entities and peoples are able to provoke the
dissolution of the State,[232] they enjoy a de facto right of secession.[233]

---

[227] A number of ethnic federations have proved to be politically unstable, including
    Nigeria, Pakistan, India, Malaysia, Canada and Belgium. The States of the former
    Soviet Empire comprised six unitary States and three ethnic federations. The six are
    now five, following the reunification of Germany. The three ethnic federations are
    now twenty-three, following the dissolution of the Union of the Soviet Socialist
    Republics (USSR), the Socialist Federal Republic of Yugoslavia and Czechoslovakia.
[228] Cf. Robert Howse and Karen Knop, 'Federalism, secession, and the limits of ethnic
    accommodation: a Canadian perspective' (1993) 1 *New Europe Law Review* 269, 296–301.
[229] James Crawford, 'State practice and international law in relation to secession' (1998)
    69 *British Year Book of International Law* 85, 92.
[230] The dissolution of a State 'means that it no longer has legal personality': Conference
    on Yugoslavia Arbitration Commission: Opinions on Questions Arising from the
    Dissolution of Yugoslavia, 31 ILM (1992) 1488, Opinion No. 8, para. 2.
[231] Examples of consensual dissolution include Norway from Sweden (1905), Iceland from
    Denmark (1944), Senegal from the Mali Federation (1961) and Singapore from Malaysia
    (1965): Musgrave, *Self-determination and minorities*, p. 111. The Czech Republic and
    Slovakia were admitted to the United Nations on 19 January 1993, following the
    dissolution of Czechoslovakia, an original member of the United Nations.
[232] This may occur, as in the Socialist Federal Republic of Yugoslavia, in the form of
    peripheral dissolution, where units beyond the centre seek to separate, or in the form
    of dissolution from the centre, where the core federal unit seeks to separate from the
    sovereign polity: Daniele Conversi, 'Central secession: towards a new analytical
    concept? The case of former Yugoslavia' (2000) 26 *Journal of Ethnic and Migration Studies*
    333, 335. Cf. Aleksandar Pavkovic, 'Recursive secessions in former Yugoslavia: too
    hard a case for theories of secession' (2000) 48 *Political Studies* 485.
[233] Cf. Alain Pellet, who describes the distinction between secession and dissolution as
    'entirely meaningless': Alain Pellet, 'Legal opinion on certain questions of

The 'Nation' States of Croatia, Slovenia, and the Former Yugoslav Republic of Macedonia, as well as the 'multi-Nation' States of Bosnia and Herzegovina and Serbia and Montenegro,[234] emerged from the dissolution of the Socialist Federal Republic of Yugoslavia,[235] which was provoked by the secessionist efforts of Croatia and Slovenia, who declared their independence on 25 June 1991. All of the States were successor States.[236] The international community did not recognise Serbia and Montenegro as the successor to the Socialist Federal Republic of Yugoslavia.[237]

On 27 August 1991, the European Community established a Peace Conference on Yugoslavia, including an Arbitration Commission, comprising five Presidents from among the various Constitutional Courts of the EC States. The Arbitration Commission was known as the Badinter Commission after its president.[238] In its Opinion No. 1, adopted on 29 November 1991, the Arbitration Commission opined that, in accordance with the principles of public international law,

international law raised by the Reference', reprinted in Bayefsky, *Self-determination in international law*, p. 85, at p. 103. See also *Reference re Secession of Quebec* [1998] 2 SCR 217, para. 88.

[234] In April 1992, Serbia and Montenegro (separate republics in the Socialist Federal Republic of Yugoslavia) joined together to form the Federal Republic of Yugoslavia. On 4 February 2003, the State changed its name to 'Serbia and Montenegro'.

[235] The Socialist Federal Republic of Yugoslavia was an ethnic federation: Slovenia was 90 per cent ethnic Slovene; Croatia 85 per cent ethnic Croat. In Serbia, Montenegro and Macedonia, two-thirds of the population were, respectively ethnic Serbian, Montenegrin and Macedonian. In Bosnia and Herzegovina, 40 per cent of the population were Muslim (Bosniac), 32 per cent Serb and 18 per cent Croat: Marc Weller, 'The international response to the dissolution of the Socialist Federal Republic of Yugoslavia' (1992) 86 *American Journal of International Law* 569, 569.

[236] Conference on Yugoslavia Arbitration Commission: Opinions on Questions Arising from the Dissolution of Yugoslavia, 31 ILM (1992) 1488, Opinion No. 9, para. 1.

[237] See SC Res. 777 (1992), para. 1; and GA Res. 47/1, adopted 22 September 1992, 'Recommendation of the Security Council of 19 September 1992', para. 1. See also GA Res. 55/12, adopted 1 November 2000, 'Admission of the Federal Republic of Yugoslavia to membership in the United Nations'. During the period when Serbia and Montenegro was not a member of the United Nations, the entity was recognised as a State with international legal rights and responsibilities, in particular for its actions in respect of the ethnic conflict in Bosnia and Herzegovina: see, Marc Weller, 'The international response to the dissolution of the Socialist Federal Republic of Yugoslavia' (1992) 86 *American Journal of International Law* 569, 596.

[238] Roland Rich, 'Recognition of states: the collapse of Yugoslavia and the Soviet Union' (1993) 4 *European Journal of International Law* 36, 40. See Alain Pellet, 'The Opinions of the Badinter Arbitration Committee: a second breath for the self-determination of peoples' (1992) 3 *European Journal of International Law* 178. See generally Matthew Craven, 'The European Community Arbitration Commission on Yugoslavia' (1995) 66 *British Year Book of International Law* 333.

'the existence or disappearance of the state is a question of fact; that the effects of recognition by other states are purely declaratory'.[239] According to the Commission, in the case of a 'federal-type state, which embraces communities that possess a degree of autonomy and, moreover, participate in the exercise of political power within the framework of institutions common to the Federation, the existence of the state implies that the federal organs represent the components of the Federation and wield effective power'.[240]

The Arbitration Commission noted that, although the Socialist Federal Republic of Yugoslavia had 'until now retained its international personality', a number of the constituent republics had expressed their desire for independence: Slovenia, Croatia and Macedonia in referendums, and Bosnia and Herzegovina in a parliamentary resolution.[241] Moreover, the 'composition and workings of the essential organs of the Federation ... no longer [met] the criteria of participation and representatives inherent in a federal state',[242] and the recourse to force in the different parts of the federation had demonstrated the federation's impotency.[243] Consequently, the Socialist Federal Republic of Yugoslavia was 'in the process of dissolution', and it was 'up to those Republics that so wish, to work together to form a new association endowed with the democratic institutions of their choice'.[244]

In Opinion No. 8, the Arbitration Commission dealt with the question as to whether the dissolution could be regarded as complete. The Commission noted a number of facts that had occurred in the intervening period since the adoption of Opinion No. 1: a referendum held in

---

[239] Conference on Yugoslavia Arbitration Commission: Opinions on Questions Arising from the Dissolution of Yugoslavia, 31 ILM (1992) 1488, Opinion No. 1, para. 1(a). The following definition of a State is provided: 'a community which consists of a territory and a population subject to an organized political authority; that such a state is characterized by sovereignty': *ibid.*, para. 1(b).

[240] *Ibid.*, para. 1(d). In a later Opinion, the Commission concluded that the existence of a federal State 'is seriously compromised when a majority of [its constituent] entities, embracing a greater part of the territory and population, constitute themselves as sovereign states with the result that federal authority may no longer be effectively exercised': Opinion No. 8, para. 2. In the case of the Socialist Federal Republic of Yugoslavia, Serbia and Montenegro, the 'rump Yugoslavia', comprised 40 per cent of the territory, and 45 per cent of the population: Yehuda Blum, 'UN membership of the "new" Yugoslavia: continuity or break?' (1992) 86 *American Journal of International Law* 830, 833. Cf. Weller, 'The international response to the dissolution of the Socialist Federal Republic of Yugoslavia', 595.

[241] Opinion No. 1, para. 2(a).   [242] *Ibid.*, para. 2(b).

[243] *Ibid.*, para. 2(c). See also Opinion No. 8, para. 1.   [244] Opinion No.1, para. 3.

Bosnia and Herzegovina had supported independence; Serbia and Montenegro had constituted themselves as a new State; most of the new States formed from the former Yugoslav republics had recognised each other's independence, thus demonstrating that the authority of the federal State no longer held sway on the territory of the newly constituted States; the common federal bodies on which all the Yugoslav republics were represented no longer existed; the former national territory and population of the Socialist Federal Republic of Yugoslavia were entirely under the sovereign authority of the new States; Bosnia-Herzegovina, Croatia and Slovenia had been admitted to membership of the United Nations; United Nations bodies referred to the '*former* Socialist Federal Republic of Yugoslavia'; and the UN had not accepted the Federal Republic of Yugoslavia (Serbia and Montenegro) as the continuer State of the Socialist Federal Republic of Yugoslavia.[245] The Arbitration Commission concluded 'that the process of dissolution of the SFRY ... is now complete and that the SFRY no longer exists'.[246]

Opinion No. 1 of the Arbitration Commission recognised a right of self-determination for the 'peoples' of the constituent republics of the Socialist Federal Republic of Yugoslavia: it was 'up to those republics that so wish, to work together to form a new association endowed with the democratic institutions of their choice'.[247] The peoples of the republics could emerge as new sovereign and independent States unilaterally or in association with other Republics. On 16 December 1991, the EC requested 'any Republic of the Socialist Federal Republic of Yugoslavia' to state whether 'they wish[ed] to be recognized as independent states'.[248] The invitation was extended only to the federal units. It was not extended to sub-federal units (Kosovo), or regions dominated by a particular ethno-cultural group (those regions of Croatia and Bosnia and Herzegovina with majority Serbian populations). The internal administrative borders both defined the 'people' to whom the right of self-determination was applied, and subsequently formed the

---

[245] Opinion No. 8, para. 3.
[246] *Ibid.*, para. 4. Whilst the Arbitration Commission referred to the process of dissolution, dissolution occurs on a particular date: see, Article 2(1)(e) of the Vienna Convention on Succession of States in respect of Treaties, adopted 22 August 1978, in force 6 November 1996, reprinted (1978) 72 *American Journal of International Law* 971.
[247] Opinion No. 1, para. 3.
[248] Declaration on Yugoslavia (Extraordinary EPC Ministerial Meeting, Brussels, 16 December 1991), reprinted (1993) 4 *European Journal of International Law* 73.

international borders between the new sovereign and independent States.[249] In its decision to limit the scope of application of the right of self-determination to the peoples of the republics, the Commission relied on the legal principle of *uti possidetis*:[250] in the absence of agreement to the contrary, 'the former boundaries become frontiers protected by international law ... The principle applies all the more readily to the Republic since the ... Constitution of the SFRY stipulated that the Republics' territories and boundaries could not be altered without their consent.'[251]

The Arbitration Commission recommended the recognition of Croatia,[252] Slovenia[253] and Macedonia.[254] The Commission did not initially recommend the recognition of Bosnia and Herzegovina.[255] No referendum on the question of independence had been held in Bosnia and Herzegovina, although the Presidency and the Government, excluding the Serbian members, supported independence. The Commission determined that the 'will of the peoples of Bosnia-Herzegovina to constitute [Bosnia and Herzegovina] as a sovereign and independent state cannot be said to have been fully established'.[256] The meaning of 'peoples' in this context is not clear, given the Arbitration Commission's decision in Opinion No. 2 (below). The Arbitration Commission determined that the assessment 'could be reviewed if appropriate guarantees were provided by the Republic applying for recognition, possibly by means of a referendum of all the citizens of [Bosnia and Herzegovina] without distinction, carried out under international supervision'.[257] Subsequently, a referendum on independence was held, in which a

---

[249] Cf. Steven Ratner, 'Drawing a better line: *uti possidetis* and the borders of new states' (1996) 90 *American Journal of International Law* 590, 605. For the objections of Serb populations to this approach, see, Kenneth Anderson, 'Illiberal tolerance: an essay on the fall of Yugoslavia and the rise of multiculturalism in the United States' (1992/3) 33 *Virginia Journal of International Law* 385, 391. See also Weller, 'The international response to the dissolution of the Socialist Federal Republic of Yugoslavia', 590. The dissolution of a State has no impact on existing international borders: Conference on Yugoslavia Arbitration Commission: Opinions on Questions Arising from the Dissolution of Yugoslavia, 31 ILM (1992) 1488, Opinion No. 3, para. 2.

[250] See Ratner, 'Drawing a better line', 609.

[251] Opinion No. 3, para. 2. Cf. Malcolm Shaw, 'Peoples, territorialism and boundaries' (1997) 8 *European Journal of International Law* 478, 489. See Ratner, 'Drawing a better line', 613.

[252] Opinion No. 5. The recommendation was accompanied by certain conditions concerning minorities. The Commission based its recommendations on the EC's 'Guidelines on the Recognition of the New States in Eastern Europe and in the Soviet Union', 31 ILM (1992) 1486. See also Musgrave, *Self-determination and minorities*, p. 112.

[253] Opinion No. 7.   [254] Opinion No. 6.   [255] Opinion No. 4.

[256] *Ibid.*, para. 4.   [257] *Ibid.*

majority of the population voted in favour of independence: 99 per cent (on a turnout of 63 per cent). The Serbian minority, some 31 per cent of the population, boycotted the vote.[258]

In the Socialist Federal Republic of Yugoslavia, the right of self-determination was not applied to 'individuals sharing common and distinctive ethnic, linguistic and cultural characteristics', but to 'those inhabiting a region whose territorial limits had previously been defined by an autonomous government and administration'.[259] Opinion No. 2 of the Arbitration Commission concerned the question as to whether 'the Serbian population in Croatia and Bosnia-Herzegovina, as one of the constituent peoples of Yugoslavia, [had] the right to self-determination'. The Arbitration Commission responded in the negative, concluding that the 'Serbian population in Bosnia-Herzegovina and Croatia is entitled to all the rights concerned to minorities and ethnic groups under international law'.[260] Thus, the Serbian population in Bosnia and Herzegovina, which had favoured the creation of a 'Common Yugoslav [i.e. Serbian] State', or the establishment of a 'Serbian Republic of Bosnia-Herzegovina',[261] did not enjoy the right to determine the international status of the territory where they formed the majority. The 'people' to whom the right of external self-determination was applied was defined by reference to a political territory, and not national, ethnic, cultural, religious or linguistic identity. Opinion No. 2 refers additionally to the human right of peoples to self-determination, which recognises that 'every individual may choose to belong to whatever ethnic, religious or language community he or she wishes'. In the view of the Arbitration Commission, 'one possible consequence of this principle might be for the members of the Serbian population in Bosnia-Herzegovina and Croatia to be recognized under agreements between the Republics as having the nationality of their choice, with all the rights and obligations which that entails with respect to the states concerned'.[262] The Commission concluded that the Republics must afford the members of minority groups 'all the human rights and fundamental freedoms recognized in international law, including,

---

[258] Rich, 'Recognition of states', 50.
[259] Weller, 'The international response to the dissolution of the Socialist Federal Republic of Yugoslavia', 606.
[260] Opinion No. 2, para. 4(i).   [261] Opinion No. 4, para. 3.
[262] Opinion No. 2, para. 3. See Karen Knop, *Diversity and self-determination in international law* (Cambridge: Cambridge University Press, 2002), p. 186.

where appropriate, the right to choose their nationality'.[263] The determination is not consistent with the contemporary right of peoples to self-determination that has emerged in international law.

'Less-than-sovereign' self-determination[264]

The Committee on the Elimination of Racial Discrimination has noted that two aspects of the right of peoples to self-determination may be distinguished: an external aspect, the right to determine the international status of the territory, and an internal aspect, 'that is to say, the rights of all peoples to pursue freely their economic, social and cultural development without outside interference'.[265]Article 1, common to the International Covenants, provides: 'All peoples have the right of self-determination. By virtue of that right they freely determine their political status and freely pursue their economic, social and cultural development.'[266] In the era of the territorial state, self-determination implies political control over territory.[267] A territorial unit that enjoys 'general or political autonomy', i.e. independence in respect of political

---

[263] *Ibid.*, para. 4(ii). Cf. Articles 3–6 of the Treaty of Peace with Poland ('Polish Minorities Treaty'), adopted at Versailles, 28 June 1919, Treaty of Peace Between the United States of America, the British Empire, France, Italy, and Japan and Poland, reprinted (1919) 13(4) Supplement, *American Journal of International Law* 423.

[264] Hannum, *Autonomy, sovereignty, and self-determination*, p. 469.

[265] Committee on the Elimination of Racial Discrimination, 'General Recommendation XXI on the right to self-determination', adopted 15 March 1996, reprinted in 'Compilation of General Comments and General Recommendations', p. 212, para. 4.

[266] Article 1(1), common to the International Covenant on Economic, Social and Cultural Rights and the International Covenant on Civil and Political Rights. Additionally: 'All peoples may, for their own ends, freely dispose of their natural wealth and resources … In no case may a people be deprived of its own means of subsistence': (common) Article 1(2).

[267] Donald Horowitz, 'The cracked foundations of the right to secede' (2003) 14 *Journal of Democracy* 5, 7. Cf. Patrick Thornberry, 'Self-determination and indigenous peoples: objections and responses', in Pekka Aikio and Martin Scheinin (eds.), *Operationalizing the right of indigenous peoples to self-determination* (Turku: Institute for Human Rights, Åbo Akademi University, 2000), p. 39, at p. 56 (footnotes omitted). In its Concluding Observations on Sweden, the Human Rights Committee expressed its concern 'at the limited extent to which the Sami Parliament can have a significant role in the decision-making process on issues affecting the traditional lands and economic activities of the indigenous Sami people, such as projects in the fields of hydroelectricity, mining and forestry, as well as the privatization of land (arts. 1, 25 and 27 of the Covenant). The State party should take steps to involve the Sami by giving them greater influence in decision-making affecting their natural environment and their means of subsistence': Concluding Observations on Sweden, UN Doc. CCPR/CO/74/SWE, 24 April 2002, para. 15.

decision-making, is an 'autonomy' for the purposes of international law.[268] The granting of cultural or religious autonomy does not constitute 'sufficient political or legal control over internal matters to constitute full autonomy as that term might be applied'.[269]

The establishment of an autonomy regime does not require that the territory should be recognised as being comparable in status to a sovereign and independent State. Few autonomies, for example, enjoy the right to control immigration, or rights of residence,[270] or limit the rights of local political participation to members of a particular group.[271] Autonomy is 'limited self-rule',[272] or 'less-than-sovereign self-determination'.[273] The extent and scope of the devolution of powers to an autonomous region will vary from State to State (and may vary between autonomous regions within a single State). Powers of self-government are normally recognised in respect of education, culture and environment.[274] Functions such as defence, foreign affairs, immigration and economic affairs often remain within the domain of the central authorities.[275]

Autonomy regimes are related to, but distinct from, regional and local government. Most democracies devolve issues relating to education, culture, the environment, local planning, natural resources, economic development, some policing functions, and housing, health and other

---

[268] Hurst Hannum and Richard Lillich, 'The concept of autonomy in international law' (1980) 74 *American Journal of International Law* 858, 860. See also Yash Ghai, 'Ethnicity and autonomy: a framework for analysis', in Yash Ghai (ed.), *Autonomy and ethnicity: negotiating competing claims in multi-ethnic states* (Cambridge: Cambridge University Press, 2000), p. 1, at p. 8.

[269] Hannum and Lillich, 'The concept of autonomy in international law', 888.

[270] Rainer Baubock, 'Why stay together? A pluralist approach to secession and federalism', in Will Kymlicka and Wayne Norman (eds.), *Citizenship in diverse societies* (Oxford: Oxford University Press, 2000), p. 366, at p. 389. Cf. *Italia Taamale v. Attorney-General* [1996] 2 *Commonwealth Human Rights Law Digest* 257.

[271] Cf. Kristian Myntti and Martin Scheinin, 'The right of domicile in the Åland Islands in the light of human rights treaties and the European integration process', in Lauri Hannikainen and Frank Horn (eds.), *Autonomy and demilitarisation in international law: the Åland Islands in a changing Europe* (The Hague: Kluwer Law International, 1997), p. 131.

[272] Ruth Lapidoth, *Autonomy: flexible solutions to ethnic conflicts* (Washington, DC: United States Institute of Peace Press, 1996), p. 33.

[273] Hannum, *Autonomy, sovereignty, and self-determination*, p. 469.

[274] See *ibid.*, p. 4. See also Will Kymlicka, 'Western political theory and ethnic relations in Eastern Europe', in Will Kymlicka and Magda Opalski (eds.), *Can liberal pluralism be exported? Western political theory and ethnic relations in Eastern Europe* (Oxford: Oxford University Press, 2001), p. 13, at p. 24.

[275] Hannum and Lillich, 'The concept of autonomy in international law', 886.

social services to regional and local government.[276] Autonomy regimes, by definition, may only be introduced for territories where a majority of the population belong to a minority group defined by a distinctive national, ethnic, cultural, religious or linguistic identity.[277] Where the regional or local self-government arrangements provide the members of the group with sufficient decision-making powers to enable the group to maintain and develop its distinctive cultural identity, the regime may be regarded as an autonomy.

The right of self-government within the autonomy must be exercised in accordance with the relevant standards established under international and regional human rights law.[278] Persons belonging to minorities within the self-government unit enjoy the right to enjoy their own culture, to profess and practise their own religion and to use their own language.[279] This protection should extend to members of the majority group in the autonomy, notwithstanding the Opinion of the Human Rights Committee in *Ballantyne and Davidson, and McIntyre* v. *Canada*. The Committee concluded that the scope of application of the rights of minorities could not extend to members of the majority group who constitute a minority in a particular region: 'the minorities referred to in Article 27 are minorities within [the] State, and not minorities within any province'.[280] The Opinion was accompanied by strong dissenting opinions, and may not be followed in future Opinions of the Committee.[281] It is not consistent with the position of other international bodies.[282]

The establishment of an autonomy regime involves the devolution of significant aspects of government authority to a territorially defined

---

[276] See, for example, the Council of Europe's European Charter of Local Self-Government, adopted at Strasbourg, 15 October 1985, in force 1 September 1988, ETS No. 122: 'local authorities are one of the main foundations of any democratic regime' (preamble).

[277] From the Greek *autos* ('self') and *nomos* ('law').

[278] See, for example, Article 50 of the International Covenant on Civil and Political Rights.

[279] Article 27, *ibid.*

[280] *Ballantyne and Davidson, and McIntyre* v. *Canada*, Communication Nos. 359/1989 and 385/1989, UN Doc. CCPR/C/47/D/359/1989, 5 May 1993, para. 11.2.

[281] Thornberry, *Indigenous peoples and international law*, p. 53.

[282] See Article 20 of the Framework Convention on National Minorities. See Opinion on Finland, ACFC/INF/OPI(2001)002, para. 17, and Opinion on Denmark, ACFC/INF/OPI(2001)005, para. 20. See also Article 13 of the Parliamentary Assembly, Recommendation 1201, adopted 1 February 1993, 'Additional protocol on the rights of national minorities to the European Convention on Human Rights (1950)'. See also SC Res. 1244 (1999), which made clear the importance of the protection of the Serb minority in Kosovo.

political unit. Powers may be devolved on a symmetrical or asymmetrical basis.[283] In cases of the symmetrical devolution of power, where the political units are accorded a high degree of self-government, and are recognised as having a share of power within the organs of the central government, the State may be regarded as a federal entity.[284] The typical federal structure consists of a central, or federal, government, with responsibility for such issues as defence, foreign affairs, immigration and economic affairs, and sub-State units, which possess a large degree of political autonomy, both from each other and from the federal authorities. The territorial division of a federal State may have no ethno-cultural basis, or some, or may closely correspond to major ethnic divisions.[285] Where all of the sub-State units are defined by reference to ethno-cultural identity, the State may be regarded as an ethnic federation (see above).

Indigenous peoples

The international community has recognised the existence of 'persons of indigenous origin',[286] 'indigenous communities',[287] and 'indigenous people',[288] where 'people' is the plural of 'person'.[289] The past decade

---

[283] On the problems created by the asymmetrical devolution of power, see Yash Ghai, 'Constitutional asymmetries: communal representation, federalism and cultural autonomy', in Andrew Reynolds (ed.), *The architecture of democracy: constitutional design, conflict management and democracy* (Oxford: Oxford University Press, 2002), p. 141, at pp. 160–1.

[284] The term 'federal', when applied to a State, has no fixed meaning, although it is generally understood to embrace two essential elements: political authority should be structurally dispersed among many centres of authority; and the federal units should possess prescribed areas of jurisdiction that cannot be invaded by the central authority: Alemante Selassie, 'Ethnic federalism: its promises and pitfalls for Africa' (2003) 28 *Yale Journal of International Law* 51, 57.

[285] Timothy Sisk, *Power sharing and international mediation in ethnic conflicts* (Washington, DC: United States Institute of Peace, 1996), p. 50.

[286] Article 29(1)(d) of the Convention on the Rights of the Child, adopted by GA Res. 44/25, 20 November 1989, in force 2 September 1990.

[287] Human Rights Committee, General Comment No. 23, 'Rights of minorities (Article 27)', para. 3.2, refers to 'indigenous communities constituting a minority'.

[288] See, for example, GA Res. 45/164, adopted 18 December 1990; 48/163, adopted 21 December 1993; and 49/214, adopted 17 February 1995, all of which concern 'the World's Indigenous People'. See also Vienna Declaration and Programme of Action (1993), 32 ILM (1993) 1661, para. I(20).

[289] Cf. Committee on Economic, Social and Cultural Rights, General Comment No. 6, 'The economic, social and cultural rights of older persons', reprinted in 'Compilation of General Comments and General Recommendations', p. 35, para. 3, which refers to

has seen the recognition of the legal category of 'indigenous peoples'. The Committee on the Elimination of Racial Discrimination has confirmed that the scope of application of the Convention on the Elimination of All Forms of Racial Discrimination concerns 'all persons who belong to different races, national or ethnic groups or to indigenous peoples'.[290] The Committee has adopted a General Recommendation on 'Indigenous peoples',[291] which calls on States parties to recognise and respect 'indigenous distinct culture, history, language and way of life',[292] and to recognise and protect the rights of indigenous peoples to own, develop, control and use their communal lands, territories and resources.[293]

The term 'indigenous' is sometimes applied to the present-day descendants of the putative original inhabitants of a particular territory,[294] or to groups that inhabited a territory prior to its colonisation by European powers.[295] In most cases, anthropologists agree that the question 'who came first' is largely meaningless.[296] Contemporary writers on the position of indigenous peoples in international law agree that the term may be applied to ethno-cultural groups which have sustained a close relationship with a particular territory over many generations, which in part gives expression to their distinctive cultural identity, and who possess a political organisation able to pursue a self-government

---

'older people'; and Committee on the Rights of the Child, General Comment No. 3, 'HIV/AIDS and the rights of the child', reprinted *ibid.*, p. 308, para. 1, which refers to 'younger people'.

[290] Committee on the Elimination of Racial Discrimination, 'General Recommendation XXIV concerning Article 1, paragraph 1 of the Convention', adopted 22 March 1993, reprinted in 'Compilation of General Comments and General Recommendations', p. 206, para. 1.

[291] Committee on the Elimination of Racial Discrimination, 'General Recommendation XXIII on the rights of indigenous peoples', adopted 18 August 1997, reprinted in 'Compilation of General Comments and General Recommendations', p. 215.

[292] *Ibid.*, para. 4(a).   [293] *Ibid.*, para. 5.

[294] Patrick Thornberry, *Indigenous peoples and international law* (Manchester: Manchester University Press, 2002), p. 39: 'ab origine, from the beginning'.

[295] According to S. James Anaya, 'the rubric of indigenous peoples or populations is generally understood to refer to culturally cohesive groups that suffer inequities within the states in which they live as the result of historical patterns of empire and conquest': S. James Anaya, *Indigenous peoples in international law* (Oxford: Oxford University Press, 1996), p. 86.

[296] Maivân Lâm, *At the edge of the state: indigenous peoples and self-determination* (Ardsley, NY: Transnational Publishers, 2000), p. 3. See also W. Michael Reisman, 'Protecting indigenous rights in international adjudication' (1995) 89 *American Journal of International Law* 350, 350.

claim.[297] They disagree as to whether the term applies only to indigenous communities that were deprived of their lands in the process of ('Western') colonisation. Patrick Thornberry identifies the following 'elements in the indigenous descriptors (not commonly found in descriptions of "minority")': precedent habitation; historical continuity; attachment to land; the communal sense and the communal right; a cultural gap between the dominant groups in a State and the indigenous; and the colonial context.[298] The UN Special Rapporteur, Martínez-Cobo, in his *Study of the problem of discrimination against indigenous populations*, defined indigenous 'communities, peoples and nations' as groups of persons, which 'having a historical continuity with pre-invasion and pre-colonial societies that developed on their territories, consider themselves distinct from other sectors of the societies now prevailing in those territories, or parts of them'. Indigenous peoples are in a 'non-dominant' position, and are 'determined to preserve, develop and transmit to future generations their ancestral territories, and their ethnic identity, as the basis of their continued existence as peoples, in accordance with their own cultural patterns, social institutions and legal systems'.[299]

Benedict Kingsbury identifies five conceptual foundations for the claims made by indigenous peoples, in relation to international law: individual human rights, and the non-discrimination norm; the rights of minorities (and in Europe, national minorities); the right of [indigenous] peoples to self-determination; the extant legal consequences of the fact of colonisation; and international agreements concluded at the time of colonisation.[300] The following sections consider the significance of the term 'peoples' in the discourse on indigenous peoples, and the right of (indigenous) peoples to territorial self-government. According to Erika-Irene Daes, former Chairman of the UN Working Group on Indigenous Peoples, 'the principal legal distinction between the rights of minorities and indigenous peoples in contemporary

---

[297] See Benedict Kingsbury, ' "Indigenous peoples" in international law: a constructivist approach to the controversy' (1998) 92 *American Journal of International Law* 414, 446.

[298] Thornberry, *Indigenous peoples and international law*, p. 55.

[299] J. Martínez-Cobo, 'Study of the problem of discrimination against indigenous populations', UN Doc. E/CN.4/Sub.2/1986/7/Add.4, para. 379, referred to in Thornberry, *Indigenous peoples and international law*, p. 49.

[300] See Benedict Kingsbury, 'Reconciling five competing conceptual structures of indigenous peoples' claims in international and comparative law', in Philip Alston (ed.), *Peoples' rights* (Oxford: Oxford University Press, 2001), p. 69.

international law is with respect to internal self-determination: the right of a group to govern itself within a recognized geographical area, without State interference'.[301]

In terms of positive international law, indigenous peoples are the subject of two international instruments adopted by the International Labour Organization (ILO): ILO Convention 107, 'Indigenous and Tribal Populations Convention' (1957),[302] and ILO Convention 169, 'Indigenous and Tribal Peoples Convention' (1989),[303] which amends the 1957 Convention.[304] Treaties concluded at the time of colonisation do not, from the perspective of international law, regulate the position of indigenous peoples.[305] Indigenous peoples may not seek to enforce the provisions of 'indigenous treaties' at the level of international law.[306]

The ILO Conventions

ILO Convention 107 concerns 'Populations'. The focus of ILO Convention 169 is 'Indigenous and Tribal Peoples'. The use of the term 'peoples' in place of 'populations' was agreed, 'because this term recognizes the existence of organized societies with an identity of their own rather than mere groupings sharing some racial or cultural

---

[301] Erika-Irene Daes and Asbjørn Eide, 'Working paper on the relationship and distinction between the rights of persons belonging to minorities and those of indigenous peoples', UN Doc. E/CN.4/Sub.2/2000/10, 19 July 2000, para. 43.

[302] Indigenous and Tribal Populations Convention (1957) (No. 107), adopted by the General Conference of the International Labour Organisation, 26 July 1957, in force 2 July 1959.

[303] Indigenous and Tribal Peoples Convention (1989) (No. 169), adopted by the General Conference of the International Labour Organisation, 27 June 1989, in force 5 September 1991.

[304] Article 36 of ILO Convention 169.

[305] See *Cayuga Indians (GB)* v. *United States* (1926) 2 RIAA 173; and *Island of Palmas Case* (1928) 2 RIAA 829. See generally Musgrave, *Self-determination and minorities*, p. 172; and W. Michael Reisman, 'Protecting indigenous rights in international adjudication' (1995) 89 *American Journal of International Law* 350, 351. In *Cherokee Nation* v. *Georgia* (1831), the US Supreme Court determined that the Cherokee Nation was a 'domestic dependent nation': *Cherokee Nation* v. *Georgia*, 30 US (5 Pet.) 1 (1831), at 17. See Charles Wilkinson and John Volkman, 'Judicial review of Indian treaty abrogation: "as long as water flows, or grass grow upon the earth" – how long a time is that?' (1975) 63 *California Law Review* 601, 613.

[306] Cf. Article 36 of the Draft Declaration on the Rights of Indigenous Peoples, UN Doc. E/CN.4/Sub.2/1994/2/Add.1 (1994). See also Article XXII of the Proposed American Declaration on the Rights of Indigenous Peoples, approved by the Inter-American Commission on Human Rights on 26 February 1997, at its 1333rd session, 95th Regular Session, OEA/Ser/L/V/II.95 Doc.6 (1997).

characteristics'.[307] In ILO Convention 169, the term 'tribal peoples' is applied to those groups 'whose social, cultural and economic conditions distinguish them from other sections of the national community, and whose status is regulated wholly or partially by their own customs or traditions or by special laws or regulations'.[308] Certain 'peoples' are 'regarded as indigenous' on account of their descent from the populations which inhabited the territory 'at the time of conquest or colonisation or the establishment of present state boundaries', and who retain some or all of their own social, economic, cultural and political institutions.[309] There is no distinction in the application of the Convention between tribal peoples and peoples regarded as indigenous. The Guide to ILO Convention No. 169 confirms that the designation of groups as 'tribal' rather than 'indigenous' resulted from political rather than legal considerations: 'the description of certain population groups as *tribal* is more easily accepted by some governments than a description of those peoples as *indigenous*.'[310]

ILO Convention 107 provides only limited protection for the distinctive cultures of indigenous and tribal populations.[311] The preamble refers to 'indigenous and other tribal and semi-tribal populations which are not *yet* integrated into the national community'.[312] The Convention obliges States parties to introduce policies for the protection of indigenous and tribal populations, 'and their progressive integration

---

[307] Manuela Tomei and Lee Swepston, 'Indigenous and tribal peoples: a guide to the ILO Convention No. 169' (Geneva: ILO, 1996). See, for example, Article 1(2) of ILO Convention 169. Cf. Article 1 of ILO Convention 107.

[308] Article 1(1)(a) of ILO Convention 169. Cf. Article 1(1)(a) of ILO Convention 107: 'members of tribal or semi-tribal populations in independent countries whose social and economic conditions are at a less advanced stage than the stage reached by the other sections of the national community, and whose status is regulated wholly or partially by their own customs or traditions or by special laws or regulations.'

[309] Article 1(1)(b) of ILO Convention 169. Cf. Article 1(1)(b) of ILO Convention 107: 'members of tribal or semi-tribal populations in independent countries which are regarded as indigenous on account of their descent from the populations which inhabited the country, or a geographical region to which the country belongs, at the time of conquest or colonisation and which, irrespective of their legal status, live more in conformity with the social, economic and cultural institutions of that time than with the institutions of the nation to which they belong.'

[310] Tomei and Swepston, 'A guide to the ILO Convention No. 169' (emphasis in original).

[311] See Articles 3 and 4 of ILO Convention 107.

[312] Preamble to ILO Convention 107. The Convention defines the term 'semi-tribal' to include groups and persons who, 'although they are in the process of losing their tribal characteristics, are not yet integrated into the national community': Article 1(2), *ibid.*

into the life of their respective countries'.[313] The underlying principles of the Convention are 'protection and integration':[314] 'indigenous societies are destined to disappear in the fullness of time'.[315] In contrast, ILO Convention 169 is 'replete with references which make sense only if [indigenous and tribal] peoples are assumed to have a continued and distinct existence'.[316] Article 2 refers to the need to promote the full realisation of the social, economic and cultural rights of indigenous and tribal peoples 'with respect for their social and cultural identity, their customs and traditions and their institutions'.[317] In applying the provisions of the Convention, 'the social, cultural, religious and spiritual values and practices of these peoples shall be recognised and protected', and 'the integrity of the values, practices and institutions of these peoples shall be respected'.[318] Additionally, ILO Convention 169 provides that indigenous and tribal peoples 'have the right to retain their own customs and institutions, where these are not incompatible with fundamental rights defined by the national legal system and with internationally recognised human rights'.[319]

ILO Convention 107 recognises the primary responsibility of governments for developing States parties' policies concerning indigenous and tribal populations.[320] By contrast, ILO Convention 169 provides that 'Governments shall have the responsibility for developing, *with the participation of the peoples concerned*, co-ordinated and systematic action to protect the rights of these peoples and to guarantee respect for their integrity'.[321] In applying the provisions of ILO Convention 169, States parties are obliged to 'consult the peoples concerned, through appropriate procedures and in particular through their representative institutions, whenever consideration is being given to legislative or administrative measures which may affect them directly'.[322] Consultations are to be undertaken in good faith, and in a form appropriate to the circumstances, 'with the objective of achieving agreement or consent to the proposed measures'.[323] Consensus is preferred, but it is not required, except in relation to the introduction of 'special

---

[313] Article 2(1) of ILO Convention 107. Cf. Article 2(2)(c) of ILO Convention 107, which prohibits 'artificial assimilation'.

[314] Thornberry, *Indigenous peoples and international law*, p. 329.   [315] *Ibid.*, p. 331.

[316] *Ibid.*, p. 345.   [317] Article 2(2)(b) of ILO Convention 169.   [318] Article 5, *ibid.*

[319] Article 8(2), *ibid.* See also Article 8(1), *ibid.*

[320] Article 2(1) of ILO Convention 107.

[321] Article 2(1) of ILO Convention 169 (emphasis added).   [322] Article 6(1)(a), *ibid.*

[323] Article 6(2), *ibid.*

measures' for safeguarding the persons, institutions, property, labour, cultures and environment of the peoples concerned.[324] In addition, States parties are required to ensure that indigenous and tribal peoples are able to participate in the formulation, implementation and evaluation of plans and programmes for national and regional development that may affect them directly.[325]

ILO Convention 169 recognises the right of indigenous and tribal peoples to their cultural security and the importance of political participation in relevant decision-making processes. A number of collective rights are recognised, which 'appear prominently in the section on land rights because that reflects the nature of the relationship of indigenous peoples to land and resources'.[326] The Convention does not recognise any right of territorial self-government for indigenous and tribal peoples. The use of the term 'peoples', the Convention provides, has no implications 'as regards the rights which may attach to the term under international law'.[327] The following section considers the extent to which indigenous peoples may rely on the right of all peoples to self-determination provided in the International Covenant on Civil and Political Rights.

Indigenous peoples and the International Covenant on Civil and Political Rights

The International Covenant on Civil and Political Rights recognises the collective right of peoples to self-determination,[328] and the rights of persons belonging to ethnic, religious or linguistic minorities to enjoy their own culture, to profess and practise their own religion and to use their own language.[329] The General Comment on Article 27 confirms that the personal scope of application of the provision includes

---

[324] Article 4(2), ibid.   [325] Article 7(1), ibid. See also Articles 16(2) and 17, ibid.

[326] Thornberry, Indigenous peoples and international law, p. 346. See, for example, Article 13(1) of ILO Convention 169: 'governments shall respect the special importance for the cultures and spiritual values of the peoples concerned of their relationship with the lands or territories, or both as applicable, which they occupy or otherwise use, and in particular the collective aspects of this relationship' (emphasis added).

[327] Article 1(3) of ILO Convention 169. The clause was included following the expression of concern by a number of governments that the use of the term peoples 'would mean that their right to secede from the countries in which they lived would be recognized in international law': Tomei and Swepston, 'A guide to the ILO Convention No. 169'. See also Thornberry, Indigenous peoples and international law, p. 344.

[328] Article 1 of the International Covenant on Civil and Political Rights.

[329] Article 27, ibid.

'members of indigenous communities constituting a minority'.[330] With regard to the exercise of cultural rights, the General Comment notes that 'culture manifests itself in many forms, including a particular way of life associated with the use of land resources, especially in the case of indigenous peoples'.[331] In its Concluding Observations on Viet Nam, the Human Rights Committee expressed its concern that information regarding the treatment of the Degar (Montagnard) indicated serious violations of Article 27 of the Covenant. The Committee noted the lack of specific information in the State party report 'concerning *indigenous peoples*, especially the Degar (Montagnard), and about measures taken to ensure that their rights under Article 27 to enjoy their cultural traditions, including their religion and language ... are respected'.[332]

In *R. L. et al.* v. *Canada*, the authors, members of the Whispering Pines Indian Band, belonging to the Shuswap Nation in south-central British Columbia, observed that they regarded themselves as 'an indigenous people rather than an "ethnic (or) linguistic minority", but that since the indigenous and minority categories overlap, indigenous peoples should also be entitled to exercise the rights of minorities'.[333] In *Chief Bernard Ominayak and the Lubicon Lake Band* v. *Canada*, the Band alleged a violation of its collective right to self-determination.[334] The Band considered that it was an 'indigenous people', having maintained its traditional economy and way of life and occupied its traditional territory since time immemorial.[335] The Committee concluded that the individual complaint mechanism was not available in respect of the collective right of peoples to self-determination,[336] but that, since the facts raised issues under Article 27, the complaints should be examined on their merits.[337] Persons belonging to indigenous peoples may not be denied the right (of persons belonging to 'minorities') to

---

[330] Human Rights Committee, General Comment No. 23, 'Rights of minorities (Article 27)', para. 3.2.

[331] *Ibid.*, para. 7.

[332] Human Rights Committee, Concluding Observations on Viet Nam, UN Doc. CCPR/CO/ 75/VNM, 26 July 2002, para. 19 (emphasis added). See also Human Rights Committee, Concluding Observations on Argentina, UN Doc. CCPR/CO/70/ARG, 3 November 2000, para. 7; and Human Rights Committee, Concluding Observations on Venezuela, UN Doc. CCPR/CO/71/VEN, 26 April 2001, para. 28.

[333] *R. L. et al.* v. *Canada*, Communication No. 358/1989, UN Doc. CCPR/C/40/D/358/1989, 28 November 1990, para. 3.7.

[334] *Chief Bernard Ominayak and the Lubicon Lake Band* v. *Canada*, Communication No. 167/ 1984, UN Doc. CCPR/C/38/D/167/1984, 10 May 1990, para. 2.1.

[335] *Ibid.*, para. 7.   [336] *Ibid.*, para. 13.3.   [337] *Ibid.*, para. 13.4.

enjoy their own culture, to profess and practise their own religion, or to use their own language.

The contemporary position of the right of peoples to self-determination, 'beyond colonialism', is expressed in Article 1, common to the International Covenants.[338] No definition of the term 'peoples' is provided, although it is clear that the term 'peoples' may be applied to the populations of sovereign and independent States, and the populations of trust and non-self-governing territories (i.e. 'colonised' peoples).[339] According to S. James Anaya: 'In its plain meaning, the term *peoples* undoubtedly embraces the multitude of indigenous groups like the Maori[,] who comprise distinct communities, each with its own social, cultural, and political attributes richly rooted in history.'[340] The following section considers whether the scope of application of the right of 'all peoples' to self-determination includes indigenous peoples.

The Committee on Economic, Social and Cultural Rights has referred to the existence of 'minorities and indigenous peoples' in States parties.[311] In relation to Article 1(2), which provides that a people may not 'be deprived of its means of subsistence', the Committee has concluded that 'States parties should ensure that there is adequate access to water for subsistence farming and for securing the livelihoods of indigenous peoples'.[342] In its Concluding Observations, the Committee has referred to the 'indigenous peoples' of States parties in Central and South America,[343] the indigenous peoples of

---

[338] Article 1, common to the International Covenant on Economic, Social and Cultural Rights and the International Covenant on Civil and Political Rights.

[339] Indigenous peoples are not 'colonised' peoples in the sense of GA Res. 1514 (XV). The 'salt-water' definition of colonialism, and application of the principle of *uti possidetis*, excluded the majority of indigenous communities within metropolitan and non-self-governing territories from the scope of application of the external aspect of the right of peoples to self-determination. The exceptions included certain of the islands of the South Pacific.

[340] S. James Anaya, *Indigenous peoples in international law* (Oxford: Oxford University Press, 1996), p. 77 (emphasis in original).

[341] Committee on Economic, Social and Cultural Rights, General Comment No. 13, 'The right to education (art. 13)', reprinted in 'Compilation of General Comments and General Recommendations', p. 71, para. 50. See also General Comment No. 15, 'The right to water (arts. 11 and 12 of the Covenant)', reprinted in 'Compilation of General Comments and General Recommendations', p. 106, para. 16.

[342] General Comment No. 15, 'The right to water', para. 7.

[343] See Committee on Economic, Social and Cultural Rights, Concluding Observations on Colombia, UN Doc. E/C.12/1/Add.74, 30 November 2001, para. 12; Guatemala, UN Doc. E/C.12/1/Add.93, 12 December 2003, para. 10; Honduras, UN Doc. E/C.12/1/Add.57,

Australia,[344] and the indigenous peoples of the Russian Federation, where the Committee noted its concern 'about the precarious situation of indigenous communities in the State party, affecting their right to self-determination under Article 1 of the Covenant'.[345] The Committee on Economic, Social and Cultural Rights recalled 'the right to self-determination enshrined in Article 1 of the Covenant, [and urged] the State party to intensify its efforts to improve the situation of the indigenous peoples and to ensure that they are not deprived of their means of subsistence'.[346]

A number of States reports to the Human Rights Committee refer to the position of 'indigenous peoples' in the section concerning the right of peoples to self-determination.[347] In its third periodic report, the Government of Australia observed that it 'has been following closely the international debates concerning self-determination in its application to indigenous peoples'.[348] The subsequent paragraph refers to the position of the Torres Strait Islanders relating to self-management and autonomy.[349] Information on indigenous persons in Australia is provided in the section of the report relating to Article 27 (rights of minorities). In its Concluding Observations, the Human Rights Committee noted the comments of the State party and the explanation given by the Australian delegation to the Committee that 'rather than the term "self-determination", the Government of Australia prefers terms such as "self-management" and "self-empowerment" to express domestically the principle of indigenous

21 May 2001, para. 29; Panama, UN Doc. E/C.12/1/Add.64, 24 September 2001, para. 12; Paraguay, UN Doc. E/C.12/1/Add.1, 28 May 1996, para. 21; Peru, UN Doc. E/C.12/1/Add.14, 16 May 1997, para. 12(f); and Venezuela, UN Doc. E/C.12/1/Add.56, 21 May 2001, para. 10.

[344] Committee on Economic, Social and Cultural Rights, Concluding Observations on Australia, UN Doc. E/C.12/1/Add.50, 1 September 2000, para. 10.

[345] Committee on Economic, Social and Cultural Rights, Concluding Observations on the Russian Federation, UN Doc. E/C.12/1/Add.94, 12 December 2003, para. 11.

[346] Ibid., para. 39.

[347] See, for example, Fifth Periodic Report (Russian Federation), UN Doc. CCPR/C/RUS/2002/5, 9 December 2002, para. 8; and Initial Report (United States of America), UN Doc. CCPR/C/81/Add.4, 24 August 1994, paras. 26 ff. The indigenous peoples of Brazil are considered under Article 27 of the International Covenant on Civil and Political Rights: Initial Report (Brazil), UN Doc. CCPR/C/81/Add.6, 2 March 1995, paras. 327 ff. Argentina deals with the position of its 'indigenous peoples' under Article 27 of the International Covenant on Civil and Political Rights: Third Periodic Report (Argentina), UN Doc. CCPR/C/ARG/98/3, 7 May 1999, paras. 277 ff.

[348] Third Periodic Report (Australia), UN Doc. CCPR/C/AUS/98/3, 22 July 1999, para. 30.

[349] Ibid., para. 31. See also Fourth Periodic Report (Australia), UN Doc. CCPR/C/AUS/98/4, 4 August 1999, paras. 133 ff.

peoples' exercising meaningful control over their own affairs'. The Committee expressed its concern that 'sufficient action has not been taken in that regard',[350] and further called on Australia to take the 'necessary steps in order to secure for the indigenous inhabitants a stronger role in decision-making over their traditional lands and natural resources (art. 1, para. 2)'.[351]

The fourth periodic report submitted by Canada deals with the issue of 'Aboriginal peoples' in the section relating to Article 27.[352] Information is provided on the implementation of the 'inherent right of Aboriginal peoples of Canada to self-government'.[353] In its Concluding Observations, the Human Rights Committee regretted that the 'concept of self-determination as applied by Canada to the aboriginal peoples' was not fully explained, and urged the State party to 'report adequately on implementation of Article 1 of the Covenant in its next periodic report'.[354] The Concluding Observations emphasised 'that the right to self-determination requires, *inter alia*, that all peoples must be able to freely dispose of their natural wealth and resources and that they may not be deprived of their own means of subsistence (art. 1, para. 2)'.[355] The Committee recommended that the practice of extinguishing inherent aboriginal rights be abandoned as 'incompatible with Article 1 of the Covenant'.[356]

Notwithstanding the position of the Governments of Australia and Canada, the Human Rights Committee has regarded the indigenous peoples of these States parties as falling within the scope of application of Article 1 of the International Covenant. In its Concluding Observations on the report by Norway, the Committee noted the positive developments in the protection of the human rights of members of the Sami indigenous people, and welcomed 'developments to ensure full consultation with the Sami in matters affecting their traditional

---

[350] Human Rights Committee, Concluding Observations on Australia, UN Doc. A/55/40, 24 July 2000, para. 506.

[351] *Ibid.*, para. 507. Article 1(2) provided that: 'All peoples may, for their own ends, freely dispose of their natural wealth and resources.'

[352] Fourth Periodic Report (Canada), UN Doc. CCPR/C/103/Add.5, 15 October 1997, paras. 286 ff.

[353] *Ibid.*, para. 299. The subsequent paragraph notes the establishment of the autonomous territory of Nunavut: *ibid.*, para. 300.

[354] Human Rights Committee, Concluding Observations on Canada, UN Doc. CCPR/C/79/Add.105, 7 April 1999, para. 7.

[355] *Ibid.*, para. 8.   [356] *Ibid.*

means of livelihood (Art. 1 and 27)'.[357] The Human Rights Committee concluded that 'As the Government and Parliament of Norway have addressed the situation of the Sami in the framework of the right to self-determination, the Committee expects Norway to report on the Sami people's right to self-determination under Article 1 of the Covenant, including paragraph 2 of that Article'.[358]

A right of self-determination is recognised for indigenous *peoples*. In the absence of agreement on the definition of the term 'indigenous peoples', the decision to recognise a community of persons as an indigenous people is essentially one for the State concerned. The Opinions of the Human Rights Committee and its Concluding Observations do not make a clear connection between the recognition of a right of self-determination for indigenous peoples and the introduction of territorial self-government, or autonomy. The right of peoples to self-determination requires both that a people may freely dispose of its natural wealth and resources, and in no case be deprived of its own means of subsistence,[359] and that they 'freely determine their political status and freely pursue their economic, social and cultural development'.[360] The final section of this chapter considers the UN Draft Declaration on the Rights of Indigenous Peoples, which recognises that 'Indigenous peoples have the right of self-determination'.[361] As a specific form of exercising this right, indigenous peoples 'have the right to autonomy or self-government'.[362]

---

[357] Human Rights Committee, Concluding Observations on Norway, UN Doc. CCPR/C/79/ Add.112, 1 November 1999, para. 10.

[358] *Ibid.*, para. 17. Finland considers the position of the Sami, an indigenous people, under the section concerning Article 27 of the International Covenant on Civil and Political Rights: see, Fifth Periodic Report (Finland), UN Doc. CCPR/C/FIN/2003/5, 24 July 2003, para. 93.

[359] Article 1(2), common to the International Covenant on Economic, Social and Cultural Rights and the International Covenant on Civil and Political Rights.

[360] Article 1(1), *ibid.*

[361] Article 3 of the Draft Declaration on the Rights of Indigenous Peoples. The right of self-determination was included following the participation of indigenous peoples in its drafting of the Declaration, because they insisted on its inclusion: Caroline Foster, 'Articulating self-determination in the Draft Declaration on the Rights of Indigenous Peoples' (2001) 12 *European Journal of International Law* 141, 142–3. The Proposed American Declaration does not use the term 'self-determination', although it recognises that indigenous peoples have the right to 'freely determine their political status and freely pursue their economic, social, spiritual and cultural development, and accordingly, they have the right to [territorial] autonomy or self-government': Article XV(1) of the Proposed American Declaration on the Rights of Indigenous Peoples.

[362] Article 31 of the Draft Declaration on the Rights of Indigenous Peoples.

The Draft Declaration on the Rights of Indigenous Peoples

The UN Working Group on Indigenous Populations adopted the Draft United Nations Declaration on the Rights of Indigenous Peoples in 1994. The draft represents, according to Patrick Thornberry, an 'emblematic synthesis of indigenous claims of right, cultural statements, and world views'.[363] The term 'tribal' is absent from the Draft Declaration, which refers throughout to 'indigenous peoples'. No definition of the term is provided,[364] although the proposed scope of application of the Draft Declaration would not appear to be limited to the descendants of populations who inhabited a territory prior to ('Western') colonisation.[365]

The preamble to the Draft Declaration refers to the need to protect the inherent rights and 'characteristics' of indigenous peoples, 'especially their rights to their lands, territories and resources, which derive from their political, economic and social structures and from their cultures, spiritual traditions, histories and philosophies'.[366] Indigenous peoples have the right not to be subjected to cultural genocide, defined to include any action which has the aim or effect of 'depriving them of their integrity as distinct peoples, or of their cultural values or ethnic identities', and 'dispossessing them of their lands, territories or resources'.[367] Indigenous peoples have the right to maintain and develop their distinct identities and characteristics,[368] to practise and revitalise their cultural traditions and customs,[369] to

---

[363] Thornberry, *Indigenous peoples and international law*, p. 26.

[364] The scope of application of the Proposed American Declaration on the Rights of Indigenous Peoples concerns 'peoples whose social, cultural and economic conditions distinguish them from other sections of the national community, and whose status is regulated wholly or partially by their own customs or traditions or by special laws or regulations': Article I(1) of the Proposed American Declaration on the Rights of Indigenous Peoples.

[365] Draft Declaration on the Rights of Indigenous Peoples, preamble: 'indigenous peoples have been deprived of their human rights and fundamental freedoms, resulting, *inter alia*, in their colonization.'

[366] *Ibid.*

[367] Article 7, *ibid*. See Article 25: 'Indigenous peoples have the right to maintain and strengthen their distinctive spiritual and material relationship with the lands … which they have traditionally owned or otherwise occupied or used.'

[368] Article 8, *ibid*.

[369] This includes the right to maintain, protect and develop the past, present and future manifestations of their cultures, such as archaeological and historical sites, artifacts, designs, ceremonies, technologies and visual and performing arts and literature, as well as the right to the restitution of cultural, intellectual, religious and spiritual property taken without their free and informed consent or in violation of their laws, traditions and customs: Article 12, *ibid*.

manifest, practise, develop and teach their spiritual and religious traditions, customs and ceremonies,[370] and to transmit to future generations
their histories, languages, oral traditions, philosophies, writing
systems and literatures.[371]

The Draft Declaration recognises the right of indigenous peoples, 'to
participate fully, if they so choose, at all levels of decision-making in
matters which may affect their rights, lives and destinies through
representatives chosen by themselves in accordance with their own
procedures, as well as to maintain and develop their own indigenous
decision-making institutions'.[372] States are required to obtain the free
and informed consent of the peoples concerned before adopting and
implementing measures that may affect them.[373] In contrast to international instruments concerning minorities, which emphasise the
importance of political participation, these rights are 'given a secondary
significance [in the Draft Declaration] and expressed as an optional
right'.[374] The emphasis is on self-government, not shared government.[375]
Indigenous peoples have the right to own, control and use the lands and
territories which they have traditionally owned or otherwise occupied
or used,[376] and to determine and develop priorities and strategies for
the development or use of their lands, territories and other resources,
'including the right to require that States obtain their free and informed
consent prior to the approval of any project affecting their lands,
territories and other resources'.[377]

The scope of application of the Draft Declaration on the Rights of
Indigenous Peoples concerns both persons belonging to indigenous
peoples and the communities themselves: indigenous peoples 'have
the collective and individual right to maintain and develop their
distinct identities and characteristics'.[378] The Draft Declaration is

---

[370] Article 13, *ibid.*   [371] Article 14, *ibid.*   [372] Article 19, *ibid.*   [373] Article 20. *ibid.*

[374] Asbjørn Eide, 'Good governance, human rights and the rights of minorities and
indigenous peoples', in Hans-Otto Sano and Gudmundur Alfredsson (eds.), *Human rights
and good governance: building bridges* (The Hague: Martinus Nijhoff, 2002), p. 47, at p. 61.

[375] The Proposed American Declaration recognises that indigenous peoples have the right
to participate 'if they so decide, in all decision-making, at all levels, with regard to
matters that might affect their rights, lives and destiny'. Additionally, indigenous
peoples have the right to maintain and develop their own indigenous decision-making
institutions: Article XV(2) of the Proposed American Declaration on the Rights of
Indigenous Peoples.

[376] Article 26 of the Draft Declaration on the Rights of Indigenous Peoples.

[377] Article 30, *ibid.* See also Article 23: 'Indigenous peoples have the right to determine and
develop all health, housing and other economic and social programmes affecting them.'

[378] Article 8, *ibid.*

concerned with communities that have the potential for self-government, in accordance with their own laws, and under their own institutions.[379] It refers to the rights of indigenous peoples to 'maintain and strengthen their distinct political, economic, social and cultural characteristics, as well as their legal systems';[380] to 'maintain and develop their own indigenous decision-making institutions';[381] and to the full recognition of their laws, traditions and customs for the development and management of resources on their land.[382] Article 3 provides that 'Indigenous peoples have the right of self-determination. By virtue of that right they freely determine their political status and freely pursue their economic, social and cultural development.'[383] As a specific form of exercising their right to self-determination, indigenous peoples 'have the right to autonomy or self-government in matters relating to their internal and local affairs, including culture, religion, education, information, media, health, housing, employment, social welfare, economic activities, land and resources management, environment and entry by non-members, as well as ways and means for financing these autonomous functions'.[384] The Draft Declaration envisages an extensive form of territorial self-government. Indigenous peoples have the collective right to determine their own citizenship in accordance with their customs and traditions,[385] to determine the structures and to select the membership of their institutions in accordance with their own procedures,[386] and to promote, develop and maintain their institutional structures and their distinctive juridical customs, traditions, procedures and practices, in accordance with internationally recognised human rights standards.[387]

---

[379] Article 9, *ibid*., recognises that particular indigenous peoples may consider themselves to be a part of a wider imagined community: 'Indigenous peoples and individuals have the right to belong to an indigenous community or nation.'

[380] Article 4, *ibid*.   [381] Article 19, *ibid*. See also Article 23.   [382] Article 26, *ibid*.

[383] Article 3, *ibid*. The right of self-determination is, according to indigenous peoples, to be understood in both its external and internal senses: Maivân Lâm, *At the edge of the state: indigenous peoples and self-determination* (Ardsley, NY: Transnational Publishers, 2000), pp. 57–60. According to Erica-Irene Daes, (then) Chairman of the UN Working Group on Indigenous Peoples, most indigenous peoples acknowledge that secession is an unrealistic goal, but see the right of secession as an important 'legal, peaceful weapon to press for genuine democracy in the States in which they live': Erica-Irene Daes, 'Discrimination against indigenous peoples: explanatory note concerning the draft declaration on the rights of indigenous peoples', UN Doc. E/CN.4/Sub.2/1993/26/Add.1, 19 July 1993, para. 28.

[384] Article 31, *ibid*.   [385] Article 32, *ibid*.

[386] *Ibid*. See also Article 43: 'All the rights and freedoms recognized herein are equally guaranteed to male and female indigenous individuals.'

[387] Article 33, *ibid*.

Conclusion

There is no objective distinction that can be made between groups recognised as minorities, national minorities, indigenous peoples and peoples. What distinguishes these groups is the nature of their political demands: simply put, minorities and national minorities demand cultural security; peoples demand recognition of their right to self-determination, or self-government.[388] In the era of the United Nations, in contrast with the earlier inter-war period, the application of the principle of self-determination of peoples recognises the right of the majority of the territory to confirm or deny the legitimacy of the authority of the governing power. The right of peoples to self-determination has been recognised for the peoples of trust and non-self-governing territories, the peoples of sovereign and independent States, peoples excluded from public life, and the peoples of the units of a federal State in the process of dissolution. Increasingly, it is recognised that the term 'peoples' may be applied to ethno-cultural groups within the State.[389]

The right of self-determination has both an external and an internal aspect. The external aspect concerns the right of the people to determine the international status of the territory. This aspect is enjoyed by the populations of trust and non-self-governing territories, the populations of sovereign and independent States, territorially concentrated populations excluded from public/political life,[390] and the populations of the constituent units of an ethnic federation in the process of dissolution. In all other cases, the recognition of the right of peoples to self-determination has no impact on the territorial integrity of sovereign and independent States. The internal aspect of the right of self-determination

---

[388] There is no correlation between the extent of putative ethnic differences and the likelihood of a particular ethnic group making secessionist or separatist claims: Nancy Bermeo, 'The import of institutions' (2002) 13 *Journal of Democracy* 96, 103. The international instruments concerning indigenous peoples recognise the right to cultural security, and provide more detail on the requirements to implement the norm, but it is the demand for self-government which differentiates the demands of (certain) indigenous peoples from those of minorities (see, Draft Declaration on the Rights of Indigenous Peoples). It therefore becomes important to distinguish the rhetorical arguments of dispossessed indigenous communities, and the particular demands of particular indigenous peoples for territorial self-government.

[389] Additional to the recognition of peoples excluded from public life, and the peoples of the units of a federal State in the process of dissolution.

[390] See the discussion above of the 'saving clause'.

recognises the right of *all* peoples to 'freely determine their political status and freely pursue their economic, social and cultural development'.[391] The internal aspect is enjoyed by the populations of sovereign and independent States, and by indigenous peoples and peoples recognised as such by the State. The internal aspect of the right of peoples to self-determination is concerned with territorial self-government. As Judge Rosalyn Higgins notes, in her Separate Opinion in *Legal Consequences of the Construction of a Wall in the Occupied Palestinian Territory*, ' "Peoples" necessarily exercise their right to self-determination within their own territory'.[392] The definition of the term 'people' in international law must include the requirement that the group demands political self-government in respect of a particular territory. Citizens who belong to groups recognised as indigenous peoples or peoples enjoy the rights of political participation both as citizens of the State and as members of their respective groups (indigenous peoples or peoples – and potentially both). The State must ensure the effective participation of all citizens in nationwide (and as appropriate regional and local) decision-making processes, and introduce (or maintain) territorial self-government for groups recognised as peoples.

A desire for self-government is not a sufficient criterion for recognising a group as a 'people'. Modern justifications for territorial self-government, that is, autonomy, concern the idea of cultural identity and integrity.[393] Territorial self-government allows a national, ethnic, cultural, religious or linguistic group to 'engage in their own competing nation-building, so as to protect and diffuse their societal culture through their traditional territory'.[394] The Bougainville Peace

---

[391] Article 1(1), common to the International Covenant on Economic, Social and Cultural Rights and the International Covenant on Civil and Political Rights.

[392] Separate Opinion of Judge Higgins, *Legal Consequences of the Construction of a Wall in the Occupied Palestinian Territory*, International Court of Justice, Advisory Opinion, 9 July 2004, 43 ILM (2004) 1009, para. 31. See also Lea Brilmayer, 'Secession and self-determination: a territorial interpretation' (1991) 16 *Yale Journal of International Law* 177, 192–3.

[393] Yash Ghai, 'Ethnicity and autonomy: a framework for analysis', in Yash Ghai (ed.), *Autonomy and ethnicity: negotiating competing claims in multi-ethnic states* (Cambridge: Cambridge University Press, 2000), p. 1, at p. 4. See also S. James Anaya, 'The capacity of international law to advance ethnic or nationality rights claims' (1990) 75 *Iowa Law Review* 837, 841; and Avishai Margalit and Joseph Raz, 'National self-determination' in Will Kymlicka (ed.), *The rights of minority cultures* (Oxford: Oxford University Press, 1995), p. 79, at pp. 89–91.

[394] Will Kymlicka, 'Western political theory and ethnic relations in Eastern Europe', in Will Kymlicka and Magda Opalski (eds.), *Can liberal pluralism be exported? Western political theory and ethnic relations in Eastern Europe* (Oxford: Oxford University Press, 2001), p. 13,

Agreement (2001), for example, establishes a self-government regime for Bougainville, in order to 'facilitate the expression and development of Bougainville identity ... [and] empower Bougainvilleans to solve their own problems, manage their own affairs and work to realize their aspirations within the framework of the Papua New Guinea Constitution'.[395] The definition of the term 'people' must include both a collective expression of a desire to be self-governing, and a distinctive ethno-cultural identity.[396] Beyond this, no criteria for defining the term 'people' can be discerned: peoples have the right to self-determination, and those ethno-cultural groups having the right to territorial self-government are to be recognised as peoples. The important fact is to recognise the value and role of territorial self-government (for 'peoples') as a tool for resolving cultural conflict.

at p. 25. See also Robert Howse and Karen Knop, 'Federalism, secession, and the limits of ethnic accommodation: a Canadian perspective' (1993) 1 *New Europe Law Review* 269, 271.

[395] Bougainville Peace Agreement, adopted 30 August 2001, para. 4, available at www.usip.org/library/pa/bougainville/pa_bougainville.html (last visited 10 January 2005). See generally Yash Ghai and Anthony Regan, 'Bougainville and the dialectics of ethnicity, autonomy and separation', in Yash Ghai (ed.), *Autonomy and ethnicity: negotiating competing claims in multi-ethnic states* (Cambridge: Cambridge University Press, 2000), p. 242; also Anthony Matthew, 'Bougainville and Papua New Guinea: complexities of secession in a multi-ethnic developing state' (2000) 48 *Political Studies* 724.

[396] On the fact that peoples are defined (in part) by their cultural identity, see UN Commission on Human Rights Res. 2003/26, adopted 22 April 2003, 'Promotion of the enjoyment of the cultural rights of everyone and respect for different cultural identities', UN Doc. E/CN.4/RES/2003/26, para. 4: 'each culture has a dignity and value which must be respected and preserved and that every people has the right and the duty to develop its culture.'

3   Democracy

The international community has recognised the rights of persons belonging to minorities to cultural security and the collective right of peoples to self-determination. It has failed to define the relevant beneficiaries of the rights, or to detail the circumstances in which measures to protect and promote cultural security should be introduced, or territorial self-government regimes established. There exists a regime of indeterminacy in relation to the position of ethno-cultural groups in international law: principles are recognised, but without detailed rules being elaborated as to how those principles are to be put into effect. States' policies concerning ethno-cultural groups – minorities, national minorities, indigenous peoples and peoples – will be decided within domestic institutions.

The traditional position of international law has been to regard the systems of government and the process of decision-making within sovereign and independent States as falling outside of the legitimate concern of the international community. The recognition of democracy as an obligation in international law changes this – for democratic States. This chapter examines the recognition of a right to democracy in the International Covenant on Civil and Political Rights. It considers the rights of political participation available to all citizens, and the particular rights of minorities to effective participation in decisions which affect them. The work recognises the limits of procedural inclusion in protecting the interests of persons belonging to national or ethnic, religious and linguistic minorities in democratic States, and considers two institutional responses proposed by writers in political science: consociational and integrative models of democracy. The extent to which these models are compatible with the principles and norms of democracy recognised in international law are examined. Finally, the chapter considers the importance of reasons and reasoned argument in democratic debate, and the emergence of the deliberative model of democracy.

Democracy in international law

Democracy is a form of government in which political power is based on the will of the people, and all citizens have the opportunity to participate equally in the political life of their societies.[1] According to the UN Vienna Declaration and Programme of Action, 'Democracy is based on the freely expressed will of the people to determine their own political, economic, social and cultural systems and their full participation in all aspects of their lives'.[2] There is no paradigmatic model of democracy to be applied in all places, at all points in time.[3] Democratic governments may take many forms, and evolve through many phases, depending on the particular characteristics and circumstances of a particular community.[4] The UN Commission on Human Rights has recognised the 'rich and diverse nature of the community of the world's democracies'.[5] A regime may be termed 'democratic' if it embodies, within its institutions and mechanisms, including its electoral system, the twin principles of political equality and popular sovereignty. Political equality requires that the votes and preferences of one citizen be accorded the same respect as those of all others. Popular sovereignty 'is the view that individual citizens bestow legitimacy upon a government through their implied or actual consent to its rule'.[6] The will of the people is the basis of legitimate government authority in a democratic State.[7]

---

[1] James Crawford, *Democracy in international law* (Cambridge: Cambridge University Press, 1994), p. 4.

[2] Vienna Declaration and Programme of Action (1993), 32 ILM (1993) 1661, para. I(8).

[3] There are a number of models of democracy in political science: see generally David Held, *Models of democracy* (2nd edn, Cambridge: Polity Press, 1996). 'Scholars have been unable to agree on the most suitable set of institutional arrangements for difficult democracies – or for democracies in general': Samuel Barnes, 'The contribution of democracy to rebuilding postconflict societies' (2001) 95 *American Journal of International Law* 86, 93.

[4] UN Secretary-General, 'Supplement to reports on democratization: agenda for democratization' (1996), UN Doc. A/51/761, 20 December 1996, para. 4.

[5] UN Commission on Human Rights Res. 57/1999, 'Promotion of the right to democracy', UN Doc. E/CN.4/RES/1999/57, adopted 28 April 1999.

[6] Gregory Fox, 'The right to political participation in international law' (1992) 17 *Yale Journal of International Law* 539, 550.

[7] See Article 21(3) of GA Res. 217 (III) A, adopted 10 December 1948, 'Universal Declaration of Human Rights'.

Following the collapse of the Soviet Empire, the introduction and maintenance of democracy became the key test of legitimacy for governments. Initially, the international community focused on institutional arrangements: the holding of periodic, multi-party elections was the defining feature of democratic government.[8] In 1990, the participating States of the Organization for Security and Co-operation in Europe adopted the Document of the Copenhagen Meeting of the Conference on the Human Dimension,[9] in part to provide a common understanding of the requirements of democratic government.[10] According to the Copenhagen Document, 'the will of the people, freely and fairly expressed through periodic and genuine elections, is the basis of the authority and legitimacy of all government'.[11] To ensure that the will of the people serves as the basis of government authority, OSCE participating States are required to hold free elections at reasonable intervals,[12] by secret ballot,[13] and by universal and equal suffrage to adult citizens.[14] Candidates who obtain the necessary number of votes are to be duly installed in office, and permitted to remain in office until their term expires, or is otherwise brought to an end in a manner that is regulated by law in conformity with democratic, parliamentary and constitutional procedures.[15] All seats in at least one chamber of the national legislature are to be freely contested in a popular vote.[16] Democratic government is representative in character, with the executive accountable to the elected legislature or the electorate.[17]

Free and fair elections are an essential element of democracy, but they are not the sole element. A focus on competitive elections, David Beetham explains, serves only to 'elevate a means into an end, [and] to

---

[8] See Susan Marks, *The riddle of all constitutions* (Oxford: Oxford University Press, 2000), p. 53.

[9] OSCE Document of the Copenhagen Meeting of the Conference on the Human Dimension ('Copenhagen Document'), 29 ILM (1990) 1318, paras. 6–8. See also OSCE/ODIHR, 'Existing Commitments for Democratic Elections in OSCE Participating States: A Progress Report', OSCE Doc. ODIHR.GAL/39/03, 30 June 2003.

[10] Henry Steiner observes that the term 'democracy' lost any descriptive power during the Cold War, when the liberal democracies of the West competed with the Socialist and People's democracies of the Soviet Union and its allies: Henry Steiner, 'Political participation as a human right' (1988) 1 *Harvard Human Rights Yearbook* 77, 89. Cf. Christian Tomuschat, 'Democratic pluralism: the right to political opposition', in Alan Rosas and Jan Helgesen (eds.), *The strength of diversity: human rights and pluralist democracy* (Dordrecht: Martinus Nijhoff, 1992), p. 27, at p. 28.

[11] Para. 6 of the OSCE Copenhagen Document. [12] Para. 7(1), *ibid*.

[13] Paras. 5(1) and 7(4), *ibid*. [14] Para. 7(3), *ibid*. [15] Para. 7(9), *ibid*. [16] Para. 7(2), *ibid*.

[17] Para. 5(2), *ibid*.

confuse an instrument with its purpose'.[18] The will of the people is
the basis of legitimate government authority in a democratic State.[19]
The UN Secretary-General has argued that there must be a 'culture of
democracy': a political culture which is fundamentally non-violent,
and in which no one party or group expects to win or lose all the time,
in which 'political opponents and minorities have a right to express
their views; and that there can be loyal and legal opposition to
the Government in power'.[20] According to the Inter-Parliamentary
Union's Universal Declaration on Democracy, adopted in 1997:
'Democracy is founded on the right of everyone to take part in the
management of public affairs; it therefore requires the existence of
representative institutions at all levels and, in particular, a Parliament
in which all components of society are represented and which has the
requisite powers and means to express the will of the people by legislating and overseeing government action.'[21] Elections must be held on the
basis of universal, equal and secret suffrage so that all voters can choose
their representatives in conditions of equality, openness and transpar-
ency that stimulate political competition. To that end, civil and political
rights are essential, including the rights to vote and to be elected, the
rights to freedom of expression and assembly, access to information
and the right to organise political parties and carry out political
activities.[22]

---

[18] David Beetham, *Democracy and human rights* (Cambridge: Polity Press, 1999), p. 3.
[19] Article 21(3) of the Universal Declaration of Human Rights.
[20] UN Secretary-General, 'Supplement to reports on democratization: agenda for
democratization' (1996), UN Doc. A/51/761, 20 December 1996, para. 21; see also UN
Secretary-General, 'Support by the United Nations system of the efforts of governments
to promote and consolidate new or restored democracies', UN Doc. A/51/512, 18
October 1996. According to Samuel Huntington, democracy is established, or
consolidated, where a political party takes power, loses a subsequent election and turns
over power to the election winners, and those election winners then peacefully turn
over power to the winners of a later election: Samuel Huntington, *The third wave:
democratization in the late twentieth century* (Norman, OK: University of Oklahoma Press,
1991), pp. 266–7. See also Report of the Secretary-General, 'The causes of conflict and
the promotion of durable peace and sustainable development in Africa', UN Doc. A/52/
871 – S/1998/318, 13 April 1998, para. 78.
[21] Inter-Parliamentary Union's Universal Declaration on Democracy, para. 11. The
Universal Declaration on Democracy was adopted without a vote by the
Inter-Parliamentary Council at its 161st session (Cairo, 16 September 1997), reprinted
(2000) 1 *Netherlands Quarterly of Human Rights* 127. The IPU, established in 1889, is the
world organisation of parliaments of sovereign States. Over a hundred national
parliaments are currently members.
[22] Universal Declaration on Democracy, para. 12.

The Warsaw Declaration, 'Towards a Community of Democracies', adopted in 2000 by the representatives of more than 100 governments, confirmed that the 'will of the people shall be the basis of the authority of government, as expressed by exercise of the right and civic duties of citizens to choose their representatives through regular, free and fair elections with universal and equal suffrage, open to multiple parties, conducted by secret ballot, monitored by independent electoral authorities, and free of fraud and intimidation'.[23] The Declaration concluded that informed participation 'by all elements of society, men and women, in a country's ... political life, including by persons belonging to minority groups, is fundamental to a vibrant and durable democracy'.[24] The Declaration reflects a shift in thinking on democracy which has taken place in recent years from a 'vote-centric' to a 'talk-centric' understanding of democracy (see below).[25]

The international community has recognised that democracy is a 'good': the UN Secretary-General has argued that the Charter of the United Nations offers a 'vision of democratic states and democracy among them',[26] whilst the General Assembly has repeatedly affirmed democracy as one of the principles enshrined in the Charter.[27] The General Assembly declared in its 'Millennium Declaration' that 'We will spare no effort to promote democracy'.[28] There is, however, no reference to democracy in the Charter, and democratic government is not a condition of membership of the organisation.[29] There is no breach of the obligations of membership by those States that are

---

[23] Warsaw Declaration: Towards a Community of Democracies, adopted 27 June 2000, 39 ILM (2000) 1306. See also 'Progress Review and Recommendations', adopted at Bucharest by the Third International Conference of the New or Restored Democracies on Democracy and Development, in which eighty states participated, UN Doc. A/52/334, 11 September 1997.

[24] Warsaw Declaration, *ibid.*

[25] Allan Patten and Will Kymlicka, 'Introduction: language rights and political theory', in Will Kymlicka and Alan Patten (eds.), *Language rights and political theory* (Oxford: Oxford University Press, 2003), p. 1, at p. 13.

[26] UN Secretary-General, 'Supplement to reports on democratization' (1996), UN Doc. A/51/761, 20 December 1996, para. 28.

[27] See, for example, GA Res. 50/133, adopted 16 February 1996, 'Support by the United Nations system of the efforts of governments to promote and consolidate new or restored democracies', preamble.

[28] General Assembly resolution 55/2, adopted 8 September 2000, 'Millennium Declaration', para. 24.

[29] 'Membership in the United Nations is open to all other peace-loving states which accept the obligations contained in the present Charter': Article 4(1) of the Charter of the United Nations, adopted 26 June 1945, in force 24 October 1945.

not democratic. No obligation to introduce democratic forms of government exists in international law for the member States of the United Nations. According to the UN Secretary-General, it is for individual societies to decide '*if* and when' to begin democratisation.[30] One in every three States is not democratic.[31] Democratic credentials are not relevant in the recognition of States,[32] or in dealings with governments.

A number of international organisations commit their member States to both introduce and maintain democratic forms of government: inter alia, the African Union,[33] the Commonwealth,[34] the European Union,[35] the Organization of American States,[36] and the participating States of the Organization for Security and Co-operation in Europe.[37] Democratic government is a condition of membership, and relevant in determining the rights of member States. In 1992, Thomas Franck

---

[30] UN Secretary-General, 'Supplement to Reports on Democratization' (1996), para. 4 (emphasis added). See *Case Concerning Military and Paramilitary Activities in and against Nicaragua (Nicaragua v. United States)*, Merits, ICJ Reports (1986), p. 14, para. 259.

[31] The US State Department considers 117 States to be democratic: see www.state.gov/g/drl/democ/ (last visited 10 January 2005). This may be contrasted with the 191 Member States of the United Nations: see www.un.org/Overview/unmember.html (last visited 10 January 2005).

[32] Sean Murphy, 'Democratic legitimacy and the recognition of states and governments', in Gregory Fox and Brad Roth (eds.), *Democratic governance and international law* (Cambridge: Cambridge University Press, 2000), p. 123, at p. 128.

[33] Article 30 of the Constitutive Act of the African Union, adopted at Lome, Togo, 11 June 2000, provides that: 'Governments which shall come to power through unconstitutional means shall not be allowed to participate in the activities of the Union.' One of the objectives of the Union is to promote 'democratic principles and institutions, popular participation and good governance': Article 3(g), *ibid*. See www.africa-union.org/About_AU/Constitutive_Act.htm (last visited 10 January 2005).

[34] 'Harare Commonwealth Declaration', issued by Heads of Government, Harare, 20 October 1991: see www.thecommonwealth.org/Templates/Internal.asp?NodeID=34457 (last visited 10 January 2005).

[35] Articles 6 and 7 of the Treaty on European Union, 37 ILM (1998) 56, provide for the imposition of sanctions in cases of serious and persistent breaches of democratic principles by a member State. See Nanette Neuwahl and Steven Wheatley, 'The EU and democracy – lawful and legitimate intervention in domestic affairs of states?', in Anthony Arnull and Daniel Wincott (eds.), *Legitimacy and accountability in the European Union after Nice* (Oxford: Oxford University Press, 2002), p. 223, at pp. 230–1.

[36] Article 1 of the OAS Inter-American Democratic Charter, adopted at Lima, 11 September 2001, 40 ILM (2001) 1289: 'The peoples of the Americas have a right to democracy and their governments have an obligation to promote and defend it.'

[37] Participating states of the OSCE have agreed to consolidate and strengthen democracy as the 'only system of government of our nations': CSCE Charter of Paris for a New Europe (1990), 30 ILM (1991) 190. See also the Document of the Moscow Meeting of the Conference on the Human Dimension, 30 ILM (1991) 1670, para. 17.

identified an 'Emerging Right to Democratic Governance'.[38] The right is constructed from the recognition of an internal aspect of the right of peoples to self-determination, and the human rights to freedom of political activity and to free and fair elections.[39] Human rights commitments concerning the rights of political participation and the holding of democratic elections exist only where the State is a signatory to the International Covenant on Civil and Political Rights and/or the relevant regional human rights instruments: the African Charter on Human and Peoples' Rights,[40] the American Convention on Human Rights[41] and the European Convention on Human Rights.[42]

The right of peoples to self-determination is a norm recognised in general international law.[43] The internal aspect of the right of peoples to self-determination recognises the right of the populations of sovereign and independent States to determine, 'when and as they wish, their internal and external political status, without external interference, and to pursue as they wish their political, economic, social and

---

[38] Thomas Franck, 'The emerging right to democratic governance' (1992) 86 *American Journal of International Law* 46.

[39] *Ibid.*, 52.

[40] See Article 13 of the African Charter on Human and Peoples' Rights, adopted at Nairobi, 27 June 1981, in force 21 October 1986, 21 ILM (1982) 58. No express right to vote and to be elected in genuine periodic elections is provided. No obligation to introduce democracy can be read into the African Charter (cf. Dominic Ayine, 'Ballots as bullets? Compliance with rules and norms providing for the right to democratic governance: an African perspective' (1998) 10 *African Journal of International and Comparative Law* (RADIC) 709, 712–21). The African Charter precludes the removal of democratically elected governments by undemocratic forces: Article 20(1). See also *Sir Dawda K. Jawara* v. *The Gambia*, Communication Nos. 147/95 and 149/96, in Thirteenth Annual Activity Report of the African Commission of Human and Peoples' Rights, 1999–2000, Annex V, ACHPR/RPT/13, para. 72; see also Resolution on Nigeria, in Eighth Annual Activity Report of the African Commission on Human and Peoples' Rights, ACHPR/RPT/8th, Annex VII.

[41] Article 23(1)(b) of the American Convention on Human Rights, adopted 22 November 1969, in force 18 July 1978, 1114 UNTS 123.

[42] Article 3 of the (First) Protocol to the Convention for the Protection of Human Rights and Fundamental Freedoms, adopted Paris, 20 March 1952, in force 18 May 1954, ETS No. 9. See *Case of Mathieu-Mohin and Clerfayt* (1987), A113, para. 50. Democracy is, according to the European Court of Human Rights, the 'only' model of government compatible with the Convention: *United Communist Party of Turkey and others* v. *Turkey*, Reports of Judgments and Decisions 1998-I, para. 45.

[43] See GA Res. 2625 (XXV), adopted 24 October 1970, 'Declaration on Principles of International Law Concerning Friendly Relations and Co-operation among States in Accordance with the Charter of the United Nations'; Vienna Declaration and Programme of Action (1993), 32 ILM (1993) 1661, para. I(2); Principle VIII of the Conference on Security and Co-operation in Europe (Helsinki) Final Act (1975), 14 ILM (1975) 1292; and Article 20(1) of the African Charter on Human and Peoples' Rights.

cultural development'.[44] The right is opposable both against external sovereignties,[45] and against the government of the relevant population. Self-determination is a right of peoples, not a right of States or governments.[46] The existence of effective control by the government and the habitual obedience of the population provide presumptive evidence that the existing government constitutes a legitimate expression of self-determination by the people of the State.[47] The presumption is rebutted where a democratically elected government is removed from power, in contravention of domestic constitutional law and relevant international standards. Where the will of the people expressed in free and fair elections has been repudiated, in places such as Haiti[48] and Sierra Leone,[49] the international community has responded by introducing measures to cajole the new government into a transition back to democratic rule.[50] A democratically elected government has the right to assume office and fulfil the term of office as legally established.[51]

---

[44] See Principle VIII of the Helsinki Final Act, *ibid*. See also Article 1(1), common to the International Covenant on Economic, Social and Cultural Rights and the International Covenant on Civil and Political Rights, GA Res. 2200A (XXI), adopted 16 December 1966, 'International Covenant on Economic, Social and Cultural Rights, International Covenant on Civil and Political Rights and Optional Protocol to the International Covenant on Civil and Political Rights'. International Covenant on Economic, Social and Cultural Rights, in force 3 January 1976; International Covenant on Civil and Political Rights, in force 23 March 1976.

[45] Military rule by an external sovereign power constitutes both a violation of the sovereign rights of the State, and the right of the people to self-determination: see, for example, GA Res. 55/85, adopted 28 February 2001, 'Universal Realization of the Right of Peoples to Self-Determination'. See Committee on the Elimination of Racial Discrimination, 'General Recommendation XXI on the right to self-determination', adopted 15 March 1996, reprinted in 'Compilation of General Comments and General Recommendations adopted by Human Rights Treaty Bodies', UN Doc. HRI/GEN/1/Rev.7, 12 May 2004 (hereafter 'Compilation of General Comments and General Recommendations'), p. 212, para. 4.

[46] Thomas Musgrave, *Self-determination and minorities* (Oxford: Oxford University Press, 2000), p. 149.

[47] Brad Roth, *Governmental illegitimacy in international law* (Oxford: Oxford University Press, 2000), p. 419.

[48] Steven Schnably, 'Constitutionalism and democratic government in the inter-American system', in Fox and Roth (eds.), *Democratic governance and international law*, p. 155, at pp. 168–71.

[49] W. Michael Reisman, 'Sovereignty and human rights in contemporary international law', in Fox and Roth (eds.), *Democratic governance and international law*, p. 239, at pp. 252–3.

[50] See Sean Murphy, 'Democratic legitimacy and the recognition of states and governments' (1999) 48 *International and Comparative Law Quarterly* 545, 580.

[51] See, for example, the Warsaw Declaration: Towards a Community of Democracies, adopted 27 June 2000, 39 ILM (2000) 1306.

The human right to democracy

The Universal Declaration of Human Rights, adopted by the General Assembly on 10 December 1948, recognises the rights of individuals to freedom of political opinion and expression,[52] and to peaceful assembly and association.[53] Article 21(1) provides that everyone has the right to take part in the government of his or her country, directly or through freely chosen representatives.[54] According to Article 21(3), the 'will of the people shall be the basis of the authority of government; this will shall be expressed in periodic and genuine elections which shall be by universal and equal suffrage and shall be held by secret vote or by equivalent free voting procedures'.[55] These democratic principles are given legal effect in the International Covenant on Civil and Political Rights.[56]

In addition to the human rights to freedom of expression,[57] peaceful assembly[58] and association,[59] the International Covenant recognises a right of all peoples to self-determination.[60] Rights of political participation for citizens are recognised in Article 25:[61] citizens have the right to (a) 'take part in the conduct of public affairs, directly or through freely chosen representatives', and (b) 'vote and to be elected at genuine periodic elections which shall be by universal and equal suffrage and shall be held by secret ballot, guaranteeing the free expression of the will of the electors'.[62] In its General Comment on Article 25, the Human Rights Committee explained the relationship between the right of peoples to self-determination and the rights of citizens to political participation: 'By virtue of the rights covered by Article 1(1), peoples have the

---

[52] Article 19 of the Universal Declaration of Human Rights.   [53] Article 20, *ibid*.
[54] Article 21(1), *ibid*.
[55] Article 21(3), *ibid*. Article 21 represents an accurate statement of general international law: see, SC Res. 556 (1984), preamble.
[56] According to Henry Steiner, the text of the Universal Declaration of Human Rights is more influenced by the ideas of liberal democracy than the International Covenant on Civil and Political Rights: Steiner, 'Political participation as a human right', 87. The text of the International Covenant on Civil and Political Rights indicates that the existence of a 'democratic society' is required in States parties: see Articles 14(1), 21 and 22(2).
[57] Article 19 of the International Covenant on Civil and Political Rights.
[58] Article 21, *ibid*.   [59] Article 22, *ibid*.
[60] Article 1(1), *ibid*.: 'All peoples have the right of self-determination.'
[61] Cf. the Council of Europe's Convention on the Participation of Foreigners in Public Life at Local Level (1992), adopted at Strasbourg, 5 February 1992, in force 1 May 1997, ETS No. 144.
[62] Article 25 of the International Covenant on Civil and Political Rights.

right to freely determine their political status and to enjoy the right to choose the form of their constitution or government. Article 25 deals with the right of individuals to participate in those processes which constitute the conduct of public affairs.'[63] Article 25 is concerned with the right of individual political participation in a system of collective decision-making. According to the Human Rights Committee, it 'lies at the core of democratic government based on the consent of the people and in conformity with the principles of the Covenant'.[64]

In a number of reports to the Human Rights Committee, State parties to the International Covenant associate the right of peoples to self-determination with a right to democratic government.[65] The report submitted by India provides: 'The internal aspects of self-determination, it is suggested, includes the right of people to choose their own form of government and the right to democracy.'[66] In its Concluding Observations on Congo, the Human Rights Committee expressed its concern that the Congolese people had been unable, owing to the postponement of general elections, 'to exercise their right to self-determination'.[67] The Committee called on Congo to organise general elections as soon as possible in order to enable its citizens to exercise their rights under Articles 1 and 25.[68] The right of peoples to self-determination, taken with the rights of citizens to political participation, creates an obligation for the 150-plus States parties to the International Covenant on Civil and Political Rights to both introduce and maintain democratic forms of government. The Committee established under the International Covenant on Economic, Social and Cultural Rights has noted that the implementation of obligations under the Covenant does not require, nor preclude, any particular form of government 'provided only that it is democratic'.[69]

---

[63] Human Rights Committee, General Comment No. 25, 'Article 25 (Participation in public affairs and the right to vote)', adopted 12 July 1996, reprinted in 'Compilation of General Comments and General Recommendations', p. 167, para. 2.

[64] *Ibid.*, para. 1.

[65] See on this point, Steven Wheatley, 'Democracy and international law: a European perspective' (2002) 51 *International and Comparative Law Quarterly* 225, 231–2.

[66] Third Periodic Report (India), UN Doc. CCPR/C/76/Add.6, 17 July 1996, para. 32.

[67] Human Rights Committee, Concluding Observations on the Second Periodic Report of the Congo, UN Doc. CCPR/C/79/Add.118, 27 March 2000, para. 20.

[68] *Ibid.*

[69] Committee on Economic, Social and Cultural Rights, General Comment No. 3, 'The nature of the States parties obligations (art. 2, para. 1)', adopted 14 December 1990, reprinted in 'Compilation of General Comments and General Recommendations', p. 15, para. 8.

Equal rights to political participation

Article 25 of the International Covenant on Civil and Political Rights recognises the right of all citizens to 'take part in the conduct of public affairs', and to 'vote and to be elected at genuine periodic elections which shall be by universal and equal suffrage and shall be held by secret ballot, guaranteeing the free expression of the will of the electors'. These rights are to be enjoyed 'without any of the distinctions mentioned in Article 2 and without unreasonable restrictions'.[70] The distinctions in Article 2 concern 'race, colour, sex, language, religion, political or other opinion, national or social origin, property, birth or other status'.[71] Persons belonging to national or ethnic, religious and linguistic minorities enjoy equal rights of political participation.[72]

The rights of political participation, including the right to stand as a candidate, are to be enjoyed without discrimination, inter alia on the ground of 'language'.[73] At the same time, the Human Rights Committee has accepted that States parties may proscribe one (or more) working language(s) for public life.[74] The question arises as to whether States parties may exclude candidates from the electoral process where they are not proficient in the official or working language(s) of the State. In *Ignatane* v. *Latvia*, the author, a Latvian citizen of Russian origin, was prevented from standing as a candidate in a local election, following a decision that she did not have the required proficiency in the Latvian language.[75] The decision was taken by a single examiner, and was not, the Committee concluded, 'based on objective criteria', or 'procedurally correct'.[76] This constituted a violation of Article 25, taken in

---

[70] Article 25 of the International Covenant on Civil and Political Rights.

[71] Article 2(1), *ibid.*

[72] See also Article 5(c) of the International Convention on the Elimination of All Forms of Racial Discrimination, adopted by GA Res. 2106 (XX), 21 December 1965, in force 4 January 1969; and Article 2(2) of GA Res. 47/135, adopted 18 December 1992, 'Declaration on the Rights of Persons belonging to National or Ethnic, Religious and Linguistic Minorities'.

[73] See Article 25(b) of the International Covenant on Civil and Political Rights, read with Article 2(1). See Fernand de Varennes, 'Equality and non-discrimination: fundamental principles of minority language rights' (1999) 6 *International Journal on Minority and Group Rights* 307, 314–17.

[74] *Ballantyne and Davidson, and McIntyre* v. *Canada*, Communication Nos. 359/1989 and 385/1989, UN Doc. CCPR/C/47/D/359/1989, 5 May 1993, para. 11.4.

[75] See *Ignatane* v. *Latvia*, Communication No. 884/1999, UN Doc. CCPR/C/72/D/884/1999, 31 July 2001, para. 7.3.

[76] *Ibid.*, para. 7.4.

conjunction with Article 2.[77] The Committee did not conclude that a language requirement for candidates was *per se* incompatible with the International Covenant.

The imposition of mandatory language requirements on candidates for elective office precludes the possibility of the electorate voting for persons from linguistic minorities not proficient in the official or working language(s) of the State. Where candidates in this position are in fact elected, it is 'either because that person represents many people who are in the same situation or, in any event, because the electorate indicated that with their votes their confidence in his or her ability to represent their interests in the legislature'.[78] Mandatory language requirements are not compatible with the primary object and purpose of Article 25(b) of the International Covenant on Civil and Political Rights: the expression of the will of the people in free and fair elections.[79] The conclusion is the same in respect of minimum education requirements for candidates, in particular where education standards are evaluated in the official or working language(s) of the State.[80]

The rights of political participation are to be enjoyed 'without unreasonable restrictions'. Persons who are otherwise eligible to stand for election should not be excluded by 'unreasonable or discriminatory requirements such as education, residence or descent, or by reason of political affiliation'.[81] Political opinion may not be used as a ground to deprive any person of the right to stand for election.[82] Political opinion includes political positions which support the introduction of policies, laws and regulations to maintain and support the ability of persons belonging to ethnic, religious or linguistic minorities to enjoy their own culture, to profess and practise their own religion, or to use their

[77] *Ibid.*, para. 7.5. See, on the same issue, *Podkolzina* v. *Latvia*, Reports of Judgments and Decisions 2002-II. The Advisory Committee on the Framework Convention for the Protection of National Minorities has concluded that language proficiency requirements for candidates in elections are 'not compatible' with Article 15 of the Framework Convention on National Minorities: Opinion on Estonia, ACFC/INF/ OPI(2002)005, para. 55. See also Opinion on the Russian Federation, ACFC/INF/ OPI(2003)005, para. 106. The OSCE/ODIHR has criticised the implementation of language requirements for presidential candidates in both Kazakhstan and the Kyrgyz Republic: see, Sally Holt and John Packer, 'OSCE Developments and Linguistic Minorities' (2001) 3(2), *MOST Journal on Multicultural Societies*, para. 2.17.

[78] De Varennes, 'Equality and non-discrimination', 317.

[79] See Human Rights Committee, General Comment No. 25, 'Article 25 (Participation in public affairs and the right to vote)', para. 21.

[80] *Ibid.*, para. 15.   [81] *Ibid.*   [82] *Ibid.*, para. 17.

own language. Political opinion also includes proposals for territorial self-government for an ethno-cultural group, including demands for separation and the establishment of a sovereign and independent State.[83]

The rights of political participation are not enjoyed by citizens advocating policies of racial discrimination – a position that applies to persons belonging to both majority and minority groups. Article 20(2) of the International Covenant on Civil and Political Rights provides: 'Any advocacy of national, racial or religious hatred that constitutes incitement to discrimination, hostility or violence shall be prohibited by law.'[84] According to the Human Rights Committee, the provision forms part of customary international law.[85] In a democratic State, the recognition of formal equality between different members of society is not a legitimate subject for political debate.

Reference to 'unreasonable restrictions' in Article 25 implies that certain restrictions on the rights of political participation are 'reasonable'.[86] According to the Human Rights Committee, restrictions are permissible where they are based on 'objective and reasonable

---

[83] See, for example, the decisions of the European Court of Human Rights in *Socialist Party and Others* v. *Turkey*, Reports of Judgments and Decisions 1998-III, para. 47; *United Communist Party of Turkey and Others* v. *Turkey*, Reports of Judgments and Decisions 1998-I, para. 55; and *Case of Stankov and the United Macedonian Organisation Ilinden* v. *Bulgaria*, Reports of Judgments and Decisions 2001-IX, para. 97.

[84] See also Article 4 of the International Convention on the Elimination of All Forms of Racial Discrimination, adopted by GA Res. 2106 (XX), 21 December 1965, in force 4 January 1969; GA Res. 55/82, adopted 26 February 2001, 'Measures to be taken against racial discrimination or ethnic exclusiveness and xenophobia, including, in particular, neo-Nazism', para. 3; and UN Commission on Human Rights Res. 2003/41, adopted 23 April 2003, 'The incompatibility between democracy and racism', UN Doc. E/CN.4/2000/40.

[85] Human Rights Committee, General Comment No. 24, 'Issues relating to reservations made upon ratification or accession to the Covenant or the Optional Protocols thereto, or in relation to declarations under Article 41 of the Covenant', adopted 4 November 1994, reprinted in 'Compilation of General Comments and General Recommendations', p. 161, para. 8. Cf. the reservation of the United States to Article 20, citing the US Constitutional right to free speech and association: see Henry Steiner and Philip Alston, *International human rights in context: law, politics, morals* (Oxford: Oxford University Press, 2000), p. 751.

[86] See Fox, 'The right to political participation in international law', 554. According to Fox, the delegates in the drafting process included the phrase to allow denial of suffrage to minors, convicts, the mentally ill and those not meeting residency requirements: *ibid.* Cf. Article 23(2) of the American Convention on Human Rights: 'The law may regulate the [right to participate in government] only on the basis of age, nationality, residence, language, education, civil and mental capacity, or sentencing by a competent court in criminal proceedings'.

criteria'.[87] They must be evaluated 'on a case-by-case basis, having regard, in particular, to the purpose of such restrictions and the principle of proportionality'.[88] The Committee has accepted that States parties may introduce minimum age limits for the right to vote,[89] and the right to stand for elective office.[90] Established mental incapacity may also be a ground for denying a person the right to vote or to hold office.[91] The right to vote may not be restricted on grounds of physical disability, or by reference to literacy, educational or property requirements.[92]

Parliamentary representation

In contemporary international law, the 'will of the people' is the basis of the legitimate authority of government. This will, according to the Universal Declaration of Human Rights, is 'expressed in periodic and genuine elections which shall be by universal and equal suffrage and shall be held by secret vote or by equivalent free voting procedures'.[93] According to the Inter-Parliamentary Union's 'Declaration on Criteria for Free and Fair Elections', a free and fair election is one in which each citizen has the right to vote, on a non-discriminatory basis,[94] and the equal opportunity to become a candidate.[95] Further, everyone has the right to

---

[87] Human Rights Committee, General Comment No. 25, 'Article 25 (Participation in public affairs and the right to vote)', para. 4. Arbitrary restrictions on the rights of political participation are not permissible: *Bwalya* v. *Zambia*, Communication No. 314/1988, UN Doc. CCPR/C/48/D/314/1988, 27 July 1993, para. 6.6. See also *Weisz* v. *Uruguay*, Communication No. 28/1978, UN Doc. CCPR/C/11/D/28/1978, 29 October 1980; and *Altesor* v. *Uruguay*, Communication No. 10/1977, UN Doc. CCPR/C/15/D/10/1977, 19 March 1982.

[88] See *Gillot et al.* v. *France*, Communication No. 932/2000, UN Doc. CCPR/C/75/D/932/2000, 26 July 2002, para. 13.2.

[89] Human Rights Committee, General Comment No. 25, 'Article 25 (Participation in public affairs and the right to vote)', para. 10. There is no consensus amongst democratic States as to the minimum age for political participation, although, given that the right is enjoyed by adult citizens, it is difficult to justify an age limit on the right to vote above eighteen: Article 1 of the Convention on the Rights of the Child, adopted by GA Res. 44/25, 20 November 1989, in force 2 September 1990.

[90] *Ibid.*, para. 15. The minimum age to vote and be elected need not be the same: *ibid.*, para. 4.

[91] *Ibid.*, para. 4.   [92] *Ibid.*, para. 10.

[93] Article 21(3) of the Universal Declaration of Human Rights.

[94] Declaration on Criteria for Free and Fair Elections, unanimously adopted by the Inter-Parliamentary Council at its 154th Session, Paris, 26 March 1994, para. 2(1). See generally Guy Goodwin-Gill, *Free and fair elections: international law and practice* (Geneva: Inter-Parliamentary Union, 1994).

[95] *Ibid.*, para. 3(1).

express political opinions, to seek, receive and impart information and to make informed choices, and to campaign on an equal basis with other political parties.[96] States should take all necessary and appropriate measures to ensure that the principle of the secret ballot is respected, and that voters are able to cast their ballots freely, without fear or intimidation.[97]

In any election, the 'will of the people' will be divided, with different levels of support evidenced for the various candidates (and their policy positions). In its General Comment on Article 25 of the International Covenant on Civil and Political Rights, the Human Rights Committee requested that States parties 'explain [in their reports] how the different political views in the community are represented in elected bodies'.[98] National parliaments should reflect the plurality of political perspectives. Democracy, according to the Universal Declaration on Democracy, requires the existence of a parliament in which 'all components of society are represented and which has the requisite powers and means to express the will of the people by legislating and overseeing government action'.[99]

The national parliament should additionally reflect the plurality of identities of the 'people' of the State. It is important, for reasons of both efficacy and legitimacy, that the legislature reflects, what the Canadian Supreme Court has called, 'the diversity of [the] social mosaic'.[100] This does not require microcosm representation, where representatives are chosen from their ethno-cultural group, normally by lottery, to represent the group.[101] It is not necessary that the legislature should mirror society. What is required is that barriers to participation for historically excluded groups are removed.[102] Non-dominant groups cannot be represented by (dominant) 'Others', who attempt to take

---

[96] *Ibid.*, para. 3(3). States should take the necessary measures to ensure that parties and candidates enjoy reasonable opportunities to present their electoral platform: *ibid.*, para. 4(4).

[97] *Ibid.*, para. 4(5).

[98] Human Rights Committee, General Comment No. 25, 'Article 25 (Participation in public affairs and the right to vote)', para. 22.

[99] Inter-Parliamentary Union's Universal Declaration on Democracy, para. 11.

[100] *Reference re Provincial Electoral Boundaries (Saskatchewan)* [1991] 2 SCR 158.

[101] Jane Mansbridge, 'What does a representative do? Communicative settings of distrust, uncrystallized interests, and historically denigrated status', in Will Kymlicka and Wayne Norman (eds.), *Citizenship in diverse societies* (Oxford: Oxford University Press, 2000), p. 99, at p. 105.

[102] See Carol Gould, 'Diversity and democracy: representing differences', in Seyla Benhabib (ed.), *Democracy and difference: contesting the boundaries of the political* (Princeton, NJ: Princeton University Press, 1996), p. 170, at p. 177.

their interests into account.[103] The Committee established under the Convention on the Elimination of Discrimination against Women has observed that policies developed and decisions made by men alone 'reflect only part of human experience and potential'.[104] The Committee concluded that societies in which women are excluded from public life and decision-making 'cannot be described as democratic'.[105]

The State is unable to take into account the interests and preferences of members of national, ethnic, cultural, religious or linguistic minorities unless persons from those groups are represented in relevant decision-making processes, including the national parliament. Representatives from minority groups are able to bring issues to the political agenda, correct factual errors and ensure that their interests and perspectives are recognised.[106] The right of peoples to self-determination requires representative government. The Committee on the Elimination of Racial Discrimination has recognised the 'internal aspect' of the right of peoples to self-determination: 'that is to say, the rights of all peoples to pursue freely their economic, social and cultural development without outside interference. In that respect there exists a link with the right of every citizen to take part in the conduct of public affairs at any level ... In consequence, Governments are to represent the whole population without distinction as to race, colour, descent or national or ethnic origin.'[107]

General Assembly Resolution 2625 (XXV), 'Declaration on Principles of International Law Concerning Friendly Relations', defines a State conducting itself in compliance with the principle of equal rights and self-determination of peoples as one 'thus possessed of a government

---

[103] According to the Committee on the Elimination of Discrimination against Women, research demonstrates that, if women's participation reaches 30 to 35 per cent (generally termed a 'critical mass'), there is a real impact on political style and the content of decisions, and political life is revitalized: Committee Established under the Convention on the Elimination of Discrimination against Women, General Recommendation No. 23, 'Political and public life', adopted 13 January 1997, reprinted in 'Compilation of General Comments and General Recommendations', p. 263, para. 16. See, on this point, Joni Lovenduski, 'Women and politics: minority representation or critical mass' (2001) 54 *Parliamentary Affairs* 743.

[104] Committee on the Elimination of Discrimination against Women, General Recommendation No. 23, 'Political and public life', *ibid.*, para. 13.

[105] *Ibid.*, para. 14.   [106] See Mansbridge, 'What does a representative do?', pp. 99–100.

[107] Committee on the Elimination of Racial Discrimination, 'General Recommendation XXI on the right to self-determination', adopted 15 March 1996, reprinted in 'Compilation of General Comments and General Recommendations', p. 212, para. 4.

representing the whole people belonging to the territory without distinction as to race, creed or colour'.[108] The clause, according to Robert Rosenstock, captures the idea of the 'necessity for governments to represent the governed'.[109] The formula was revised in the UN Vienna Declaration and Programme of Action to make clear that the government must represent the whole people belonging to the territory 'without distinction of any kind'.[110] Two aspects of representative government may be identified: the legislative and other measures of the State should not arbitrarily favour, or disfavour, any particular group of persons; and the character of the government should be 'representative' of the heterogeneous people of the State. The members of the government, including its elected members, should reflect the national, ethnic, cultural, religious and linguistic diversity of the population.[111] The purpose of democratic elections to a national parliament is both to provide a coherent expression of the 'will of the people', and to produce a representative assembly.[112]

Human rights law offers no guidelines for the selection of the electoral system in democratic States.[113] No preference is expressed in the International Covenant on Civil and Political Rights for a proportional or a majority system of voting.[114] Article 25 makes 'allowance for the coexistence of various types of democratic system'.[115] There must be regular elections, which are free and fair, with universal and equal suffrage, open to multiple parties, conducted by secret ballot,

---

[108] GA Res. 2625 (XXV), 'Declaration on Principles of International Law Concerning Friendly Relations and Co-operation among States in Accordance with the Charter of the United Nations', adopted 24 October 1970.

[109] Robert Rosenstock, 'The Declaration on Friendly Relations' (1971) 65 *American Journal of International Law* 713, 732.

[110] Vienna Declaration and Programme of Action (1993), 32 ILM (1993) 1661, para. I(2).

[111] The Committee on the Elimination of Racial Discrimination has commented favourably where minority groups have been represented in Parliament in proportion to their representation in the wider society (Concluding Observations on Islamic Republic of Iran, UN Doc. A/54/18 (1999), para. 300), and expressed its concern where minority groups are under-represented (Concluding Observations on Georgia, UN Doc. A/56/18 (2001), para. 95; Concluding Observations on India, UN Doc. A/51/18 (1996), para. 362; Concluding Observations on Croatia, UN Doc. A/57/18 (2002), para. 96; and Concluding Observations on Armenia, UN Doc. A/57/18 (2002), para. 278).

[112] Elections must both 'reflect fairly faithfully the opinions of the people, and ... channel currents of thought so as to promote the emergence of a sufficiently clear and coherent political will': *Case of Mathieu-Mohin and Clerfayt* (1987), A113, para. 54.

[113] Steiner, 'Political participation as a human right', 108.

[114] Fox, 'The right to political participation in international law', 556.

[115] Steiner, 'Political participation as a human right', 91–2.

monitored by independent electoral authorities, and free of fraud and intimidation. The principle of 'one person, one vote' must apply, and the electoral system must guarantee and give effect to the 'free expression of the will of the electors'.[116]

Where a national, ethnic, cultural, religious or linguistic minority is under-represented in the national parliament, in relation to its proportion of the population, a number of policy options are available to the authorities. The State may introduce measures which seek to encourage greater participation by members of a minority group in the existing democratic system, for example by encouraging voter registration and turnout, or by providing information on the electoral system and the importance of the electoral process, and its consequences.[117] The State may amend the electoral system to ensure that the representation of persons from minority groups is maximised. Measures may include the removal of requirements that political parties achieve a minimum percentage of the popular vote for representation in the national parliament, or requirements for political parties representing territorially concentrated minority groups to have offices or members in all parts of the State in order to stand in general elections, or to receive State funding for political activities.

The electoral system will have a significant influence on the outcome of any election. Depending on the territorial distribution of a minority group, and the extent to which its members are politically organised, both first-past-the-post and proportional systems of voting may facilitate greater minority representation. Where members of a minority community are concentrated in a particular geographical region, candidates from ethno-cultural minorities are likely to be elected in a first-past-the-post system of voting.[118] For those groups that are not concentrated in one or more geographical areas, the introduction of relative pure systems of proportional representation, where the percentage of seats in the legislature is roughly equivalent to the percentage of votes received, will facilitate greater representation.[119] Where members of minority groups are politically organised (i.e. where political parties are

---

[116] Human Rights Committee, General Comment No. 25, 'Article 25 (Participation in public affairs and the right to vote)', para. 21.

[117] See *ibid.*, paras. 11 and 12.

[118] See generally David Brockington *et al.*, 'Minority representation under cumulative and limited voting' (1998) 60 *Journal of Politics* 1108, 1109.

[119] See Pippa Norris, 'Ballots not bullets: testing consociational theories of ethno conflict, electoral systems, and democratisation' in Andrew Reynolds (ed.), *The architecture of*

established to represent the interests of the group), the use of relatively pure systems of proportional representation will provide for a 'representative' presence of persons from minorities in the national parliament.

Where an electoral system relies on constituency representation, the State may establish 'minority-majority' constituencies, in which a majority of the electorate are members of a minority group, thus enhancing opportunities for representation. This may be achieved by drawing the electoral boundaries around the minority community, but without deviating significantly from the average number of voters in a constituency. This is not problematic. In the case of smaller minorities, the creation of a 'minority-majority' constituency may require that the total number of voters in the constituency be significantly reduced, to ensure that members of the minority group do in fact constitute a majority of the electorate. In *Mátyus* v. *Slovakia*, the Human Rights Committee concluded that, where there was a substantial difference between the number of inhabitants per elected representative, there would be a violation of Article 25 of the International Covenant on Civil and Political Rights 'in the absence of any reference by the State party to factors that might explain the differences in the number of inhabitants or registered voters per elected representative'.[120] Deviations from absolute voter parity may be justified to provide for more effective representation. Factors such as community history, community interests and minority representation may be taken into account to ensure that the legislative assembly represents the social diversity.[121]

The State may respond to the problem of under-representation of minority groups by reserving seats for representatives from minorities in the national parliament. Tom Hadden and Ciarán Maoláin identify the use of reserved seats in Venezuela, Romania, Ethiopia, India, Jordan, Niger, Slovenia, Colombia and Croatia.[122] The Advisory Committee on the Framework Convention has recognised that electoral arrangements

democracy: constitutional design, conflict management and democracy (Oxford: Oxford University Press, 2002), p. 206, at pp. 213–14.

[120] *Mátyus* v. *Slovakia*, Communication No. 923/2000, UN Doc. CCPR/C/75/D/923/2000, 26 July 2002, para. 9.2.

[121] See, for example, *Reference re Provincial Electoral Boundaries (Saskatchewan)* [1991] 2 SCR 158.

[122] Tom Hadden and Ciarán Maoláin, 'Integrative approaches to the accommodation of minorities', paper prepared for the Working Group on Minorities (Seventh Session, Geneva, 14–18 May 2001), UN Doc. E/CN.4/Sub.2/AC.5/2001/WP.6.

for parliamentary representation are a domain where, from the point of view of international standards, States enjoy a broad margin of appreciation.[123] The Committee has though emphasised the importance of national minority representation in legislative bodies, especially the national parliament,[124] and expressed concern where barriers to representation exist for persons belonging to national minorities: for example, where laws require that political parties achieve a minimum percentage of the popular vote in order to achieve parliamentary representation,[125] or that political parties have branches in all parts of the State.[126] In its Opinion on Romania, the Advisory Committee 'strongly welcome[d] the fact that organisations of citizens belonging to a national minority are given participation rights through a constitutionally guaranteed representation in Parliament'.[127] In its Opinion on Ukraine, the Advisory Committee noted that, whereas in 1994 the Crimean Tatars had reserved seats in the legislature in the Autonomous Republic of Crimea, 'the present legislation provides no such guarantees and as a result their presence has been drastically reduced. The Advisory Committee [found] the resulting situation regrettable.'[128]

Where reserved seats are provided, citizens do not compete equally for political representation. Candidates from certain minorities (defined by reference to identity) are guaranteed representation in the national parliament. Candidates from groups representing other interests are not. Rights of political participation may only be limited in order to protect fundamental democratic principles, or to facilitate a more effective democratic system. Many States, for example, exclude public servants from the rights of political participation. There is no automatic right of exclusion.[129] The restriction is justified only where it can be shown that it is necessary to protect the rights of others, i.e. the electorate, to an effective political

---

[123] Opinion on Hungary, ACFC/INF/OPI(2001)004, para. 49.

[124] See inter alia, Opinion on Croatia, ACFC/INF/OPI(2002)003, para. 60; and Opinion on Czech Republic, ACFC/INF/OPI(2002)002, para. 70.

[125] Opinion on Germany, ACFC/INF/OPI(2002)008, para. 63. Cf. Opinion on Serbia and Montenegro, ACFC/INF/OPI(2004)002, para. 102; and Opinion on Italy, ACFC/INF/OPI(2002)007, para. 75.

[126] Opinion on Russian Federation, ACFC/INF/OPI(2003)005, para. 105.

[127] Opinion on Romania, ACFC/INF/OPI(2002)001, para. 65.

[128] Opinion on Ukraine, ACFC/INF/OPI(2002)010, para. 70. See also Opinion on Croatia, ACFC/INF/OPI(2002)003, paras. 61 and 62.

[129] *Aduayom et al.*, Communications Nos. 422/1990, 423/1990 and 424/1990, UN Doc. CCPR/C/57/D/422/1990, 19 August 1996, para. 7.5.

democracy.[130] The democratic principles of political equality and popular sovereignty may be balanced against each other to produce a more democratic system. The use of reserved seats is justified on the basis that it produces a more accurate reflection of the will of the people, ensuring the inclusion of otherwise excluded (national or ethnic, religious and linguistic minority) interests and perspectives. Their use in a democracy should 'be a last resort and temporary option for representing otherwise excluded representatives'.[131]

Where a State reserves parliamentary seats for members of minority groups, the authorities may simply appoint the required number of minority representatives, although this practice will undermine the claims of those persons to represent the group. Alternatively, the authorities may devolve responsibility for appointing minority representatives to a minority association, which may or may not rely on democratic procedures. Ideally, persons belonging to the relevant national, ethnic, cultural, religious or linguistic group should elect their own representatives at the time of the general election. Citizens belonging to minority groups have the right, in common with other citizens, to participate in free and fair general elections. Reserved seats provide an additional, not an alternative, opportunity for person belonging to minorities to be represented in the national Parliament.

The right to vote in elections for candidates in reserved seats must be restricted to persons belonging to the minority, to avoid the 'cuckoo-problem' identified in Hungary: persons not belonging to the minority are, through the openness of the electoral system, able to vote and get themselves elected as representatives of that minority.[132] The Advisory Committee has called for 'creative solutions' to the problem, 'whilst not going as far as to introduce a form of ethnic registration'.[133]

---

[130] See, for example, *Debreczeny v. The Netherlands*, Communication No. 500/1992, UN Doc. CCPR/C/53/D/500/1992, 4 April 1995, para. 9.3. Likewise, limits may be placed on campaign expenditure, to ensure that the 'free choice of voters is not undermined or the democratic process distorted by the disproportionate expenditure on behalf of any candidate or party': Human Rights Committee, General Comment No. 25, 'Article 25 (Participation in public affairs and the right to vote)', para. 19.

[131] Iris Marion Young, *Inclusion and democracy* (Oxford: Oxford University Press, 2000), p. 150.

[132] See Andrea Krizsán, 'The Hungarian minority protection system: a flexible approach to the adjudication of ethnic claims' (2000) 26 *Journal of Ethnic and Migration Studies* 247, 256–7.

[133] Opinion on Hungary, ACFC/INF/OPI(2001)004, para. 52. In Slovenia, persons are only included on the separate minority voter register where they are accepted as a member of the minority by the group itself: see, Tamas Korhecz, 'Democratic legitimacy and

Participation in the conduct of public affairs

Article 25 of the International Covenant on Civil and Political Rights provides both a right to vote and be elected at genuine periodic elections,[134] and the right to 'take part in the conduct of public affairs, directly or through freely chosen representatives'.[135] The conduct of public affairs concerns the exercise of political power, in particular the exercise of legislative, executive and administrative powers, and the formulation of policy.[136] Citizens participate directly in the conduct of public affairs when they exercise power as members of legislative bodies, hold executive office, decide public issues through referendums or other electoral process, and take part in formal consultation processes established by government.[137]

In *Mikmaq Tribal Society* v. *Canada*, the representatives of the group complained that they had been excluded from conferences considering proposed amendments to the Canadian Constitution.[138] As a general rule, constitutional conferences were attended only by the elected leaders of the federal (i.e. central) and provincial governments of Canada. When questions concerning the rights of indigenous populations were considered, representatives of four national (indigenous) associations were invited to take part. The Mikmaq tribal society was not invited. In its Opinion, the Human Rights Committee concluded that Article 25 could not be read as providing a right for each citizen to 'determine either to take part directly in the conduct of public affairs or to leave it to freely chosen representatives':[139]

---

election rules of national ethnic minority bodies and representatives: reflections on legal solutions in Hungary and Slovenia' (2002) 9 *International Journal on Minority and Group Rights* 161, 177. In relation to the Nordic States' Sami Parliaments, the rights to vote and to stand as a candidate are restricted to those who meet the criteria established for membership of the Sami group: see, Kristian Myntii, 'The Nordic Sami Parliaments', in Pekka Aikio and Martin Scheinin (eds.), *Operationalizing the right of indigenous peoples to self-determination* (Turku: Institute for Human Rights, Åbo Akademi University, 2000), p. 203.

[134] Article 25(b) of the International Covenant on Civil and Political Rights.
[135] Article 25(a), *ibid.*
[136] Human Rights Committee, General Comment No. 25, 'Article 25 (Participation in public affairs and the right to vote)', para. 5.
[137] *Ibid.*, para. 6.
[138] *Mikmaq Tribal Society* v. *Canada*, Communication No. 205/1996, UN Doc. CCPR/C/43/D/205/1986, 3 December 1991, para. 3.2.
[139] *Ibid.*, para. 5.4.

It must be beyond dispute that the conduct of public affairs in a democratic State is the task of representatives of the people, elected for that purpose, and public officials appointed in accordance with the law. Invariably, the conduct of public affairs affects the interest of large segments of the population or even the population as a whole, while in other instances it affects more directly the interests of more specific groups of society. Although prior consultations, such as public hearings or consultations with the most interested groups may often be envisaged by law or have evolved as public policy in the conduct of public affairs, Article 25(a) of the Covenant cannot be understood as meaning that any directly affected group, large or small, has the unconditional right to choose the modalities of participation in the conduct of public affairs.[140]

Article 25 does not provide a right for all concerned citizens to 'take part' in democratic debates in decision-making bodies. Citizens participate in the conduct of public affairs 'directly or through freely chosen representatives'.[141] In the majority of cases, they will be represented in decision-making forums by others, who should ensure that their opinions, interests and preferences are taken into account.[142] Citizens also take part in the conduct of public affairs 'by exerting influence through public debate and dialogue with their representatives or through their capacity to organize themselves'.[143] They must be free to debate public affairs, hold peaceful demonstrations and meetings, criticise and oppose, publish political material, campaign for election and advertise their own political ideas.[144] The right to freedom of political expression is protected by the right to freedom of expression,[145] contained in Article 19 of the International Covenant on Civil and Political Rights.[146] Citizens must be free to 'criticize or openly and publicly evaluate their Governments without fear of interference or punishment'.[147] An individual may, in

---

[140] *Ibid.*, para. 5.5.
[141] Article 25(a) of the International Covenant on Civil and Political Rights.
[142] See Young, *Inclusion and Democracy*, p. 134.
[143] Human Rights Committee, General Comment No. 25, 'Article 25 (Participation in public affairs and the right to vote)', para. 8.
[144] *Ibid.*, para. 25.
[145] See *Dergachev* v. *Belarus*, Communication No. 921/2000, UN Doc. CCPR/C/74/D/921/2000/ Rev.1, 2 April 2002, para. 8.
[146] Article 19(3) provides: 'The right to freedom of expression may therefore be subject to certain restrictions, but these shall only be such as are provided by law and are necessary: (a) For respect of the rights or reputations of others; (b) For the protection of national security or of public order (*ordre public*), or of public health or morals.'
[147] *Aduayom et al.*, Communications Nos. 422/1990, 423/1990 and 424/1990, UN Doc. CCPR/ C/57/D/422/1990, 19 August 1996, para. 7.4.

'no case', be subject to restrictions in their rights of political expression and activity 'solely because of his or her political opinion'.[148]

Minorities and political participation

The Human Rights Committee concluded in its General Comment on Article 27 of the International Covenant on Civil and Political Rights that the rights of persons belonging to minorities 'may require ... measures to ensure the effective participation of members of minority communities in decisions which affect them'.[149] The Optional Protocol to the International Covenant provides a procedure under which persons belonging to minorities can claim that their rights to enjoy their own culture, to profess and practise their own religion, or to use their own language have been violated.[150] In its Opinions concerning Article 27, the formulation hardens to 'measures *must be taken* "to ensure the effective participation of members of minority communities in decisions which affect them"'.[151] In those Opinions, the Human Rights Committee pays particular attention to the extent to which a minority group has been involved in relevant decision-making processes, and the extent to which its interests and perspectives have been taken into account.

In *Länsman et al.* v. *Finland (No. 1)*, the Human Rights Committee concluded that the quarrying of stone on the flank of the Etelä-Riutusvaara mountain, and its transportation through reindeer-herding territory, did not constitute a denial of the authors' right to enjoy their own culture, which was based on reindeer husbandry. In the Opinion, the Committee noted that 'the interests of the Muotkatunturi Herdsmens' Committee and of the authors were considered during the proceedings leading to the delivery of the quarrying permit, that the authors *were*

---

[148] See *Pietraroia* v. *Uruguay*, Communication No. 44/1979, UN Doc. CCPR/C/12/D/44/1979, 9 April 1981, para. 16.

[149] Human Rights Committee, General Comment No. 23, 'Rights of minorities (Article 27)', adopted 8 April 1994, reprinted in 'Compilation of General Comments and General Recommendations', p. 158, para. 7.

[150] Article 1 of the Optional Protocol to the International Covenant on Civil and Political Rights, adopted by GA Res. 2200A (XXI), 16 December 1966, in force 23 March 1976. These rights are set out in Part III of the Covenant, Articles 6 to 27, inclusive.

[151] *Länsman et al.* v. *Finland (No. 1)*, Communication No. 511/1992, UN Doc. CCPR/C/52/D/511/1992, 8 November 1994, para. 9.5 (emphasis added). See also *Länsman et al.* v. *Finland (No. 2)*, Communication No. 671/1995, UN Doc. CCPR/C/58/D/671/1995, 22 November 1996, para. 10.4.

consulted during the proceedings, and that reindeer herding in the area does not appear to have been adversely affected by such quarrying as has occurred'.[152] According to Martin Scheinin, *Länsman (No. 1)* introduces a two-part test: the first part concerning the continued economic sustainability of the indigenous community, and the second, the question of 'effective consultation with the community concerned in determining when interference with nature-based traditional forms of economic life amounts to "a denial" of the persons' right to enjoy their own culture'.[153]

In *Mahuika* v. *New Zealand*, members of the Maori people of New Zealand complained that the Government's actions threatened their way of life and the culture of their tribes, in violation of Article 27.[154] In 1992, the Government of New Zealand had agreed to pay NZ$150 million to the Maori for the purchase of Sealords, the largest fishing company in Australia and New Zealand, in final settlement of all claims by Maori in respect of commercial fishing.[155] The settlement was enacted in the Treaty of Waitangi (Fisheries Claims) Settlement Act 1992. The Human Rights Committee accepted that the Act, and its mechanisms, limited the right of the authors to enjoy their own culture,[156] which included the use and control of fisheries, as an essential element of their culture.[157] The question was whether the measures amounted to a denial of the rights protected by Article 27.[158]

The Opinion noted that, in its case law under the Optional Protocol, 'the Committee has emphasised that the acceptability of measures that affect or interfere with the culturally significant economic activities of a minority depends on whether the members of the minority in question have had the opportunity to participate in the decision-making process in relation to these measures and whether they will continue to benefit

---

[152] *Länsman et al.* v. *Finland (No. 1)*, para. 9.6 (emphasis in original). In *Länsman et al.* v. *Finland (No. 2)*, the Committee again declined to find a violation of Article 27, noting that the Herdsmen's Committee had been consulted in the process of drawing up the logging plans and had 'not react[ed] negatively'. There was evidence that the authorities had gone through a process of weighing the minority's interests against the general economic interest: *Länsman et al.* v. *Finland (No. 2)*, para. 10.5. See also *Äärelä and Näkkäläjärvi* v. *Finland*, Communication No. 779/1997, UN Doc. CCPR/C/73/D/779/1997, 7 November 2001, para. 7.6.

[153] Martin Scheinin, 'State responsibility, good governance and indivisible human rights', in Hans-Otto Sano and Gudmundur Alfredsson (eds.), *Human rights and good governance: building bridges* (The Hague: Martinus Nijhoff, 2002), p. 29, at p. 42.

[154] *Mahuika et al.* v. *New Zealand*, Communication No. 547/1993, UN Doc. CCPR/C/70/D/547/1993, 15 November 2000, para. 6.2.

[155] *Ibid.*, para. 5.12.   [156] *Ibid.*, para. 9.5.   [157] *Ibid.*, para. 9.3.   [158] *Ibid.*, para. 9.4.

from their traditional economy'.[159] Maori communities and national Maori organisations were consulted on the proposals for the settlement of claims by Maori in respect of commercial fishing. Their responses did affect the design of the final agreement, which was only enacted following evidence of substantial Maori support.[160] Special attention was paid to the cultural and religious significance of fishing for the Maori, inter alia by securing the possibility of Maori individuals and communities engaging in non-commercial fishing activities. The Human Rights Committee concluded that, whilst it was a matter of concern that the settlement and its process had contributed to divisions amongst Maori, the State party had 'by engaging itself in the process of broad consultation before proceeding to legislate, and by paying specific attention to the sustainability of Maori fishing activities, taken the necessary steps to ensure that the [relevant measures were] compatible with Article 27'.[161]

The Opinions of the Human Rights Committee demonstrate the need for States parties to ensure that the interests and preferences of persons belonging to minorities are effectively represented in relevant decision-making processes. The Committee has yet to conclude that the absence of political participation, ipso facto, constitutes a violation of Article 27. The Committee's Opinion in *Hopu and Bessert* v. *France*, nominally concerning the rights to family and privacy,[162] suggests that the failure of a State party to take into account the interests of persons belonging to a minority on issues which affect the ability of those persons to enjoy their own culture, to profess and practise their own religion, or to use

---

[159] *Ibid.*, para. 9.5 (footnotes omitted).   [160] *Ibid.*, para. 9.6.

[161] *Ibid.*, para. 9.8. The Committee noted that 'the State party continues to be bound by Article 27 which requires that the cultural and religious significance of fishing for Maori must deserve due attention ... [In] order to comply with Article 27, measures affecting the economic activities of Maori must be carried out in a way that the authors continue to enjoy their culture, and profess and practice their religion in community with other members of their group': *ibid.*, para. 9.9.

[162] Articles 17 and 23 of the International Covenant on Civil and Political Rights. The Human Rights Committee accepted that, upon accession to the International Covenant, France made a valid reservation to Article 27: *H.K.* v. *France*, Communication No. 222/1987, UN Doc. CCPR/C/37/D/222/1987, 8 December 1989, paras. 8.5–8.6. The issues in *Hopu and Bessert* could not be addressed directly under Article 27. Cf. *Hopu and Bessert* v. *France*, Communication No. 549/1993, UN Doc. CCPR/C/60/D/549/1993/Rev.1, 29 December 1997, individual opinion by Committee members David Kretzmer and Thomas Buergenthal, co-signed by Nisuke Ando and Lord Colville, para. 5: 'The reference by the Committee to the authors' history, culture and life, is revealing. For it shows that the values that are being protected are not the family, or privacy, but cultural values ... These values, however, are protected under Article 27 of the Covenant and not the provisions relied on by the Committee.'

their own language will constitute a violation of the provision. The authors had complained that the construction of a hotel complex would destroy their ancestral burial grounds, constituting an unjustified interference in the right to respect for family life. The majority of the Human Rights Committee accepted that cultural traditions could be taken into account when defining the term 'family', and noted that the relationship between the applicants, who were Polynesian inhabitants of Tahiti, and their ancestors was 'an essential element of their identity', and played an important role in their family life.[163] The Committee concluded that the construction of a hotel complex on the authors' ancestral burial grounds interfered with their right to family and privacy:

The State party has not shown that this interference was reasonable in the circumstances, and *nothing in the information before the Committee shows that the State party duly took into account the importance of the burial grounds for the authors*, when it decided to lease the site for the building of a hotel complex. The Committee concludes that there has been an *arbitrary interference* with the authors' right to family and privacy.[164]

The right of effective political participation for minorities is parasitic to the rights recognised in Article 27. In relation to issues that do not directly affect the culture of the group, persons belonging to minorities enjoy the same rights as other citizens to participate in democratic deliberations, but the State is under no obligation to ensure that their interests and preferences are directly represented in decision-making processes.

The importance of political participation for minorities is reflected in General Assembly Resolution 47/135, 'Declaration on the Rights of Persons belonging to National or Ethnic, Religious and Linguistic Minorities'.[165] Article 2(2) provides: 'Persons belonging to minorities have the right to participate effectively in ... public life.' This includes the right to vote and stand in elections, and to hold public office.[166] Through the exercise of the right of public/political participation,

---

[163] *Hopu and Bessert* v. *France*, Communication No. 549/1993, UN Doc. CCPR/C/60/D/549/1993/Rev.1, 29 December 1997, para. 10.3.

[164] *Ibid*, (emphasis added).

[165] GA Res. 47/135, adopted 18 December 1992, 'Declaration on the Rights of Persons belonging to National or Ethnic, Religious and Linguistic Minorities'.

[166] Asbjørn Eide, 'Commentary to the Declaration on the Rights of Persons Belonging to National or Ethnic, Religious and Linguistic Minorities', UN Doc. E/CN.4/Sub.2/AC.5/2001/2, 2 April 2001, para. 35.

persons belonging to national, ethnic, cultural, religious or linguistic minorities are able to 'promote their interests and values ... and to contribute to political change in the larger society'.[167] Article 2(3) provides that persons belonging to minorities 'have the right to participate effectively in decisions on the national and, where appropriate, regional level concerning the minority to which they belong or the regions in which they live, in a manner not incompatible with national legislation'.[168] As a minimum, according to Asbjørn Eide, this includes the right to have their opinions heard and fully taken into account before decisions that concern them are adopted.[169] The Declaration further requires that policies and programmes are planned and implemented with 'due regard for the legitimate interests of persons belonging to minorities'.[170] The requirement for States to give 'due regard' to the interests of minorities requires, according to Eide, that their interests are given 'reasonable weight' compared with other legitimate interests that a government must take into consideration.[171]

There are a number of ways in which the democratic State may ensure the inclusion of the interests and preferences of persons belonging to minorities in decision-making processes. Which are best will depend on 'the political situation, on the nature of the structural cleavages of the polity, possible trade-offs with other political values, and the institutional context for representation'.[172] It is possible for the authorities to engage directly with members of national or ethnic, religious and linguistic groups, including indigenous peoples.[173] The Alaska Native Review Commission, for example, visited sixty villages and numerous fishing camps in rural Alaska, allowing 1,450 of the 60,000 Alaskan Native population to speak on relevant issues.[174] In most cases, the authorities will engage with representatives from the minority groups. According to

---

[167] *Ibid.*   [168] Article 2(3) of GA Res. 47/135, 'Declaration on the Rights of Minorities'.

[169] Asbjørn Eide, 'Commentary to the Declaration on the Rights of Persons Belonging to National or Ethnic, Religious and Linguistic Minorities', para. 42.

[170] Article 5(1) of GA Res. 47/135, 'Declaration on the Rights of Minorities'.

[171] Asbjørn Eide, 'Commentary to the Declaration on the Rights of Persons Belonging to National or Ethnic, Religious and Linguistic Minorities', para. 73.

[172] Iris Marion Young, *Inclusion and democracy* (Oxford: Oxford University Press, 2000), p. 149.

[173] See also Indigenous and Tribal Peoples Convention, 1989 (No. 169), adopted by the General Conference of the International Labour Organisation, 27 June 1989, in force 5 September 1991.

[174] John Dryzek, *Discursive democracy: politics, policy and political science* (Cambridge: Cambridge University Press, 1990), p. 127.

Eide, 'effective participation requires representation in legislative, administrative and advisory bodies and more generally in public life'.[175]

The rights of political participation of national minorities in Europe

Article 15 of the Framework Convention on National Minorities provides: 'The Parties shall create the conditions necessary for the effective participation of persons belonging to national minorities in cultural, social and economic life and in public affairs, in particular those affecting them.'[176] Public participation requires the inclusion of persons from national minorities in relevant decision-making processes, in particular where issues affecting the national minority are under consideration.[177] The Explanatory Report on the Framework Convention makes clear that no particular mechanism is envisaged by Article 15, but the principle of public/political participation must be given effect. Appropriate mechanisms range from consultation, in particular, through representative institutions, to the effective participation of persons belonging to national minorities in elected bodies, to decentralised or local forms of government.[178]

In a number of Opinions, the Advisory Committee on the Framework Convention has affirmed the importance of establishing formal advisory or consultative bodies as one mechanism by which the rights of political participation for national minorities may be given effect.[179] The

---

[175] Asbjørn Eide, 'Commentary to the Declaration on the Rights of Persons Belonging to National or Ethnic, Religious and Linguistic Minorities', para. 44. The Commentary on this provision draws extensively on the Lund Recommendations on the Effective Participation of National Minorities in Public Life (below).

[176] Article 15 of the Framework Convention for the Protection of National Minorities, adopted at Strasbourg, 1 February 1995, in force 1 February 1998, ETS No. 157.

[177] See generally J. A. Frowein and Roland Bank, 'The participation of minorities in decision-making processes', Council of Europe Doc. DH-MIN(2000)1 (2000).

[178] Explanatory Report on the Framework Convention on National Minorities, para. 80.

[179] See, for example, the following: 'in a number of countries in Europe, special representative bodies in the form of Councils of National Minorities have been successfully established to further the dialogue and to ensure the effective participation of persons belonging to national minorities': Opinion on Albania, ACFC/INF/OPI(2003)004, para. 69; '[the] Advisory Committee would hope ... that, for example, a consultative committee for minorities be created, to institutionalise the consultation between the Government and minority representatives': Opinion on Cyprus, ACFC/INF/OPI(2002)004, para. 42; 'bodies established by the Government to deal with minority issues ... are important from the perspective of the implementation of

Opinions of the Advisory Committee provide an important contribution to understanding how such bodies should operate. The scope of concern of these bodies should not be cast too narrowly. It should not be confined to cultural and educational issues.[180] Advisory or consultative bodies should be consulted 'on all issues specifically affecting minorities'.[181] Article 15 obliges States parties to create the conditions necessary for the effective participation of persons belonging to national minorities in public affairs, 'in particular those affecting them'.

All of the State's minorities must be represented on advisory or consultative bodies, or on a single body.[182] The advisory or consultative bodies must provide a 'permanent consultation structure':[183] 'occasional meetings and *ad hoc* consultations' are not sufficient.[184] They must meet regularly, in order to promote consultation and dialogue between the State and national minority groups.[185] Sufficient staff and other resources should be provided.[186] The Advisory Committee has suggested that a majority of participants on an advisory or consultative body should be from national minority groups.[187] It may be possible to hold elections to determine the representatives from national minority groups.[188] Where representatives are appointed by the State, the choice of minority representatives should not be controversial, and should not

Article 15 of the Framework Convention': Opinion on Romania, ACFC/INF/OPI(2002)001, para. 65; and national councils of national minorities, which participate in the decision-making in respect of official use of language, education, information in the language of the national minority and culture, 'may become a central tool in the implementation of Article 15 of the Framework Convention': Opinion on Serbia and Montenegro, ACFC/INF/OPI(2004)002, para. 107.

[180] Opinion on Moldova, ACFC/INF/OPI(2003)002, para. 88.

[181] Opinion on Romania, ACFC/INF/OPI(2002)001, para. 66.

[182] The Advisory Committee has commented on the importance of 'involving all national minorities, including the numerically smallest ones': Opinion on Norway, ACFC/INF/OPI(2003)003, para. 61.

[183] *Ibid.*   [184] Opinion on Sweden, ACFC/INF/OPI(2003)006, para. 64.

[185] The Advisory Committee noted that the Council of Representatives of Public Organisations of National Minorities in Ukraine 'is convened only rarely, and it does not constitute a forum for regular and frequent consultation and dialogue on issues pertaining to national minorities': Opinion on Ukraine, ACFC/INF/OPI(2002)010, para. 72. See also Opinion on Azerbaijan, ACFC/INF/OPI(2004)001, para. 73.

[186] Opinion on Czech Republic, ACFC/INF/OPI(2002)002, paras. 68–9.

[187] See Opinion on Slovakia, ACFC/INF/OPI(2001)001, para. 46. Cf. Opinion on Germany, ACFC/INF/OPI(2002)008, para. 65.

[188] The Finnish Sami Parliament, for example, has elected members: Opinion on Finland, ACFC/INF/OPI(2001)002, para. 50. See Kristian Myntii, 'The Nordic Sami Parliaments', in Pekka Aikio and Martin Scheinin (eds.), *Operationalizing the right of indigenous peoples to self-determination* (Turku: Institute for Human Rights, Åbo Akademi University, 2000), p. 203.

be contested by a majority of the group in question.[189] The representatives from national minority groups should not, though, be 'perceived as the sole and exclusive interlocutor of the authorities in minority questions'.[190] Advisory or consultative bodies must be open to representations from other interested parties, and other members of the national minority groups.[191] There is no single group perspective that can be represented by one individual, or group of individuals.

Advisory or consultative bodies provide a formal structure for consultation and deliberation between the State authorities and representatives of national minority groups. They should ensure the effective inclusion of the interests and preferences of persons belonging to national minorities in relevant decision-making processes; provide representatives of national minorities with the opportunity to contribute to the development of policies, and influence the outcomes of decision-making processes; and allow the State the opportunity to provide reasoned explanations to national minority representatives as to why particular policies, opposed by the group, have been introduced, or why proposals put forward by the group have not been accepted. In its report on Romania, the Advisory Committee noted that the views of the Council of National Minorities were sometimes disregarded without explanation by State agencies. The Advisory Committee concluded that the government should give 'reasons whenever the authorities do not accept its views'.[192]

In the Copenhagen Document, the participating States of the Organization for Security and Co-operation in Europe recognised that the 'questions relating to national minorities can only be satisfactorily resolved in a democratic political framework'.[193] They agreed to respect the right of persons belonging to national minorities to effective participation in public affairs, including participation in the affairs relating to the protection and promotion of the identity of such minorities.[194] The participating States committed themselves to protect the ethnic, cultural,

---

[189] See Gaetano Pentassuglia, 'Minority rights and the role of law: reflections on themes of discourse in Kymlicka's approach to ethnocultural identity' (2002) *Journal on Ethnopolitics and Minority Issues in Europe*, at www.ecmi.de/jemie/download/ Focus4-2002_Pentassuglia_Kymlicka.pdf (last visited 14 June 2005). In Austria, members of the advisory councils for national minorities are appointed by the government on the basis of proposals made by minorities' organisations, political parties and the churches. Opinion on Austria, ACFC/INF/OPI(2002)009, para. 68.

[190] Opinion on Serbia and Montenegro, ACFC/INF/OPI(2004)002, para. 109.

[191] See, for example, Opinion on Romania, ACFC/INF/OPI(2002)001, para. 67.

[192] Opinion on Romania, ACFC/INF/OPI(2002)001, para. 66.

[193] OSCE Copenhagen Document, para. 30.   [194] *Ibid.*, para. 35.

linguistic and religious identity of national minorities on their territory and to create conditions for the promotion of that identity, and agreed to take the necessary measures to that effect 'after due consultations, including contacts with organizations or associations of such minorities, in accordance with the decision-making procedures of each State'.[195]

An important contribution to the elaboration of OSCE commitments, in respect of national minorities and political participation, was provided with the adoption of the 'Lund Recommendations' on 'Effective Participation of National Minorities in Public Life', by a group of international experts. John Packer has argued that the Recommendations represent an 'authoritative interpretation of the relevant international standards' on political participation and minorities.[196] Recommendation 1 provides that 'in order to promote [political] participation, governments often need to establish specific arrangements for national minorities'.[197] Opportunities should exist for national minorities to have an 'effective voice' at the level of the central government.[198] This may require special representation for representatives of national minorities, for example through a reserved number of seats in parliament; formal or informal understandings for allocating cabinet posts, and other positions in government, to members of national minorities; mechanisms to ensure that minority interests are considered within relevant government departments; and special measures for minority participation in the civil service.[199] Additionally, the Recommendations argue that 'States should establish advisory or consultative bodies ... to serve as channels for dialogue between governmental authorities and national minorities'.[200]

---

[195] *Ibid.*, para. 33.

[196] John Packer, 'The origin and nature of the Lund Recommendations on the Effective Participation of National Minorities in Public Life' (2000) 11 *Helsinki Monitor* 29, 41.

[197] Recommendation 1, Lund Recommendations on the Effective Participation of National Minorities in Public Life (The Hague: Foundation on Inter-Ethnic Relations, 1999). The text of the Recommendations appears as an annex to Packer, 'The origin and nature of the Lund Recommendations'. See also www.osce.org/hcnm/documents/recommendations/lund/index.php3 (last visited 10 January 2005).

[198] Lund Recommendation 6.   [199] *Ibid.*

[200] Lund Recommendation 12. OSCE participating States have committed themselves to intensify their efforts to ensure the right of persons belonging to national minorities to participate fully in the political life of their countries 'including through democratic participation in decision-making and *consultative bodies* at the national, regional and local level, inter alia, through political parties and associations': Declaration and Decisions from Helsinki Summit (1992), 31 ILM (1992) 1385, Chapter IV, para. 24 (emphasis added).

These bodies should be able to raise issues with decision-makers, prepare recommendations, formulate legislative and other proposals, monitor developments and provide views on proposed governmental decisions that may directly or indirectly affect minorities. Governmental authorities should consult these bodies regularly regarding minority-related legislation and administrative measures in order to contribute to the satisfaction of minority concerns and to the building of confidence. The effective functioning of these bodies will require that they have adequate resources.[201]

The Explanatory Note to the Lund Recommendations considers that such bodies may be 'standing or ad hoc, part of or attached to the legislative or executive branch or independent therefrom'. In order for them to be effective, 'these bodies should be composed of minority representatives and others who can offer special expertise, provided with adequate resources, and given serious attention by decisionmakers'. Good governance 'requires positive steps on the part of the authorities to engage established advisory and consultative bodies, to refer to them as needs may arise and to invite their input'.[202]

Citizens belonging to national, ethnic, cultural, religious or linguistic minorities enjoy the same rights of political participation as all other citizens. Additionally, the right to cultural security (Article 27 of the International Covenant on Civil and Political Rights) requires that persons belonging to minorities are consulted on any proposal or measures that might impact on the right of the members of the group to enjoy their own culture, to profess and practise their own religion, or to use their own language. The experience in Europe suggests that the most effective mechanism for ensuring that the interests and preferences of persons from minority groups are included in relevant decision-making processes is the establishment of formal advisory or consultative bodies. The inclusion of persons from minority groups in decision-making processes will produce better, more informed, decisions. This should increase the legitimacy of legislative and other measures that emanate from law-making

---

[201] Lund Recommendation 13.
[202] Explanatory Note to the Lund Recommendations on the Effective Participation of National Minorities in Public Life. See also the Flensburg Proposals, adopted by a group of international experts, which call for decision-makers to 'proactively consult and seek input from those to be affected by public decisions, ... and create opportunities for effective contribution from such groups'. They, likewise, recommend the establishment of advisory or consultative bodies within appropriate institutional frameworks: Proposals of the European Centre for Minority Issues Seminar, 'Towards Effective Participation of Minorities', UN Doc. E/CN.4/Sub.2/AC.5/1999/WP.4, 5 May 1999, para. 12.

bodies from the perspective of persons belonging to minority groups.[203] The practice of democracy, in the contemporary age, recognises the importance of procedural inclusion.[204]

The limits of procedural inclusion

National or ethnic, religious and linguistic minorities are political minorities. Cultural conflicts concern political differences on 'questions of culture'. In a democracy, the majority/dominant ethno-cultural group will dictate the relevant convention. The fact of procedural inclusion is unlikely to alter the outcomes of decision-making processes. In deeply divided societies, political differences between ethno-cultural groups extend beyond questions of culture to encompass all political issues.[205] Differences between the groups are couched in the language of political argument.[206] Political debate is limited to bargaining over the distribution of public goods: public expenditure, employment opportunities, housing, etc., and a benefit to 'them' is considered a loss for 'us'. Democratic debate does not promote mutual understanding. It increases tensions, leading to the possibility of violent conflict.[207] In these circumstances, the application of majoritarian conceptions of democracy becomes highly problematic.[208] Majority rule assumes the possibility of oppositions becoming governments, and of shifting public opinions.[209] In a democracy, citizens find themselves in the majority on certain issues, but not on others. This creates 'cross pressures' from membership of different groups, leading to the adoption of moderate policies.

---

[203] Cf. Pippa Norris, 'Ballots not bullets: testing consociational theories of ethno conflict, electoral systems, and democratisation', in Reynolds (ed.), *The architecture of democracy*, p. 206, at p. 214.

[204] See Jürgen Habermas, *Between facts and norms: contributions to a discourse theory of law and democracy* (trans. William Rehg, Cambridge, MA: MIT Press, 1996), p. 303.

[205] Donald Horowitz, *Ethnic groups in conflict* (Berkeley: University of California Press, 1985), p. 8.

[206] Ian Lustick, 'Stability in deeply divided societies: consociationalism versus control' (1979) 31 *World Politics* 325, 325.

[207] Arend Lijphart, 'Consociational democracy' (1969) 21 *World Politics* 207, 220. See also Harry Anastasiou, 'Communication across conflict lines: the case of ethnically divided Cyprus' (2002) 39 *Journal of Peace Research* 581, 583.

[208] There are, according to Lijphart, no unambiguous cases of successful majoritarian democracy in deeply divided societies: Arend Lijphart, 'Definitions, evidence, and policy: a response to Matthijs Bogaards' critique' (2000) 12 *Journal of Theoretical Politics* 425, 428.

[209] Horowitz, *Ethnic groups in conflict*, p. 86.

Where the political culture is deeply divided, the pressures to moderate are absent.[210] Political parties representing the majority govern – permanently – in the interests of the majority. In response to the problem of majority rule in deeply divided societies, Arend Lijphart proposes the introduction of consociational, or power-sharing, democracy.[211]

Consociational democracy

There are four central features in a consociational democracy: a grand coalition (or power-sharing executive), proportionality in public life, a minority veto and segmental autonomy.[212] The consociational model may be applied generally within the State, or in a particular region.[213] A consociational arrangement was introduced for Bosnia and Herzegovina in the General Framework Agreement for Peace in Bosnia-Herzegovina (Dayton Peace Agreement).[214] The Agreement provides both that Bosnia and Herzegovina shall be a 'democratic state … with free and democratic elections',[215] and for the sharing of power between 'Bosniacs, Croats, and Serbs', as the 'constituent peoples'.[216]

---

[210] Lijphart, 'Consociational democracy', 208–9.

[211] See, for example, Lijphart, 'Consociational democracy'; Lijphart, 'Self-determination versus pre-determination of ethic minorities in power-sharing systems'; and Lijphart, 'The wave of power-sharing democracy', in Reynolds (ed.), *The architecture of democracy*, p. 37. The consociational model is only one model of power sharing, albeit the most influential. Timothy Sisk defines power sharing to include any practices and institutions that result in broad-based governing coalitions generally inclusive of all major ethnic groups in society: Timothy Sisk, *Power sharing and international mediation in ethnic conflicts* (Washington, DC: United States Institute of Peace, 1996), p. vii.

[212] Lijphart, 'Self-determination versus pre-determination of ethic minorities in power-sharing systems', p. 278.

[213] Examples include Dagestan (Russian Federation), Northern Ireland (United Kingdom) and South Tyrol (Italy).

[214] The General Framework Agreement for Peace in Bosnia-Herzegovina, 35 ILM (1996) 89. Pugh and Cobble describe the Accord as the 'awkward child of the marriage between the realities of power on the ground and the international ideal of a unitary multi-ethnic state': Michael Pugh and Margaret Cobble, 'Non-nationalist voting in Bosnian municipal elections: implications for democracy and peacebuilding' (2001) 38 *Journal of Peace Research* 27, 29. According to Patrice McMahon, whilst Bosnia and Herzegovina 'did not appear to meet even the minimum requirements for the success of [a consociational] arrangement, the concept was nonetheless exported and imposed on the country by the international community': Patrice McMahon, 'Rebuilding Bosnia: a model to emulate or to avoid?' (2004/5) 119 *Political Science Quarterly* 569, 585.

[215] Article I(2) of Annex 4, 'Constitution', to the General Framework Agreement for Peace in Bosnia-Herzegovina, *ibid*.

[216] Preamble, *ibid*. The Agreement also created the Office of the High Representative (Annex 10, 'Civilian Implementation of Peace Settlement'). The OHR has increasingly

A three-member Presidency is established, consisting of one Bosniac, one Croat and one Serb member. The strict proportionality requirement is applied to the parliament.[217] Each member of the Presidency, as well as representatives in the Parliamentary Assembly, can block legislation which they consider to be 'destructive of a vital interest' of their group.[218] The State of Bosnia and Herzegovina is divided into two largely autonomous entities: the Federation of Bosnia and Herzegovina (the Bosniac and Croat part of the State), and Republika Srpska (a Serb entity).[219] Central government enjoys defined and limited areas of competence, inter alia, in areas of foreign policy, monetary policy, immigration, and inter-entity issues, such as criminal law enforcement and transportation.[220] Most government functions are the responsibility of the two entities, thus providing the Serbs in Republika Srpska with a large degree of autonomy.[221]

The following sections examine the features of consociational democracy to consider the extent to which they are compatible with international law,[222] and consequently available to policy-makers concerned to enhance the political participation of persons belonging to minorities in democratic States. Relevant features include an insistence on a heterogeneous executive, proportionality in public life, autonomy arrangements, and procedural measures to protect minorities from the application of bare majority voting.

implemented a 'trusteeship model' of governance in Bosnia and Herzegovina: Patrice McMahon, 'Rebuilding Bosnia: a model to emulate or to avoid?' (2004/5) 119 *Political Science Quarterly* 569, 587.

[217] The upper House of Peoples comprises, specifically, 'five Croats', 'five Bosniacs' and 'five Serbs': Article IV(1). The three-member Presidency consists of 'one Bosniac and one Croat', directly elected from the territory of the Federation, and 'one Serb' directly elected from the territory of Republika Srpska: Article V(1). In Parliament, two-thirds of the forty-two members of the (lower) House of Representatives are elected from the territory of the Federation and the remaining one-third from Republika Srpska (Article IV(2)). Representatives for the (upper) House of Peoples, comprising five Croats, five Bosniacs and five Serbs are selected, respectively, by the Croat or Bosniac delegates to the House of Peoples of the Federation and the delegates of the National Assembly of the Republika Srpska: Article IV(4).

[218] Respectively, Article IV (Parliamentary Assembly) and Article V (Presidency).

[219] The war ended with Bosniac and Croat forces in alliance against the Serbs.

[220] Article III(1) of Annex 4, 'Constitution', to the General Framework Agreement for Peace in Bosnia-Herzegovina.

[221] Cf. Decision of the Constitutional Court of Bosnia and Herzegovina, U 5/98 III of 1 July 2000 (the 'Constituent Peoples Decision').

[222] On the question of the compatibility of consociational arrangements with international law, see David Wippman, 'Practical and legal constraints on internal power sharing', in David Wippman (ed.), *International law and ethnic conflict* (Ithaca: Cornell University Press, 1998), p. 211.

Power-sharing executives

The central feature of a consociational democracy is the sharing of power by all significant groups within the polity.[223] Coalition governments are common where the State is faced with external threats, at times of war, for example. It follows, according to Arend Lijphart, that a government of national unity is 'the appropriate response to the internal crisis of fragmentation into hostile subcultures'.[224] A consociational agreement can spell out in advance those groups that are to share power.[225] The 1960 Cyprus Constitution is an example of such a 'pre-determined' consociation.[226] The Constitution provided for a Greek Cypriot President and a Turkish Cypriot Vice-President, elected, respectively, by the Greek and Turkish communities,[227] and an appointed Council of Ministers comprising seven Greek Cypriot and three Turkish Cypriot members.[228] The elected unicameral legislature was to have fifty members: thirty-five elected by the Greek community and fifteen by the Turkish community.[229]

Pre-determined consociational arrangements are not compatible with the human rights of political participation,[230] in particular when taken with the non-discrimination norm.[231] A constitutional requirement that the holder of a given political office be a member of a certain national, ethnic, cultural, religious or linguistic group is an act of direct discrimination, prohibited by international human rights instruments.[232] A State constitution may require that a plurality of identities

---

[223] Lijphart, 'The wave of power-sharing democracy', p. 39.

[224] Lijphart, 'Consociational democracy', 215. One such example is the 'Government of National Unity' in the Former Yugoslav Republic of Macedonia established in 2001: see, Farimah Daftary, 'Conflict resolution in FYR Macedonia: power-sharing or "civic approach"' (2001) 12 *Helsinki Monitor* 291, 297.

[225] Lijphart, 'Self-determination versus pre-determination of ethnic minorities in power-sharing systems', p. 280.

[226] *Ibid.*, 283. See also Jon Fraenkel, 'Minority rights in Fiji and the Solomon Islands', UN Doc. E/CN.4/Sub.2/AC.5/2003/WP.5, 5 May 2003.

[227] Article 1 of the Constitution of Cyprus 1960.   [228] Article 54, *ibid.*

[229] Article 61, *ibid.* Shortly after the founding of the Republic, serious differences arose between the two communities about the implementation and interpretation of the Constitution: see, Thomas Musgrave, *Self-determination and minorities* (Oxford: Oxford University Press, 2000), pp. 225–6.

[230] Article 25 of the International Covenant on Civil and Political Rights.

[231] Articles 2(1) and 26, *ibid.*

[232] Persons may not be excluded from the rights of political participation on 'unreasonable or discriminatory' criteria such as 'descent': Human Rights Committee, General Comment No. 25, 'Article 25 (Participation in public affairs and the right to vote)', para. 15.

be represented in the executive, but it cannot specify that the President or the Prime Minister should be a member of a particular group. Moreover, pre-determined consociational arrangements require 'invidious comparisons and discriminatory choices' in deciding which groups are allowed to participate, and which not (Lijphart's words).[233] They often exclude smaller minorities.[234] This is not compatible with the right of all citizens to political equality.[235]

In preference to pre-determined arrangements, Lijphart identifies a model of 'self-determined' consociational government.[236] The outcome of any election in a deeply divided society may be a coalition government involving parties representing the interests of all significant ethno-cultural groups. In the practice of democracy, this is unlikely, in the absence of external pressures.[237] The creation of multi-ethnic coalitions requires that political parties representing the majority see greater common cause with parties representing the minority than with other parties representing the majority group. In deeply divided societies, political accommodation with 'Others' is likely to result in electoral losses, and the defection of supporters to more extreme political parties (those opposing any form of accommodation). Given that voters will not switch their support to political parties representing the interests of other ethnic groups, the imperative is for political parties to consolidate their core vote.[238] The only coherent political idea likely to find general support is the promotion of their group, and most likely the denigration of other groups. In the practice of consociational democracy, there is a logic of political extremism, making the emergence of a self-determined

---

[233] Lijphart, 'Self-determination versus pre-determination of ethnic minorities in power-sharing systems', 284–6.

[234] The Roma of Bosnia and Herzegovina do not appear in the General Framework Agreement for Peace in Bosnia-Herzegovina.

[235] The Human Rights Committee has noted 'with concern that every Lebanese citizen must belong to one of the religious denominations officially recognized by the Government, and that this is a requirement in order to be eligible to run for public office. This practice *does not comply* with the requirements of Article 25 of the Covenant': Human Rights Committee, Concluding Observations on Lebanon, UN Doc. CCPR/C/79/Add.78, 1 April 1997, para. 23.

[236] Lijphart, 'Self-determination versus pre-determination of ethnic minorities in power-sharing systems', 281–2.

[237] See, for example, Martin Brusis, 'The European Union and interethnic power-sharing arrangements in accession countries' (2003) *Journal on Ethnopolitics and Minority Issues in Europe*, at www.ecmi.de/jemie/download/Focus1-2003_Brusis.pdf (last visited 14 June 2005).

[238] Horowitz, *Ethnic groups in conflict*, p. 318.

consociational arrangement unlikely, and, where they do emerge, highly unstable. Successful consociational government, one which avoids serious violence,[239] requires the existence of a cartel of political leaders committed to the survival of the polity through a series of bargaining and compromise.[240] At the same time those political leaders must ensure that they maintain the support of members of their own ethnic group.[241] These contradictory and conflicting requirements make consociational democracies highly unstable in practice.[242]

A constitutional arrangement may exclude the possibility of a homogenous executive, composed exclusively by persons belonging to the dominant/majority group. The right of peoples to self-determination requires representative government. Under the Dayton Peace Agreement, no more than two-thirds of all ministers in Bosnia and Herzegovina may be appointed from the territory of the Federation, ensuring that one-third of ministerial posts will go to Serbs.[243] A more sophisticated arrangement exists in Northern Ireland (at the time of writing, devolved government in Northern Ireland is suspended).[244] The Agreement Reached in the Multi-Party Negotiations avoids direct

[239] Lijphart, 'The wave of power-sharing democracy', 41–2.
[240] Ian Lustick, 'Stability in deeply divided societies: consociationalism versus control' (1979) 31 *World Politics* 325, 328.
[241] Lijphart, 'Consociational democracy', 221. Michael Hudson has described consociationalism as 'government by a cartel of ethnosectarian elites, which can manage their respective "flocks" and get along with each other': Michael Hudson, 'Trying again: power-sharing in post-civil war Lebanon' (1997) 2 *International Negotiation* 103, 105.
[242] See Arend Lijphart, 'The puzzle of Indian democracy: a consociational interpretation' (1996) 90 *American Political Science Review* 258, 263: 'pleasing other elites will tend to displease their own supporters, and vice versa'. Joseph Ruane and Jennifer Todd have described the Agreement Reached in the Multi-Party Negotiations (below) as resting on contradictory foundations and inherently unstable: 'The politics of transition? Explaining political crises in the implementation of the Belfast Good Friday Agreement' (2001) 49 *Political Studies* 923, 938.
[243] Article V(4)(b) of Annex 4, 'Constitution' to the General Framework Agreement for Peace in Bosnia-Herzegovina, 35 ILM (1996) 89. See also the Arusha Peace and Reconciliation Agreement for Burundi, adopted 28 August 2000, Protocol II: Democracy and Good Governance, Article 15(12) (below); and the 1994 Constitution of the Russian Federation Republic of Dagestan: see, Robert Bruce Ware and Enver Kisriev, 'Ethnic parity and democratic pluralism in Dagestan: a consociational approach' (2001) 53 *Europe–Asia Studies* 105, 111–12.
[244] On the Agreement Reached in the Multi-Party Negotiations and consociationalism, see Brendan O'Leary, 'The nature of the Agreement' (1999) 22 *Fordham International Law Journal* 1628; and Brendan O'Leary, 'The protection of human rights under the Belfast Agreement' (2001) 72 *Political Quarterly* 353.

reference to ethno-cultural identity in the establishment of the power-sharing executive. The executive comprises a First Minister and a Deputy First Minister, and an inclusive executive committee comprising up to ten ministers with departmental responsibilities, filled by the d'Hondt proportional allocation mechanism.[245] Candidates for the office of First Minister and Deputy First Minister must stand jointly, and be elected by an absolute majority of members of the legislative assembly, and by a majority of the designated nationalists voting and a majority of the designated unionists.[246] The rule effectively guarantees that one member from each community will be elected. Brendan O'Leary has described this as a 'coalition government without a coalition agreement'.[247] The d'Hondt system of allocating executive seats is designed to favour the main, ethnically based, political parties.[248] The system produces an executive that is representative of the two communities (but not other interests).

In a democratic society, governments emerge from an electoral process that constitutes an expression of the 'will of the people'. The State may facilitate a more representative executive through its choice of electoral system, or constitutional rules on the allocation of cabinet seats. The idea of democracy does not allow for political leaders to decide in advance who will share power.[249] Consociational democracy is not compatible with the human right to democracy recognised in the Universal Declaration of Human Rights[250] and in the International Covenant on

---

[245] Agreement Reached in the Multi-Party Negotiations, Belfast, 10 April 1998, 37 ILM (1998) 751, 'Strand One: Democratic Institutions in Northern Ireland', paras. 15 and 16. See also section 18 of the Northern Ireland Act 1998, 39 ILM (2000) 927.

[246] Section 16(2) of the Northern Ireland Act 1998. See Agreement Reached in the Multi-Party Negotiations, Belfast, 'Strand One: Democratic Institutions in Northern Ireland', para. 15. There is no obligation for representatives in the Legislative Assembly to designate themselves.

[247] Brendan O'Leary, 'The nature of the Agreement', 1633. Cf. Colin Harvey, 'The politics of rights and deliberative democracy: the process of drafting a Northern Irish bill of rights' (2001) 1 European Human Rights Law Review 48, 54: 'My argument is that the Agreement reflects a strong commitment to participation and thus the realisation of the rights and other political values which make effective engagement possible. If the Agreement has a nature (and this is open to some debate) then it is a mixture of consociational and deliberative democracy.'

[248] Brian Thompson, 'Transcending territory: towards an agreed Northern Ireland?' (1999) 6 International Journal on Minority and Group Rights 235, 254.

[249] Cf. Lijphart, 'Consociational democracy', 214.

[250] Article 21(3) of the Universal Declaration of Human Rights: 'The will of the people shall be the basis of the authority of government; this will shall be expressed in periodic and genuine elections.'

Civil and Political Rights.[251] Power-sharing is appropriate only in the initial transition from conflict to democracy.[252] Consociational democracy can only be justified by reference to ideas of transitional justice: the conception of justice that emerges in periods of transition 'is contextualized and partial: What is deemed just is contingent and informed by prior injustice.'[253] Justice, in the transitional period, demands that a minority systematically excluded from public life is recognised as having a right to share power in the process of democratisation.[254]

Proportionality in public life

Proportionality in public life has two aspects: the proportionate allocation of public goods, including public funding and employment in the public or State sectors, and proportionality in political representation. Any policy that deliberately favours one part of the population in the allocation of public goods, without reasonable and objective criteria, is contrary to the international norm prohibiting discrimination on grounds of 'race, colour, descent, or national or ethnic origin'.[255] The right of access to employment in the public sector is protected by Article 25 of the International Covenant on Civil and Political Rights.[256] The right is to be enjoyed 'without distinction of any kind, such as race, colour, sex, language, religion, political or other opinion, national or social origin, property, birth or other status'.[257] Article 25 protects citizens from their removal from employment in the public sector, without good reason.[258] Ethnic, linguistic or religious identity does not constitute a good reason.

[251] Article 25 of the International Covenant on Civil and Political Rights: Every citizen shall have the right and the opportunity, without distinction: (a) to take part in the conduct of public affairs, directly or through freely chosen representatives; and (b) to vote and to be elected at genuine periodic elections which shall be by universal and equal suffrage.

[252] Timothy Sisk explains: 'power sharing may be appropriate as a transitional, confidence-building mechanism but not as a permanent solution to ethnic conflict management through democratic institutions': Sisk, *Power sharing and international mediation in ethnic conflicts*, p. 116.

[253] Ruti Teitel, *Transitional justice* (Oxford: Oxford University Press, 2000), p. 6.

[254] For majorities systematically excluded from public life, the application of the 'one person, one vote' principle will remedy the previous injustice.

[255] See Article 1(1) of the International Convention on the Elimination of All Forms of Racial Discrimination.

[256] *Karakurt* v. *Austria*, Communication No. 965/2000, UN Doc. CCPR/C/74/D/965/2000, 29 April 2002, para. 8.2.

[257] Article 25 of the International Covenant on Civil and Political Rights, taken with Article 2(1).

[258] *Vargas-Machuca* v. *Peru*, Communication No. 906/2000, UN Doc. CCPR/C/75/D/906/2000, 26 July 2002.

In deeply divided societies, the exclusion of minority groups from public life may be particularly marked, and the need to facilitate a more representative civil service and public sector particularly important. Measures of positive discrimination, to remedy the consequences of past discrimination, for example by reserving positions in the civil service or the wider public/State sector, are often controversial, but they are not contrary to the non-discrimination principle.[259] The application of strict proportionality rules, or quotas, in consociational arrangements is unusual.[260] In most cases, multi-ethnic constitutional arrangements agree on the objective of equitable representation,[261] and/or specify the measures necessary to promote a more representative public sector.[262] In a post-conflict context, there may be a need to ensure that the mechanisms of domination, the police and the military, are not filled exclusively by one section of the population. In Burundi, the Tutsi minority exercised control over the majority Hutu population largely through the military. The Arusha Peace and Reconciliation Agreement contains an interim provision which provides that not more than 50 per cent of the national defence force can be drawn from any one ethnic group. The measure is specifically designed to prevent future acts of genocide, and the possibility of a military *coup d'état*.[263]

There are a number of practical difficulties in ensuring equitable representation for minorities in public appointments. A further complication is added to the issue of proportionality in political

[259] See Article 8(3) of GA Res. 47/135, adopted 18 December 1992, 'Declaration on the Rights of Persons belonging to National or Ethnic, Religious and Linguistic Minorities'; also Article 1(4) of the International Convention on the Elimination of All Forms of Racial Discrimination.

[260] See, for example, the power-sharing agreement in South Tyrol. The Advisory Committee on the Framework Convention has noted that 'the system of allocating posts strictly according to the size of the Italian-speaking, German-speaking and Ladin communities, has helped to make the participation of these minorities more effective, since each group's representation in the civil service now approximates to its demographic profile': Advisory Committee on the Framework Convention, Opinion on Italy, ACFC/INF/OPI(2002)007, para. 66.

[261] See, for example, para. 4 of the Framework Agreement (Macedonia), 13 August 2001, www.president.gov.mk/prilozi/dokumenti/180/FRAMEWORK%20AGREEMENT.pdf (last visited 10 January 2005).

[262] See, for example, Agreement Reached in the Multi-Party Negotiations, 'Rights, Safeguards and Equality of Opportunity', para. 3. Introduced, in a slightly modified form, in section 75(1) of the Northern Ireland Act 1998.

[263] Arusha Peace and Reconciliation Agreement for Burundi, adopted 28 August 2000, Protocol II: Democracy and Good Governance, Article 11(4)(d) (below).

representation: the democratic exercise. It is not possible to dictate to the electorate whom they should elect. One possibility is to divide the electorate along 'ethnic' lines, and allow the members of each group to elect their own representatives.[264] The use of 'communal rolls' requires that each citizen be allocated to one or other electoral roll on the basis of their ethnic identity.[265] This position is not compatible with the international instruments concerning the rights of persons belonging to minorities. Membership of a minority group is a matter of individual choice.[266] Additionally, the use of communal rolls will deny the right to vote to those citizens who refuse to be allocated to one or other ethnic identity, and those citizens whose ethnic identity is not recognised in the electoral system. Where an individual is denied the right to vote because they are not allocated, or refuse to be allocated, this will constitute a violation of their rights to political participation without discrimination. States enjoy a wide margin of discretion in establishing rules concerning the conduct of elections to national parliaments, but these rules may not have the effect of excluding citizens who would otherwise be eligible to vote from the rights of political participation.[267] The use of communal rolls for voting in general elections is not compatible with the rights of political participation, which are to be enjoyed without discrimination.

Ensuring proportionality in political representation in most plural democracies is problematic. In deeply divided societies, however, the outcomes of elections are highly predictable. Each ethno-cultural group

---

[264] The electoral system in the Russian Republic of Dagestan relies on communal candidates. Thus, for example, in an 'Avar district', only a candidate from the Avar community can stand for election, although voters of all national groups may select from amongst any number of Avar candidates. See Ware and Kisriev, 'Ethnic parity and democratic pluralism in Dagestan', 113. The system is not compatible with the right to political participation without discrimination. See Advisory Committee on the Framework Convention, Opinion on Russian Federation, ACFC/INF/OPI(2003)005, para. 104.

[265] Communal representation was the cornerstone of the British colonial system. At independence, most former colonies abolished the system of separate representation, the outstanding exceptions being Fiji and Cyprus. See Yash Ghai, 'Constitutional asymmetries: communal representation, federalism and cultural autonomy', in Reynolds (ed.), *The architecture of democracy*, p. 141, at p. 145. See also Vernon van Dyke, 'The individual, the State and ethnic communities in political theory' (1977) 29 *World Politics* 343, 352.

[266] See, for example, Article 3(2) of GA Res. 47/135, adopted 18 December 1992, 'Declaration on the Rights of Persons belonging to National or Ethnic, Religious and Linguistic Minorities'.

[267] See, for example, *Aziz* v. *Cyprus*, App. No. 69949/01, judgment 22 June 2004, para. 28.

will have its own political party,[268] whose primary function is to represent the interests of its members (and not 'Others').[269] Elections are less of a measure of the popular will than a 'census of the population'.[270] Provided that relatively pure systems of proportional representation are employed, the composition of the legislative assembly will reflect that of the wider society. The system of elections to the Northern Ireland Legislative Assembly relies on a relatively pure system of proportional representation. The 2001 census reported that the population was 53 per cent Protestant and 44 per cent Catholic. Elections to the Legislative Assembly in November 2003 returned 55 per cent of the Members of the Legislative Assembly from Protestant/unionist political parties, and 39 per cent from Catholic/nationalist parties.[271] The under-representation of Catholics/nationalists can, in part, be explained by demographic factors, given that a greater proportion of Catholics are of non-voting age.

Minority veto

The third feature of Arend Lijphart's consociational model is the minority veto, a measure designed to protect minority communities from the application of laws with majority support. The minority veto may be recognised in the form of a constitutional convention or a legally guaranteed right to reject a decision or proposal made by a law-making body.[272] It is, according to Lijphart, the 'ultimate weapon' required by minorities, because, even when their vital interests are at stake, the majority group can outvote them.[273]

The minority veto applies only to those issues which are vital to the interests of the minority. In a deeply divided polity, where most issues will have a political dimension, it will not always be clear which issues should be designated as 'vital'. Self-designation ensures that all issues

---

[268] Or more usually political parties.

[269] Arend Lijphart, 'Self-determination versus pre-determination of ethnic minorities in power-sharing systems', in Will Kymlicka (ed.), *The rights of minority cultures* (Oxford: Oxford University Press, 1995), p. 275, at p. 276.

[270] Horowitz, *Ethnic groups in conflict*, p. 86.

[271] In the June 1998 election, the respective figures were 54 per cent (Protestant/unionist) and 39 per cent (Catholic/nationalist).

[272] The veto, according to Arend Lijphart, usually consists of 'merely an informal understanding that minorities can effectively protect their autonomy by blocking any attempts to eliminate or reduce it': Arend Lijphart, 'The puzzle of Indian democracy: a consociational interpretation' (1996) 90 *American Political Science Review* 258, 261.

[273] Lijphart, 'Self-determination versus pre-determination of ethnic minorities in power-sharing systems', 278.

which the minority regards as vital will be designated. A dissenting member of the three-member Presidency of Bosnia and Herzegovina may declare a decision to be 'destructive of a vital interest of the Entity from the territory from which he was elected'.[274] In Northern Ireland, 'key decisions', those that must be taken on a cross-community basis, may be designated as such by a vote of just 30 of the 108 Members of the Legislative Assembly.[275] Self-designation has the benefit of protecting minorities from a failure to designate important issues as vital, but it does allow the possibility that a minority group might unjustifiably bargain hard for preferential treatment in the knowledge that no decision can be reached without its support.

An alternative to self-designation is to delimit 'vital' issues in advance. The Framework Agreement concerning the government of Macedonia provides that 'a majority of the votes of Representatives claiming to belong to the communities not in the majority in the population of Macedonia' are required for the adoption of Constitutional amendments and in respect of laws concerning culture, language and education.[276] Where there is a dispute as to whether an issue does in fact concern the cultural security of the group, the question is referred to a Committee on Inter-Community Relations for resolution.[277] The Committee consists of seven members chosen from amongst the Macedonian representatives, seven from amongst the

---

[274] Article V(2)(d) of Annex 4, 'Constitution', to the General Framework Agreement for Peace in Bosnia-Herzegovina, 35 ILM (1996) 89. If this declaration is supported by two-thirds of the National Assembly of the Republika Srpska (if the declaration was made by the member from that territory), or of the Bosniac Delegates of the House of Peoples of the Federation (if made by the Bosniac member), or two-thirds of the Croat Delegates of that body (where made by the Croat member), then the challenged Presidency decision does not take effect. See also the veto powers of members of the Parliamentary Assembly: Article IV(3)(e), *ibid*.

[275] Agreement Reached in the Multi-Party Negotiations, Belfast, 10 April 1998, 37 ILM (1998) 751, 'Strand One: Democratic Institutions in Northern Ireland', para. 5(d).

[276] Paras. 5.1 and 5.2 of the Framework Agreement (Macedonia). The Definitive (Final) Constitution for Burundi adopted under the Arusha Agreement provides that constitutional amendments will require the support of a four-fifths majority in the Burundi National Assembly, and a two-thirds majority in the Senate: Arusha Peace and Reconciliation Agreement for Burundi, adopted 28 August 2000, Protocol II: Democracy and Good Governance, Article 6(5). It is estimated that the electoral system will yield a National Assembly in which over 38 per cent of the representatives come from minority groups; and the Senate will have (roughly) equal numbers of Hutu and Tutsi members (see below).

[277] Article 69(2) (revised) of the Constitution: Framework Agreement (Macedonia).

Albanian representatives, and five from amongst the Turks, Vlachs, Romanies and two other communities.[278]

There is no basis to recognise a right of veto for the majority ethnocultural group. So-called 'mutual vetoes' require that we conceive of democracy as an accommodation between homogenous and cohesive sub-groups, and politics as the process by which elites conclude bargains as to the distribution of public goods. In Northern Ireland, 'key decisions' require either 'parallel consent', an overall majority within the legislature and a majority of the unionist and nationalist designations present and voting, or a 'weighted majority', 60 per cent voting in favour, with at least 40 per cent of each of the nationalist and unionist designations present and voting.[279] Representatives from the majority unionist community have an effective right of veto. They will only invoke this right where majority support exists for a particular legislative proposal – in an Assembly in which they constitute the majority. Just over half of the representatives of the unionist community can veto any measure or initiative, even where it has the support of the remaining unionist representatives and all the representatives of the nationalist community and all others.

The problem of plurality is mirrored in the minority community: a bare majority of the representatives from the minority nationalist group may veto legislative initiatives. The justification for recognising a right of veto for minority groups is more compelling: it is possible for measures to be adopted (with majority support) where there is a consensus amongst the representatives from the minority group that the measure is destructive to its vital interests. Minority opposition to policy proposals exists because members of the group have not been persuaded by the merits of the policy, at least not as they concern the group. There is a deficit of democratic deliberation. In a number of consociational arrangements, the minority veto operates to require further deliberation. In Bosnia and Herzegovina, the dissent of a member of the Presidency leads to further discussion on the relevant issue in either the National Assembly of the Republika Srpska or in the House of Peoples of the Federation.[280] Proposed decisions of the Parliamentary Assembly may be declared to be 'destructive of a vital interest' of one

---

[278] Article 78, *ibid.*

[279] Agreement Reached in the Multi-Party Negotiations, 'Strand One: Democratic Institutions in Northern Ireland', para. 5(d).

[280] Article V(2)(d) of Annex 4, 'Constitution', to the General Framework Agreement for Peace in Bosnia-Herzegovina.

of the groups represented in the House of Peoples (Serbs, Croats and Bosniacs) by as few as two of the fifteen Delegates.[281] When this determination is made, it may be objected to by a majority of one or more of the Delegates from other groups. The Chair of the House of Peoples is then required to convene a commission comprising three Delegates, one from each of the recognised groups, to resolve the issue. If they fail to do so within five days, the matter is referred to the Constitutional Court.[282]

Further discussion might produce a change in the position of one or more of the participants to the democratic debate, or may elucidate a new position acceptable to all parties. There is no guarantee, however, that it will result in an outcome that is more favourable, or satisfactory, to the representatives from minority groups. There comes a point when democratic institutions must make decisions, and where they do they rely on the principle of majority rule. This ensures that the government is not paralysed, or subject to undue and unjustified influence by a minority of representatives. The application of majority rule is a procedural device that allows decisions to be made. There is no reason why a legislative body could not decide to adopt measures by consensus.[283] In many democracies, majorities in excess of 50 per cent plus one are required where constitutional amendments are proposed (both in legislative assemblies and in plebiscites). In deeply divided polities, there is no reason why issues concerning cultural security, identified by bodies with appropriate minority representation, should not require majorities in excess of a bare majority. The particular majority can be set at a level to require the support of a reasonable section of the minority group.

---

[281] Article IV(3)(e), taken with Article IV(1)(b), *ibid*.

[282] Article IV(3)(f), *ibid*. See also the 1972 South Tyrol Autonomy Statute.

[283] The Polish Diet, from 1652 until 1791, was characterised by the *Liberum Veto*, under which the dissent of one deputy could paralyse proceedings. The aim was to ensure consensus for proposed measures. The procedure was undermined by deputies with corrupt motives for its use. See Joseph Jaconelli, 'Majority rule and special majorities' (1989) *Public Law* 587, 590. Under Article 81 of the Dagestan Constitution, the objection of a single dissenting representative to the People's Assembly can block the passage of any legislation that significantly affects the member's ethnic group. The determination requires an override of a two-thirds majority. See Ware and Kisriev, 'Ethnic parity and democratic pluralism in Dagestan', 118–19. This is not a de facto veto (the largest group in Dagestan, the Avars, constitute 25 per cent of the population), but a super-majority, requiring higher levels of support, where the interests of a minority group are at stake.

Autonomy

The consociational model of democracy provides one institutional response to the problem of majority rule in deeply divided polities. Minority groups are guaranteed a share of power at the level of the central government through participation in the executive (power sharing) and the legislature (proportionality in public life), and through the provision of a veto on measures that threaten their vital interests. The consociational model further provides for authority to be devolved to minority groups through the introduction of autonomy regimes. According to Arend Lijphart, autonomy, or self-government, may be exercised on a territorial or cultural basis.[284] Cultural autonomy concerns the devolution of power to a group over an aspect of state policy, but within a territory over which the minority group does not enjoy legislative or regulatory autonomy.[285] Territorial autonomy involves the devolution of authority to a district or region in which the minority group forms the majority.[286] The issue of territorial autonomy is considered in chapter 2. Suffice it to say that there are no principled objections to the introduction of territorial autonomy as a mechanism for accommodating diversity within a divided polity.

Cultural autonomy concerns the devolution of authority to a minority group over an aspect of State policy, for example education, providing an opportunity for 'self-government' by the group in relation to the issue in question. Karl Renner first proposed the idea of cultural autonomy in the early part of the twentieth century. Renner sought to develop a mechanism by which non-territorial groups could enjoy autonomy in areas such as education, whilst at the same time participating in the overall decision-making processes of the State.[287] Bodies elected by the minorities themselves would regulate social and cultural life, whilst matters concerning more than one group would fall under

---

[284] Lijphart, 'Self-determination versus pre-determination of ethnic minorities in power-sharing systems', 278.

[285] See Hurst Hannum and Richard Lillich, 'The concept of autonomy in international law' (1980) 74 *American Journal of International Law* 858, 883.

[286] The General Framework Agreement for Peace in Bosnia-Herzegovina (Dayton Peace Agreement) provides the Serbs in Republika Srpska with a high degree of territorial autonomy on domestic issues within Bosnia and Herzegovina: Article III(1) of Annex 4, 'Constitution', to the General Framework Agreement for Peace in Bosnia-Herzegovina.

[287] Karl Renner, *Das Selbstbestimmungsrecht der Nationen in Besonderer Anwendung auf Östereich* (1918), referred to in Lapidoth, *Autonomy*, p. 39.

the responsibility of common State institutions.[288] The objective of the scheme was to localise ethno-cultural issues, in order to ensure that political parties based on class or ideology would contest national politics.[289]

Past examples of cultural autonomy include the *millet* system of the Ottoman Empire,[290] and the inter-war Estonian regime of cultural autonomy, under which certain minorities enjoyed the rights to establish their own schools and cultural institutions, governed by elected councils with law-making and tax-raising powers.[291] Contemporary examples include the Estonian Law on Cultural Autonomy for National Minorities 1993, and the Hungarian 1993 Act LXXVII 'On the Rights of National and Ethnic Minorities'.[292] Additionally, a number of States recognise the authority of religious courts in family law matters,[293] or require that ordinary courts take into account the religious identity of parties to legal proceedings.[294] In a number of States, local or traditional leaders are able to adjudicate civil claims arising under customary law and to try minor criminal offences under common and customary law.[295]

The devolution of authority over policies to associations representing the interests of persons belonging to national or ethnic, religious and

---

[288] Thomas Franck, *The empowered self: law and society in the age of individualism* (Oxford: Oxford University Press, 2001), p. 247.

[289] Andrea Krizsán, 'The Hungarian minority protection system: a flexible approach to the adjudication of ethnic claims' (2000) 26 *Journal of Ethnic and Migration Studies* 247, 250 (reference omitted).

[290] *Millets* were responsible for education, enjoyed the right to levy taxes on members and to adjudicate in disputes between them. The head of the *millet* was chosen by the community, albeit confirmed by the sultan: Michael Hechter, *Containing nationalism* (Oxford: Oxford University Press, 2000), p. 72.

[291] Lapidoth, *Autonomy*, pp. 93 ff.

[292] Krizsán, 'The Hungarian minority protection system', 253. See also Kristian Myntti, 'The Nordic Sami Parliaments', in Pekka Aikio and Martin Scheinin (eds.), *Operationalizing the right of indigenous peoples to self-determination* (Turku: Institute for Human Rights, Åbo Akademi University, 2000), p. 203.

[293] See Yash Ghai, 'Constitutional asymmetries: communal representation, federalism and cultural autonomy' in Andrew Reynolds (ed.), *The architecture of democracy: constitutional design, conflict management and democracy* (Oxford: Oxford University Press, 2002), p. 141, at pp. 164–6.

[294] In India, the application of certain 'personal laws', in the area of family law, depends on the individual's religion: see, Duncan Derrett, *Religion, law and the state in India* (Delhi: Oxford University Press, 1999), p. 39. See also Lijphart, 'The puzzle of Indian democracy', 260.

[295] See, for example, N. Olivier *et al.*, *Indigenous law* (Durban: Butterworths, 1995), pp. 100–4.

linguistic minorities is not problematic. Most democratic States devolve responsibility for deciding policy issues to expert bodies (arts councils being one example). What is not permitted is the devolution of authority over persons. The issue was addressed by the European Court of Human Rights in *Refah Partisi and Others* v. *Turkey*. The Refah Partisi (Welfare Party) was proscribed, in part, because its political platform included proposals for the introduction of an extensive form of cultural autonomy for the Islamic population of Turkey. A plurality of legal systems would have been established, with each individual required to choose the religious movement to which they wished to belong. They would then be subject to the rights and obligations incumbent on members of the particular religious community. Each religious movement would be able to set up its own courts, with the ordinary courts obliged to apply the law according to the religion of those appearing before them.[296] The decision of the Grand Chamber of the European Court of Human Rights confirmed the earlier Chamber decision, that the establishment of a plurality of legal systems, as proposed by the Refah Partisi, was not compatible with the Convention system.[297] The Grand Chamber quoted the following passage from the chamber judgment:

70. ... the Court considers that Refah's proposal that there should be a plurality of legal systems would introduce into all legal relationships a distinction between individuals grounded on religion, would categorise everyone according to his religious beliefs and would allow him rights and freedoms not as an individual but according to his allegiance to a religious movement.

The Court takes the view that such a societal model cannot be considered compatible with the Convention system, for two reasons.

Firstly, it would do away with the State's role as the guarantor of individual rights and freedoms and the impartial organiser of the practice of the various beliefs and religions in a democratic society, since it would oblige individuals to obey, not rules laid down by the State in the exercise of its above-mentioned functions, but static rules of law imposed by the religion concerned ...

Secondly, such a system would undeniably infringe the principle of non-discrimination between individuals as regards their enjoyment of public freedoms, which is one of the fundamental principles of democracy. A difference in treatment between individuals in all fields of public and private law according to their religion or beliefs manifestly cannot be justified under the Convention.[298]

---

[296] See *Refah Partisi and Others* v. *Turkey*, App. Nos. 41340/98 and 41342–4/98, judgment 31 July 2001, para. 69.

[297] *Case of Refah Partisi (The Welfare Party) and Others* v. *Turkey*, Reports of Judgments and Decisions 2003-II, para. 119.

[298] *Ibid.* (references omitted).

Self-government may be recognised for persons belonging to minorities (individual autonomy and exemption rights) and for minority groups in certain policy areas, notably in relation to education and language policies. Moreover, persons belonging to minorities may accept the authority of other individuals within the group as a form of alternative dispute resolution. Self-government may not be recognised for minority groups in relation to the putative 'members' of the group: in the age of the territorial State, authority may only be devolved over persons in respect of territory in the form of central, regional and local government.

Integrating diversity

The conflict in Bosnia and Herzegovina has been explained in terms of 'primordialism': the idea that ethnic hatred is embedded deeply within the history and culture of the Balkans.[299] Kenneth Anderson has referred to the idea that the war in the former Yugoslavia was 'nothing less than the massive, geological conjunction of pre-modern ethnic hatreds unleashed when modernist institutions failed'.[300] Where ethno-cultural groups are seen as possessing immutable characteristics, including an antagonistic relationship with other groups, there appears (to proponents of consociational thought) no alternative but to hand power to political elites in order to avoid future conflict. Where they are introduced, consociational arrangements entrench ethnic differences,[301] and there is no possibility to moving to a more open, liberal, integrated and normal political life.[302] The role of the ordinary citizen is largely passive: it is the 'elites, not ordinary people, who interact and

---

[299] Marcus Cox, 'The Dayton Agreement in Bosnia-Herzegovina: a study of implementation strategies' (1998) 69 *British Year Book of International Law* 201, 207. See also Ian Shapiro, 'Group aspirations and democratic politics', in Harold Koh and Ronald Slye, *Deliberative democracy and human rights* (New Haven: Yale University Press, 1999), p. 143, at pp. 149–51.

[300] Kenneth Anderson, 'Illiberal tolerance: an essay on the fall of Yugoslavia and the rise of multiculturalism in the United States' (1992/3) 33 *Virginia Journal of International Law* 385, 388.

[301] Asbjørn Eide, 'Good governance, human rights and the rights of minorities and indigenous peoples', in Hans-Otto Sano and Gudmundur Alfredsson (eds.), *Human rights and good governance: building bridges* (The Hague: Martinus Nijhoff, 2002), p. 17, at p. 66.

[302] Rainer Bauböck, 'Why stay together? A pluralist approach to secession and federalism', in Will Kymlicka and Wayne Norman (eds.), *Citizenship in diverse societies* (Oxford: Oxford University Press, 2000), p. 366, at p. 390.

make compromises with each other'.[303] There may be a number of background features which favour the introduction of consociational democracy,[304] but the key to stability is the willingness of political elites to share power.[305] It is not possible, then, with any degree of certainty, to identify those situations where the introduction of consociational democracy will assist in the resolution of ethnic conflict.[306]

There are other, more contingent, explanations for group conflict, which see ethnic relations as contextual, fluid and a function of the structural conditions of society.[307] The conflict in Bosnia and Herzegovina has also been explained in terms of 'elite manipulation',

---

[303] Richard Bellamy, 'Dealing with difference: four models of pluralist politics' (2000) 53 *Parliamentary Affairs* 198, 208.

[304] According to Arend Lijphart, there are nine background features that favour the introduction of successful consociational rule: (1) the absence of a dominant majority group; (2) the absence of major socio-economic differences; (3) a small, rather than a large, number of sub-groups (the existence of the latter makes negotiations more complex); (4) rough equivalence in group size; (5) a relatively small total population; (6) the existence of external threats, which promote internal unity; (7) the existence of certain symbols, institutions, ideals or values, to which all groups have a common loyalty; (8) the geographical concentration of certain sub-groups, allowing for the introduction of regimes of territorial autonomy; and (9) traditions of compromise and accommodation: Arend Lijphart, 'The puzzle of Indian democracy: a consociational interpretation' (1996) 90 *American Political Science Review* 258, 262–3. Ulrich Schneckener identifies the following, additional, favourable factors: (1) the existence of political or other cleavages (i.e. differences) that cut across ethno-national or linguistic lines; (2) the existence of more than one political party seeking to represent the interests of each sub-group; (3) a political leadership in each group capable of commanding internal support for any compromises; (4) the commitment of all parties to the status quo, i.e. no group seeking a hegemonic position, or change in territorial borders; (5) historical experiences of conflict management; (6) the involvement and inclusion of all groups and all political parties in the consociational agreement; and (7) the development of the consociational arrangement by the groups themselves, and not by external actors: Ulrich Schneckener, 'Making power-sharing work: lessons from successes and failures in ethnic conflict regulation' (2002) 39 *Journal of Peace Research* 203, 211–17.

[305] Lijphart, 'Consociational democracy', 212. See also Dominique Arel, 'Political stability in multinational democracies: comparing language dynamics in Brussels, Montreal and Barcelona', in Alain Gagnon and James Tully (eds.), *Multinational democracies* (Cambridge: Cambridge University Press, 2001), p. 65, at p. 66; and John McGarry and Brendan O'Leary, 'Introduction: the macro-political regulation of ethnic conflict', in John McGarry and Brendan O'Leary (eds.), *The politics of ethnic conflict regulation* (London: Routledge, 1993), p. 1, at pp. 36–7.

[306] Matthijs Bogaards, 'The favourable factors for consociational democracy: a review' (1998) 33 *European Journal of Political Research* 475, 488.

[307] Sisk, *Power sharing and international mediation in ethnic conflicts*, p. 12. See also Hurst Hannum, *Autonomy, sovereignty, and self-determination: the accommodation of conflicting rights* (Philadelphia: University of Pennsylvania Press, 1990), p. 4.

that is, individuals were manipulated by political elites to define themselves primarily by reference to ethnicity, and to see their group as threatened by others,[308] and by reference to 'political economy', that is, political elites recognised that, once communism had collapsed, nationalism was the only force capable of mobilising support for these regional elites who continued to dominate the political scene.[309] In other cases, it has been argued that ethnic conflict results from the pursuit of essentially economic interests.[310] If conflict is contingent on the presence or absence of certain factors, then it might be possible to design a democratic system which seeks to move citizens away from their positions of ethnic antagonisms.[311] According to this approach, the citizen, and not any political elite, should be placed at the centre of democratic debate. Members of minority groups, Donald Horowitz argues, are protected in a democracy when political leaders need their support.[312]

There is no model of integrative democracy, but a number of integrative responses to the realities of multi-cultural democratic polities: creating a mixed, or non-ethnic, federal structure; establishing an inclusive, centralised unitary State; adopting majoritarian but ethnically neutral, or non ethnic, executive, legislative and administrative decision-making bodies; adopting a semi-majoritarian or semi-proportional electoral system that encourages the formation of pre-election coalitions across ethnic divides; and devising 'ethnicity-blind' public policies.[313] Donald Horowitz favours two of these approaches: territorial autonomy (discussed in chapter 2), and designing the electoral system to reward political integration between sub-groups. The electoral system,

---

[308] Cox, 'The Dayton Agreement in Bosnia-Herzegovina', 207.   [309] *Ibid.*, 208.

[310] Sisk, *Power sharing and international mediation in ethnic conflicts*, p. 12.

[311] Political conflict between ethnic groups is only one manifestation of an antagonistic relationship between sub-groups. There is no guarantee that a more integrated democratic system will produce a more integrated society: Eiki Berg and Wim van Meurs, 'Borders and orders in Europe: limits of nation- and state-building in Estonia, Macedonia and Moldova' (2002) 18 *Journal of Communist Studies and Transition Politics* 51, 61. On the limited utility of elections in promoting democracy in a post 'ethnic' conflict scenario, see Christine Bell, *Peace agreements and human rights* (Oxford: Oxford University Press, 2002), pp. 178–9; and Michael Pugh and Margaret Cobble, 'Nonnationalist voting in Bosnian municipal elections: implications for democracy and peacebuilding' (2001) 38 *Journal of Peace Research* 27, 28. In Northern Ireland, a variety of conflict resolution and peace-building activities are used to promote civil society and attempt to move away from group conflict to political deliberation: Sean Byrne, 'Consociational and civic society approaches to peacebuilding in Northern Ireland' (2001) 38 *Journal of Peace Research* 327, 341–2.

[312] Horowitz, *Ethnic groups in conflict*, p. 596.

[313] Sisk, *Power sharing and international mediation in ethnic conflicts*, p. xi.

Horowitz explains, can be harnessed to the goal of ethnic accommodation in one of five ways: (1) it can fragment the support of one or more ethnic groups, especially a majority group, to prevent the creation of a permanent majority; (2) it can induce an ethnic group, especially a majority, to behave moderately towards another group, by for example requiring a successful Presidential candidate to enjoy broad territorial support; (3) it can encourage the formation of multi-ethnic coalitions, often resulting from the need to secure a majority of seats in the legislature; (4) it can preserve a measure of fluidity or multi-polar balance among several groups to prevent bifurcation and the permanent exclusion of the resulting minority; and (5) it can reduce any disparity between the votes won and the seats won, so as to reduce the possibility of a minority group obtaining a majority of seats.[314] The key is to move away from the 'winner-take-all' view of democracy. The electoral system should create incentives for political parties to broaden their appeal in order to attract votes from all communities, so that representatives have a broad base of support.[315]

The Arusha Peace and Reconciliation Agreement for Burundi does not seek to entrench a power-sharing government, but to recognise difference in an integrated model of pluralist democracy.[316] The Security Council has affirmed its 'full support for the process of the [Agreement]', and called on all the Burundian parties to fully honour their commitments.[317] The Security Council has also authorised the deployment of a peacekeeping operation in Burundi (United Nations Operation in Burundi (ONUB)) 'in order to support and help to implement the efforts undertaken by Burundians to restore lasting peace and bring about national reconciliation, as provided under the Arusha Agreement'.[318] ONUB is authorised to use all necessary means to contribute to the successful completion of the electoral process stipulated in the Arusha Agreement, by ensuring a secure environment in which free, transparent and peaceful elections can take place.[319]

---

[314] Horowitz, *Ethnic groups in conflict*, p. 632. See also Yash Ghai, 'Constitutional asymmetries: communal representation, federalism and cultural autonomy', in Reynolds (ed.), *The architecture of democracy*, p. 141, at p. 154.

[315] Donald Horowitz, 'Constitutional design: proposals versus processes', in Reynolds (ed.), *The architecture of democracy*, p. 15, at p. 23. See also Sisk, *Power sharing and international mediation in ethnic conflicts*, p. ix.

[316] Arusha Peace and Reconciliation Agreement for Burundi, adopted 28 August 2000, available at www.usip.org/library/pa/burundi/pa_burundi_08282000_toc.html (last visited 8 January 2005).

[317] SC Res. 1545 (2004), preamble.   [318] *Ibid.*, para. 2.   [319] *Ibid.*, para. 5.

Protocol I to the Arusha Peace and Reconciliation Agreement argues that the causes of the conflict in Burundi are a legacy of colonialism, a period characterised by a strategy of 'divide and rule', during which the colonial administration injected and imposed a caricatured, racist vision of Burundian society.[320] Identity cards were introduced, which indicated ethnic origin, thus reinforcing ethnic awareness to the detriment of national awareness. Identity cards also enabled the coloniser to accord specific treatment to each designated ethnic group in accordance with its own theories of racial and ethnic difference.[321] Rejecting these constructed and imposed identities, the Agreement concludes that the conflict between Hutu and Tutsi groups in Burundi 'is fundamentally political', albeit with important ethnic dimensions: 'It stems from a struggle by the political class to accede to and/or remain in power.'[322]

The Arusha Agreement establishes an interim political arrangement, and a longer-term constitutional settlement. The transitional agreement provides that the President and Vice-President should come from different ethnic groups.[323] Under the Agreement, President Buyoya, a Tutsi, gave way to Vice-President Ndayizeye, a Hutu, halfway through the three-year interim period.[324] The Definitive, or Final, Constitution provides for an electoral system that will attempt to facilitate integration. There will be a President with executive powers, and a bicameral legislature consisting of a National Assembly and Senate. The President is to be elected by direct universal suffrage.[325] He or she will be assisted by two Vice-Presidents, appointed by the President, but with the support of a majority of both the National Assembly and the Senate. The Vice-Presidents must belong to different ethnic groups and political parties.[326] The President, after consultation with the two Vice-Presidents, will appoint the members of the government.[327] Political

---

[320] Arusha Peace and Reconciliation Agreement for Burundi, adopted 28 August 2000, Protocol I: Nature of the Burundi Conflict, Problems of Genocide and Exclusion and their Solutions, Article 2(2).

[321] *Ibid.*, Article 2(3).   [322] *Ibid.*, Article 4.

[323] Arusha Peace and Reconciliation Agreement for Burundi, adopted 28 August 2000, Protocol II: Democracy and Good Governance, Article 15(12).

[324] The Agreement further provides, during the transitional period, for a government of national unity in which more than half but less than three-fifths of the portfolios are to be allocated amongst the principal Hutu political parties: Arusha Peace and Reconciliation Agreement for Burundi, adopted 28 August 2000, Protocol II. Democracy and Good Governance, Article 15(13).

[325] Arusha Peace and Reconciliation Agreement for Burundi, adopted 28 August 2000, Protocol II: Democracy and Good Governance, Article 7(1).

[326] *Ibid.*, Article 7(4).   [327] *Ibid.*, Article 7(5).

parties with 5 per cent of the popular vote are entitled to at least the same proportion of the total number of ministers as their proportion of members in the National Assembly.[328] There is no specific requirement for an ethnically balanced, or mixed, cabinet.

In deeply divided societies, the use of a relatively pure system of proportional representation in elections for national parliaments and a rule requiring that political parties should be represented in the executive in the same proportion as the legislature will produce an inclusive and representative executive, without explicit reference to ethnicity (and without limiting the rights of political participation to groups defined by reference to ethno-cultural identity).[329] South Africa's Interim Constitution (1993) provided that any political party with at least 20 per cent of the seats in the National Assembly was entitled to designate an Executive Deputy President,[330] and that political parties with twenty or more seats in the National Assembly, a mere 5 per cent, were entitled to participate in the 'government of national unity'. Political parties would receive seats in the cabinet on a proportionate basis to their representation in the Assembly.[331] The Interim Constitution provided for a coalition government based on the idea of inclusivity and co-operation.[332] The 'final' South African Constitution (1996) firmly rejects the consociational model.[333]

---

[328] *Ibid.*, Article 7(6).

[329] One of the functions of the legislature is to hold the executive to account. The inclusion of all significant political parties in the executive is likely to remove the possibility of effective opposition.

[330] Section 84(1) of the Constitution of the Republic of South Africa (1993) (the 'Interim Constitution'). In the 1994 elections, the African National Congress (ANC) (with 62 per cent of the seats) and the National Party (NP) (20 per cent) designated Deputy Presidents.

[331] *Ibid.*, section 88(2). The twenty-seven Cabinet posts were allocated to the ANC (eighteen), the NP (six) and the Inkhata Freedom Party (IFP) (three).

[332] Dion Basson, *South Africa's interim constitution*, p. 136. According to Timothy Sisk, political parties responded to the incentives imbedded in the electoral system to moderate their campaign rhetoric. The two main vote-getters, the ANC and the National Party, deliberately structured their candidate lists to appear racially inclusive: Sisk, *Power sharing and international mediation in ethnic conflicts*, p. 63.

[333] Gloppen, *South Africa: the battle over the constitution*, p. 215. Arend Lijphart's concept of power sharing is particularly tainted in South Africa following the introduction of a 'sham' system of power sharing under the 1983 Constitution: see, Dion Basson, *South Africa's interim constitution* (revised edn, Kenwyn: Juta, 1995), p. 135; and Siri Gloppen, *South Africa: the battle over the constitution* (Aldershot: Dartmouth, 1997), p. 93. Cf. Arend Lijphart, 'The puzzle of Indian democracy: a consociational interpretation' (1996) 90 *American Political Science Review* 258, 258.

Under the Arusha Peace and Reconciliation Agreement, Members of the National Assembly will be elected under a system of proportional representation. Political parties must be open to all Burundians and be national in character and leadership.[334] Parties receiving as little as 2 per cent of the popular vote may achieve representation in the National Assembly.[335] The electoral system will operate by way of a system of party lists, which are required to be multi ethnic in character: 'For each three names in sequence on a list, only two may belong to the same ethnic group, and for each five names at least one shall be a woman.'[336] This electoral system, it is estimated, will yield a National Assembly in which over 38 per cent of the representatives come from minority groups.[337] Given that those political parties are entitled to the same proportion of government ministers as seats in the National Assembly, the Agreement effectively guarantees the establishment of a multi-ethnic and representative executive and legislature without attempting to pre-determine the outcome of the democratic processes. The Senate will comprise two delegates from each province, elected by an electoral college comprising members of the commune councils in the province in question, 'from different ethnic communities and shall be elected in separate ballots'.[338] Tutsis, who comprise 14 per cent of the total population, will be guaranteed parity of representation with Hutus in the Senate.[339] In the longer term, these arrangement for the Senate are on the borderlines of acceptability.

The Arusha Peace and Reconciliation Agreement highlights certain necessary features of any effective integrative approach in a deeply divided polity. First, there should be a separation of powers between the different branches of government. Secondly, the electoral system should reduce the importance of success in any one election. Where power is concentrated, for example in the hands of an executive President, those groups who do not believe they have a chance of winning that election have little incentive to participate in the democratic system. Thirdly, democratic

---

[334] Arusha Peace and Reconciliation Agreement for Burundi, adopted 28 August 2000, Protocol II: Democracy and Good Governance, Article 4(4).

[335] *Ibid.*, Article 20(6).   [336] *Ibid.*, Article 20(8).

[337] Arusha Peace and Reconciliation Agreement for Burundi, adopted 28 August 2000, Explanatory Commentary on Protocol II (Democracy and Good Governance), para. 2.

[338] Arusha Peace and Reconciliation Agreement for Burundi, adopted 28 August 2000, Protocol II: Democracy and Good Governance, Article 6(14).

[339] The importance of the Senate lies in its ability to block constitutional changes and the adoption of important laws. Constitutional amendments require the support of two-thirds of the votes in the Senate: *ibid.*, Article 6(5). Other important legislation, including electoral laws, cannot be adopted without the approval of the Senate: *ibid.*, Article 6(6).

institutions should be as representative as possible. There is a clear rela-tionship between representativeness and stability.[340] Fourthly, the consti-tutional arrangement should ensure that the plurality of identities within the polity is represented in each branch of government: the legislature, judiciary, executive and civil service. Where possible, this should be achieved without direct reference to ethnicity. Fifthly, a relatively pure system of proportional representation must be used in elections, to ensure the representation of a broad range of political parties. Sixthly, executive authority should rest with an executive body whose members are drawn proportionately from the legislature. Finally, there should be a strong and independent judiciary, with the power to implement directly relevant international and regional human rights standards.[341]

Democratic decision-making

The chapter has highlighted the importance of political participation for persons belonging to national, ethnic, cultural, religious or linguistic minorities. The inclusion of otherwise excluded minority perspectives increases the possibility that the interests and preferences of persons from minority groups may influence relevant decision-making processes. Guarantees of procedural inclusion are, however, insufficient in them-selves to protect the group from the introduction of policies deleterious to its way of life.[342] No right of veto may be recognised for minority groups, beyond the protection afforded by human rights regimes. There is no reason to consider the perspective of persons belonging to the minority any more valid than that of those belonging to the majority. Indeed, in a democracy, the presumption must be that the perspective of a minority of citizens is less valid than that of a majority. The only possibility, within a democratic context, for minorities to exercise a decisive influence on policy outcomes is for decisions to be 'based not only on the counting of votes but also on the sharing of reasons'.[343]

---

[340] See Marta Reynal-Querol, 'Ethnicity, political systems, and civil wars' (2002) 46 *Journal of Conflict Resolution* 29, 35.

[341] See Arusha Peace and Reconciliation Agreement for Burundi, adopted 28 August 2000, Protocol II: Democracy and Good Governance, Article 3.

[342] See Susan Marks, *The riddle of all constitutions* (Oxford: Oxford University Press, 2000), p. 101.

[343] Melissa Williams, 'The uneasy alliance of group representation and deliberative democracy', in Will Kymlicka and Wayne Norman (eds.), *Citizenship in diverse societies* (Oxford: Oxford University Press, 2000), p. 124, at pp. 124–5 (footnotes omitted).

In a democracy, the will of the people is the basis of the legitimate authority of government.[344] Where the will of the people is divided, 'aggregative' models of democracy dictate that the majority should determine the relevant policy position. The will of the people is identified by aggregating the preferences of equal citizens, each of whom is the best judge of their own interests and preferences, to identify where the majority lies on a particular issue. Majority rule is consistent with equality of voting rights, and ensures that one single policy position is adopted.[345] The body politic, according to John Locke, should 'move that way whither the greater force carries it'. The only alternative would be the consent of each individual, but 'such consent is next impossible ever to be had'.[346]

Aggregative models of democracy focus on competitive elections. Citizens express individual preferences through the act of voting, or by lobbying elected politicians.[347] Aggregative models ignore, or underplay, the importance of the political deliberation and debate that precedes the act of decision-making.[348] The UN Commission on Human Rights has observed that 'in a democracy the widest participation in the democratic dialogue by all sectors and actors of society must be promoted in order to come to agreements on appropriate solutions to the social, economic and cultural problems of a society'.[349] Moreover,

---

[344] See Article 21(3) of GA Res. 217 (III) A, adopted 10 December 1948, 'Universal Declaration of Human Rights'.

[345] Joseph Jaconelli, 'Majority rule and special majorities' (1989) *Public Law* 587, 595–6. On majority rule, see Elias Berg, *Democracy and the majority principle* (Stockholm: Svenska, 1966); and Willmore Kendall, *John Locke and the doctrine of majority-rule* (Urbana: University of Illinois Press, 1966). See also Russell Miller, 'Self-determination in international law and the demise of democracy' (2003) 41 *Columbia Journal of Transnational Law* 601, 641–2.

[346] John Locke, *Two treatises of government* (Cambridge: Cambridge University Press, 1964), Part II, p. 96, at p. 350.

[347] Cf. Joseph Schumpeter, *Capitalism, socialism and democracy* (5th edn, London: Allen and Unwin, 1976), pp. 284–5: the people do not actually rule in any obvious sense of the terms 'people' and 'rule'. Democracy is rule by the elected politician: the role of the citizen is to determine who will hold power.

[348] Iris Marion Young, *Inclusion and democracy* (Oxford: Oxford University Press, 2000), p. 22.

[349] UN Commission on Human Rights Res. 1995/60, adopted 7 March 1995, 'Ways and means of overcoming obstacles to the establishment of a democratic society and requirements for the maintenance of democracy', UN Doc. E/CN.4/RES/1995/60, preamble. As explained by the Canadian Supreme Court in *Reference re Secession of Quebec*: 'No one has a monopoly on truth, and our [democratic] system is predicated on the faith that in the marketplace of ideas, the best solutions to public problems will rise to the top ... [A] functioning democracy requires a continuous process of

citizens are not the passive recipients of political argument. They inter-act with political debate, both directly, in deliberations with politicians and other citizens, and indirectly, through the coverage of politics in the media. Citizens accept that their existing political positions may be revised in this interaction with political debate.[350]

In the contemporary age, democratic legitimacy is increasingly seen in terms of the 'ability or opportunity to participate in effective deliber-ation on the part of those subject to collective decisions'.[351] The UN 'Millennium Declaration' refers to '[d]emocratic and participatory gov-ernance based on the will of the people'.[352] The understanding of democracy in international law must expand beyond an institutional and procedural one to recognise the importance of political participa-tion, in particular for marginalised groups. This is necessary in order to give genuine effect to the underlying principles of democracy: popular sovereignty and political equality.[353]

The recognition of the importance of democratic deliberation has led a number of writers to articulate a conception of deliberative democ-racy, which they claim elucidates some aspects of the logic of the contemporary practice of democracy better than other models of democracy, albeit in imperfect form.[354] The deliberative model has been described as a 'pure form of participatory democracy':[355] citizens deliberate with a view to reaching a consensus on the political questions of the day. Julia Black outlines the requirements of deliberative democracy:

[T]he equal and uncoerced participation of all ... All issues have to be open to question; all opinions voiced in conditions of equality and free from domina-tion. Decision processes have to be conditioned by the desire of participants to reach agreement in the absence of coercion or threat of coercion. To this end

---

discussion ... [T]he need to build majorities necessitates compromise, negotiation, and deliberation': *Reference re Secession of Quebec* [1998] 2 SCR 217, para. 68.

[350] John Rawls, *The law of peoples, with 'The idea of public reason revisited'* (Cambridge, MA: Harvard University Press, 1999), pp. 138–9.

[351] John Dryzek, *Deliberative democracy and beyond: liberals, critics, contestations* (Oxford: Oxford University Press, 2000), p. 1.

[352] GA Res. 55/2, adopted 8 September 2000, 'Millennium Declaration', para. 6.

[353] Susan Marks, *The riddle of all constitutions*, p. 109.

[354] Seyla Benhabib, 'Toward a deliberative model of democratic legitimacy', in Seyla Benhabib (ed.), *Democracy and difference: contesting the boundaries of the political* (Princeton: Princeton University Press, 1996), p. 67, at p. 84. See also Maeve Cooke, 'Five arguments for deliberative democracy' (2000) 48 *Political Studies* 947, 955.

[355] David van Mill, 'The possibility of rational outcomes from democratic discourse and procedures' (1996) 58 *Journal of Politics* 734, 738.

each has to put forward reasons that others could reasonably accept, and seek acceptance for their reasons, and reject proposals on the basis that insufficiently good reasons have been offered for them: the requirement of public reason. The only influence thus exercised is the force of the better argument.[356]

In ideal deliberative conditions, laws and regulations emerge from a process of reasoned deliberation amongst equal citizens, who reach a consensus as to what is to be done.[357] This is the 'metanorm' of deliberative democracy.[358] For a law to be legitimate it must enjoy the 'united and consenting will of all'.[359] The purpose of democratic deliberation is to reach a consensus amongst participants to democratic deliberations as to relevant policy positions.[360] The right of political autonomy is understood to involve not only the right to participate in political deliberation, but also to decide whether a law should in fact be adopted: 'The great right of every man, the right of rights, is the right of having a share in the making of the laws, to which the good of the whole makes it his duty to submit'.[361] Given that self-interested arguments will not convince others to change their positions,[362] participants must rely on arguments supported by reasons. A valid reason constitutes a moral, economic, political, scientific, institutional or social argument that materially supports a policy position.[363]

A reliance on reasoned deliberation to resolve cultural disputes has been criticised for forcing persons belonging to ethno-cultural minorities to enter democratic debate on the terms of the liberal State, given that rational discourse derives from the ruling institutions of the

---

[356] Julia Black, 'Proceduralizing regulation: part I' (2000) 20 *Oxford Journal of Legal Studies* 597, 609.

[357] Habermas, *Between facts and norms*, p. 158.

[358] Seyla Benhabib, *The claims of culture: equality and diversity in the global era* (Princeton, Princeton University Press, 2002), p. 107.

[359] Immanuel Kant, *Metaphysical elements of justice* (1965), p. 78, referred to in Jürgen Habermas, 'Popular sovereignty as procedure', in James Bohman and William Rehg (eds.), *Deliberative democracy: essays on reason and politics* (Cambridge, MA: MIT Press, 1997), p. 35, at p. 45.

[360] Joshua Cohen, 'Deliberation and democratic legitimacy', in Bohman and Rehg (eds.), *Deliberative democracy*, p. 67, at pp. 74–5.

[361] William Cobbet, *Advice to Young Men and Women, Advice to a Citizen* (1829), quoted in Jeremy Waldron, *Law and disagreement* (Oxford: Clarendon Press, 1999), p. 232.

[362] Jon Elster, 'The market and the forum: three varieties of political theory', in Bohman and Rehg (eds.), *Deliberative democracy*, p. 3, at pp. 11–12. Participants will not accept the self-interested bargaining positions of others: see, Habermas, *Between facts and norms*, p. 309.

[363] Luc Tremblay, 'Deliberative democracy and liberal rights' (2001) 14 *Ratio Juris* 424, 445.

West: scientific debate, modern parliaments and courts.[364] Evidence demonstrates, however, that individuals from different cultures do not reason in fundamentally different ways.[365] The assumption that certain groups represent 'the other of reason' is, according to Seyla Benhabib, a species of 'exoticism'.[366] Differences in culture, religion and language are impediments to communication and understanding, not insurmountable barriers.[367]

Where members of different language groups deliberate, they must choose the language of political deliberation, or agree on the use of translators. Additionally, they must agree a procedure for the resolution of disputes as to the interpretation of subsequently agreed terms in the different languages.[368] There may be circumstances where there is no corresponding term or concept in both languages.[369] This may be a particular problem in deliberations involving indigenous peoples.[370] In other cases, there may be a common recognition of relevant concepts or terms, but disagreement as to their (cultural) value. The economic and social benefits of an economic development in the territories of an indigenous people cannot be directly balanced against the spiritual value of the territory to the group.[371] A democratic mechanism for decision-making must accommodate the fact that, in a democracy, all individual perspectives are intrinsically important (even if they should not always be accommodated).[372]

---

[364] See Iris Marion Young, 'Communication and the other: beyond deliberative democracy', in Benhabib (ed.), *Democracy and difference*, p. 120, at p. 123.

[365] Lawrence Rosen, 'The right to be different: indigenous peoples and the quest for a unified theory' (1997) 107 *Yale Law Journal* 227, 253.

[366] Benhabib, *The claims of culture*, p. 139.

[367] See James Tully, *Strange multiplicity: constitutionalism in an age of diversity* (Cambridge: Cambridge University Press, 1995), p. 134.

[368] See Julia Black, 'Proceduralizing regulation: part II' (2001) 21 *Oxford Journal of Legal Studies* 33, 45–8.

[369] *Ibid.*, 48.

[370] See, for example, Rex Adhar, 'Indigenous spiritual concerns and the secular State: some developments' (2003) 23 *Oxford Journal of Legal Studies* 611.

[371] See, for example, *Lyng* v. *Northwest Indian Cemetery Protection Association*, 485 US 439 (1988), before the US Supreme Court, where American Indians objected to the building of a paved road through federal land, which had historically been used by certain American Indians for religious rituals that depend upon privacy, silence and an undisturbed natural setting: 485 US 439, 453 (1988).

[372] Chandran Kukathas, 'Are there any cultural rights?', in Will Kymlicka (ed.), *The rights of minority communities* (Oxford: Oxford University Press, 1995), p. 228, at p. 246, relying on Loren Lomansky, *Persons, rights and the moral community* (Oxford: Oxford University Press, 1997). See also Jeremy Waldron, 'Cultural identity and civic responsibility', in

Conclusion

This chapter has examined the implications for persons belonging to minorities of the emergence of a norm of democracy in international human rights law. It has examined the rights of political participation, and the requirement for the State to ensure that democratic institutions are representative of its heterogeneous people. The particular right of minorities to participate directly in the making of decisions which affect the ability of members of the group to enjoy their own culture, to profess and practise their own religion, or to use their own language was considered. The right of political participation does not guarantee that persons belonging to minorities will be able to affect the outcomes of decision-making processes, in particular where issues concerning the cultural security of the group are under consideration. Where democracy is defined primarily by reference to majority rule, numerical (national or ethnic, religious and linguistic) minorities are unlikely to have their cultural interests and preferences recognised by the State. Alternative understandings of democracy suggest different conclusions. Where minorities are recognised as having a share of power and a right of veto on those issues which are vital to the interests of the minority, cultural security is guaranteed. Consociational models of democracy are not, however, compatible with the concept of democracy recognised in the international instruments. The democratic system may legitimately seek to integrate persons belonging to minorities into the democratic process. The inclusion of minority interests and preferences may ensure better decision-making, but it cannot guarantee that the interests and preferences of persons belonging to minorities are recognised, in particular where democracy is defined by, or associated with, the principle of majority rule.

The protection of minorities in democratic States does not depend on the particular institutional arrangements extant in any particular society. Cultural differences are respected and protected where the procedures for decision-making approximate to the ideal conditions of a deliberative democracy: inclusion, reasoned political debate and an attempt to reach a consensus amongst all participants on relevant policy positions. In particular, the State should be reluctant to regulate cultural practice in the face of opposition from the

---

Will Kymlicka and Wayne Norman (eds.), *Citizenship in diverse societies* (Oxford: Oxford University Press, 2000), p. 155, at p. 170; see also Robert Baker, 'Negotiating international bioethics' (1998) 8 *Kennedy Institute of Ethics Journal* 423, 442.

representatives of national or ethnic, religious or linguistic minorities. Where the State does regulate cultural conduct it must accept that others, including those in the international community, may question the legitimacy of the relevant measure – and the State's treatment of its minorities.

Conclusion: the accommodation of diversity

This work has examined the relevance of international law to cultural disputes in democratic States. It has shown that minorities, national minorities, indigenous peoples and peoples are defined primarily by their cultural differences to a dominant/majority culture and by their political demands. International law recognises a right of persons belonging to minorities to enjoy their own culture, to profess and practise their own religion, or to use their own language, and a right of peoples to self-determination. The principles of cultural security and self-determination are recognised, but without detailed rules being elaborated as to how those principles are to be put into effect. According to Antonio Cassese, the adoption of principles rather than rules is 'the expression and result of conflicting views of States on matters of crucial importance'. When States cannot agree on 'definite and specific standards of behaviour' but require some 'basic guideline for their conduct', they formulate legal principles rather than legal rules.[1]

States policies concerning ethno-cultural groups will emerge through domestic decision-making procedures, in accordance with the principles recognised by the international community: cultural security for minorities and self-determination for peoples. In democratic States, these policies will be adopted in accordance with the principles of democracy: popular sovereignty and political equality. Legislative and other measures will enjoy limited legitimacy where those who will be subject to the law have been excluded from the process of democratic

---

[1] Antonio Cassese, *Self-determination of peoples: a legal reappraisal* (Cambridge: Cambridge University Press, 1995), p. 128. Cf. Karen Knop, *Diversity and Self-determination in international law* (Cambridge: Cambridge University Press, 2002), pp. 30–8.

deliberation and decision-making.[2] Additionally, citizens (and others) will enjoy the protection of international and domestic human rights norms, which proscribe unjustified interferences with the right of all persons to moral autonomy: the right to a particular 'way of life'. Interferences must be justified by reference to reasons, and the justification must demonstrate a reasoned argument in support of the interference: arbitrary interferences are not permitted by human rights regimes. The reasons and argument should constitute a 'sufficient justification' for the interference.[3] Where the issue concerns a central aspect of individual identity, the State should provide compelling evidence in support of any interference.[4]

In relation to the rights of persons belonging to minorities, courts may consider arguments concerning the application of the non-discrimination principle, and claims that policies, laws and regulations have the effect of denying persons belonging to minorities the right to enjoy their own culture, to profess and practise their own religion, or to use their own language.[5] Judicial bodies may also evaluate the extent to which the interests and perspectives of persons belonging to minorities have been represented in the decision-making processes, and may overturn decisions that result from a defective process.[6] Courts are not, however, competent to determine whether the authorities have unjustifiably regulated minority cultural practices, or have failed to introduce the necessary positive measures to maintain and support minority cultures.[7] The question, for example, as to whether

[2] Seyla Benhabib, *The claims of culture: equality and diversity in the global era* (Princeton: Princeton University Press, 2002), p. 37.

[3] Luc Tremblay, 'Deliberative democracy and liberal rights' (2001) 14 *Ratio Juris* 424, 447.

[4] See Joshua Cohen, 'Democracy and liberty', in Jon Elster (ed.), *Deliberative democracy* (Cambridge: Cambridge University Press, 1998), p. 185, at p. 220. The European Court of Human Rights has, for example, referred to the need for the State to adduce 'very weighty reasons' to justify a difference in treatment on the grounds of sex and sexuality: see, *Case of Abdulaziz, Cabales and Balkandali* (1985) A94, para. 78, and *Smith and Grady* v. *United Kingdom*, Reports of Judgments and Decisions 1999-VI, para. 89.

[5] See, for example, *Länsman et al.* v. *Finland (No. 1)*, Communication No. 511/1992, UN Doc. CCPR/C/52/D/511/1992, 8 November 1994, para. 9.4.

[6] See Tom Campbell, 'Legal positivism and deliberative democracy' (1998) 51 *Current Legal Problems* 65, 83.

[7] The European Court of Human Rights has concluded, for example, that 'the complexity and sensitivity of the issues involved in policies balancing the interests of the general population ... and the interests of a minority with possibly conflicting requirements, renders the Court's role a strictly supervisory one': *Chapman* v. *UK*, Reports of Judgments and Decisions 2001-I, para. 94. See generally Duncan Kennedy, *A critique of adjudication* (Cambridge, MA: Harvard University Press, 1997), p. 317. See Rainer Bauböck, 'Cultural

it is appropriate, in all the (financial, practical and other) circumstances to fund minority schools is one of individual moral judgment. There is no reason to privilege those who would claim the title of 'philosopher king',[8] simply because they sit in a judicial capacity.[9]

The rights of minorities are not 'legal rights', rooted in legal principle, but 'political rights'. The distinction is made in *Société des Acadiens* v. *Association of Parents* before the Canadian Supreme Court, concerning whether the right to be heard by a court in one of two languages included the right to be understood by the judge.[10] The judgment of Beetz *et al.* distinguished between 'legal rights', and rights, such as language rights, 'founded on political compromise'.[11] Legal rights may be judicially recognised, and evolve by judicial interpretation. Political rights emerge from political institutions: competent legislative and administrative bodies. The procedural correctness of decisions concerning political rights may be examined by the courts, but the substance of decisions which emerge from proper procedures should not be challenged.

On 'questions of culture', the members of the dominant/majority ethno-cultural group do not have the right to dictate the relevant convention simply because they constitute a majority of the population.[12] In a democracy, the will of the majority does not ipso facto determine the 'will of the people'.[13] The 'right' answer (according to theories of deliberative democracy) is the one that commands the support of all citizens.[14] In the practice of democracy, where a consensus cannot be reached, the view of the majority may

---

citizenship: minority rights and political community', in Burton Leiser and Tom Campbell (eds.), *Human rights in philosophy and practice* (Aldershot: Ashgate, 2001), p. 235, at p. 236; see also Jürgen Habermas, *Between facts and norms: contributions to a discourse theory of law and democracy* (trans. William Rehg, Cambridge, MA: MIT Press, 1996), p. 132.

[8] In a heterogeneous society, 'many seek the crown of philosopher king and hence the inevitability of the right answer depends from which segment of the community one comes': Dennis Davis, *Democracy and deliberation* (Kenwyn: Juta, 1999), p. 10.

[9] Cf. John Rawls, *Political liberalism* (New York: Columbia University Press, 1993), p. 231; see also Ronald Dworkin, *Freedom's law: the moral reading of the American Constitution* (Oxford: Oxford University Press, 1996), p. 31.

[10] *Société des Acadiens* v. *Association of Parents* [1986] 1 SCR 567.

[11] *Ibid.*, paras. 63 and 64, per Beetz *et al.*

[12] See David Miller, 'Doctrinaire liberalism versus multicultural democracy' (2002) 2 *Ethnicities* 261, 263.

[13] See Andreas Føllesdal, 'Indigenous minorities and the shadow of injustice past' (2000) 7 *International Journal on Minority and Group Rights* 19, 28.

[14] Julia Black, 'Proceduralizing regulation: part I' (2000) 20 *Oxford Journal of Legal Studies* 597, 609. See also Dryzek, *Discursive democracy*, p. 17.

prevail.[15] Where, following reasoned democratic deliberation, a majority of participants agree that policy proposal A should be adopted, there
is a presumption that the policy is legitimate.[16] In the practice of
democracy, episodic injustices are unlikely to raise serious questions
as to the legitimate (moral) authority of government rule.[17] Citizens
accept the validity of laws which they did not, and do not, support. They
expect to find themselves part of the minority on some issues, and part
of the majority on others.[18] In contrast, on questions of culture, a
reliance on majority rule is inherently problematic. The absence of
consensus is not the result of a lack of time for effective deliberation,
or insufficiently compelling reasoned argument. Cultural disputes
result from a fundamental moral disagreement: reasonable persons
hold irreconcilable positions,[19] and they are not willing to relinquish
that part of their individual identity conditioned by membership of a
national, ethnic, cultural, religious or linguistic group.[20] A decision to
regulate a minority group's cultural practices will not be accepted by
those against whom it will be applied.

The international community has recognised that the differences in
culture, language, history, institutional and political circumstance
between one State and another may be taken into account when
applying the principles of international human rights law.[21] The UN

---

[15] Joshua Cohen, 'Deliberation and democratic legitimacy', in Bohman and Rehg (eds.),
Deliberative democracy, p. 67, at p. 75. Reliance of majority rule is required to avoid an
implicit decision in favour of the status quo.

[16] Seyla Benhabib, 'Toward a deliberative model of democratic legitimacy', in Benhabib
(ed.), *Democracy and difference*, p. 67, at p. 72. See also Luc Tremblay, 'Deliberative
democracy and liberal rights' (2001) 14 *Ratio Juris* 424, 436.

[17] Brad Roth, *Governmental illegitimacy in international law* (Oxford: Oxford University Press,
2000), p. 17. Cf. Amy Gutmann, 'The challenge of multiculturalism in political ethics'
(1993) 22 *Philosophy and Public Affairs* 171, 191–2.

[18] Richard Bellamy, 'Dealing with difference: four models of pluralist politics' (2000) 53
Parliamentary Affairs 198, 202–3.

[19] See Gutmann, 'The challenge of multiculturalism in political ethics', 196.

[20] See Angel Oquendo, 'Deliberative democracy in Habermas and Nino' (2002) 22 *Oxford
Journal of Legal Studies* 189, 217. Cf. David van Mill, 'The possibility of rational outcomes
from democratic discourse and procedures' (1996) 58 *Journal of Politics* 734, 736; and
Rawls, 'The idea of public reason revisited', 138–9. Identity concerns the defining
characteristics of an individual's understanding of who they are as a person: Charles
Taylor, 'The politics of recognition', in Amy Gutmann (ed.), *Multiculturalism: examining
the politics of recognition* (Princeton: Princeton University Press, 1994), p. 25, at p. 25.

[21] See Paolo Carozza, 'Subsidiarity as a structural principle of international human rights
law' (2003) 97 *American Journal of International Law* 38, 71. See also Bhikhu Parekh, 'The
cultural particularity of liberal democracy' (1992) 40 (Special Issue) *Political Studies* 160, 169.

Declaration on the Rights of Persons belonging to National or Ethnic, Religious and Linguistic Minorities provides that States shall create favourable conditions to enable persons belonging to minorities to express their characteristics and to develop their culture, language, religion, traditions and customs, 'except where specific practices are in violation of national law and contrary to international standards'.[22] The regulation of cultural conduct may legitimately differ from one State to the next. This is problematic, given that national laws will reflect the cultural values, practices and beliefs of the dominant/ majority group.

No right of veto may be recognised for the members of the minority group on questions of culture. There is no reason to consider the perspective of the minority any more valid than that of the majority. A more deliberative understanding of democracy provides a basis upon which individual societies can begin to resolve the complex questions of culture in a way that is compatible with the international human rights instruments. There must be formal, inclusive and reasoned democratic deliberation. Regulations introduced on an arbitrary and discriminatory basis should not be permitted.[23] The fact that cultural conflict results from the existence of a fundamental moral disagreement between members of majority and minority groups creates strong pressures against the enforcement of the dominant/majority group's cultural values, beliefs and practices at the expense of those of the minority, given that the members of the minority group would not freely consent to those regulations.[24] The default position must be against the regulation of cultural conduct.

---

[22] See Article 4(2) of GA Res. 47/135, adopted 18 December 1992, 'Declaration on the Rights of Persons belonging to National or Ethnic, Religious and Linguistic Minorities'.

[23] See, for example, *Church of Lukumi Babalu Aye* v. *City of Hialeah*, 508 US 520 (1993), where the US Supreme Court struck down a law targeting the practice of animal sacrifice by the adherents of the Santeria religion, in part, because the city council had not likewise regulated analogous non-religious conduct. The only reason for the regulation was dislike of the Santeria religion, and that was not a reason to which adherents to that religion could be expected to give reasonable consideration.

[24] Joshua Cohen, 'Democracy and liberty', in Jon Elster (ed.), *Deliberative democracy* (Cambridge: Cambridge University Press, 1998), p. 185, at p. 220. See also Joshua Cohen, 'Procedure and substance in deliberative democracy', in Seyla Benhabib (ed.), *Democracy and difference*, p. 95, at p. 103. Cf. Brian Barry, *Culture and equality: an egalitarian critique of multiculturalism* (Cambridge, MA: Harvard University Press, 2001), p. 32: the application of uniform rules creates identical choices for all individuals, who may make different choices, depending on their own preferences, tastes and opinions. Some of these preferences, tastes and opinions may be conditioned by an individual's membership

Where the State decides to regulate cultural practices, it must demonstrate a sufficient justification for the regulation, and appeal to reasoned argument which is either explicitly non-cultural, or which reflects cultural values generally recognised in the international community: the protection of the environment and endangered species, the protection of children, the importance of education, etc.[25] In relation to the positive aspect of the right to cultural security, the State must demonstrate that its policies concerning minorities have resulted from a process of formal inclusive deliberation, in which minority groups have been able to put their case, and have been provided with a reasoned explanation as to why their policy preferences have not been accepted. No citizen may reasonably expect that all of his or her political demands will be met by the State. At the same time, no group of citizens expects all of its reasonable demands on cultural issues to be rejected. Where the State refuses to engage in a reasonable accommodation with its ethno-cultural minorities, the legitimacy of its democratic rule may be challenged by the members of the group, and the wider international community.

The political demands of ethno-cultural groups for territorial self-government should be met, not where the group is recognised as a 'nation', but where the differences between the dominant/majority group and the minority are 'so profound that it is simply not possible for them to co-operate in the practices of deliberative democracy'.[26] Where the minimum community that democratic decision-making requires is lacking with no prospect of constructing it. In such cases, the 'best option' is to redraw the political boundaries to reflect the fact that there are two political communities, not one.[27] This does not (necessarily) require the establishment of a new sovereign and independent State for the territory of the minority group (although that is one possibility).

of a religious, ethnic or cultural group, but 'this has no significance … justice is guaranteed by equal opportunities'. See also Jean-Christophe Merle, 'Cultural minority rights and the rights of the majority in the liberal state' (1998) 11 *Ratio Juris* 259, 270.

[25] See generally Jeremy Waldron, 'Cultural identity and civic responsibility', in Will Kymlicka and Wayne Norman (eds.), *Citizenship in diverse societies* (Oxford: Oxford University Press, 2000), p. 155, at p. 167.

[26] Allen Buchanan, 'Democracy and secession', in Margaret Moore (ed.), *National self-determination and secession* (Oxford: Oxford University Press, 1998), p. 14, at p. 23.

[27] *Ibid.*, p. 24. Cf. Allen Buchanan, 'Towards a theory of secession' (1991) 101 *Ethics* 322, 324. See also Robert Dahl, *On democracy* (New Haven: Yale University Press, 1998), p. 149.

Democratic deliberation may be problematic for linguistic minorities where there is one language of public life (that of the dominant/majority group) and few members of the minority group are able to communicate in that language. For religious minorities democratic deliberations are difficult where the State refuses to recognise religion as a personal matter for the individual, and seeks to introduce legislative and other measures in accordance with the religious values, practices and beliefs of the dominant/majority group. In cases of ethnic groups, cultural differences (absent language and religious differences) would not normally justify the introduction of territorial self-government regimes from the perspective of democratic legitimacy.[28] An exception might be recognised in circumstances where the cultural differences between the State and the minority group are so profound as to make effective democratic deliberation impossible. This may particularly be the case in democratic deliberations involving some indigenous peoples.[29]

The regime concerning the position of ethno-cultural groups in international law does not propose a uniform solution to the 'question of minorities' in each State. The international community has detailed few normative commitments concerning the treatment of ethno-cultural groups: minorities, national minorities, indigenous peoples and peoples. The international instruments concerning these groups do not provide a solution to the questions of culture and differences, but they do recognise the political tools necessary for the resolution of cultural conflicts: cultural security for persons belonging to minorities and self-determination for peoples. It is for the peoples of sovereign and independent States to agree the particular arrangements for their respective societies. In the resolution of cultural conflicts, 'we cannot escape the risks and responsibilities of practical judgment'.[30]

The democracy norm, recognised by the international community, emphasises the importance of effective political participation. Democracy is not understood simply as majority rule, but by its underlying principles of popular sovereignty ('the will of the people') and political equality. In a democracy, the authority of government should

---

[28] Internal constitutional values might recognise a moral claim to self-government in these circumstances.

[29] See generally James Tully, *Strange multiplicity: constitutionalism in an age of diversity* (Cambridge: Cambridge University Press, 1995), p. 131.

[30] Robert Post, 'Law and cultural conflict' (2003) 78 *Chicago-Kent Law Review* 485, 508.

enjoy the support of all citizens, irrespective of national or ethnic, religious and linguistic identity. Cultural conflicts in a democratic State should be resolved in a way that is either acceptable or defensible and defeasible to all citizens, including persons belonging to ethno-cultural minorities.

Index